THE DAY ROMMEL
WAS STOPPED

The Battle of Ruweisat Ridge, 2 July 1942

MAJOR FRANCIS RONALD 'JEPH' JEPHSON, MC, TD
AND CHRIS JEPHSON

CASEMATE

Oxford & Philadelphia

Published in Great Britain and the United States of America in 2017 by
CASEMATE PUBLISHERS
The Old Music Hall, 106–108 Cowley Road, Oxford OX4 1JE, UK
and
1950 Lawrence Road, Havertown, PA 19083, US

Hardcover Edition: ISBN 978-1-61200-558-4
Digital Edition: ISBN 978-1-61200-559-1

A CIP record for this book is available from the British Library

Printed and bound in the United Kingdom by TJ International Ltd

For a complete list of Casemate titles, please contact:

CASEMATE PUBLISHERS (US)
Telephone (610) 853-9131
Fax (610) 853-9146
Email: casemate@casematepublishers.com
www.casematepublishers.com

CASEMATE PUBLISHERS (UK)
Telephone (01865) 241249
Fax (01865) 794449
Email: casemate-uk@casematepublishers.co.uk
www.casematepublishers.co.uk

Contents

Preamble

My father was inspired to start work on the research for this book by a number of events, not least the 25th anniversary of the First Battle of Alamein in 1967. On 2 July 2017 it will be 75 years since the battle and that only reinforces the desire to see my father's work finally published.

As an amateur historian, he was concerned about being accurate, something that as a trained actuary he probably needed to worry less about than he did. As a person who could generally complete the challenging *Times* crossword puzzle in less than ten minutes, he was also probably the right person to try and unravel this quite complex story. I am sure that he would agree with Professor Mary Beard when she wrote in her book *SPQR* on the history of Rome that: 'Reconstructing the history of this period is an intriguing and sometimes tantalising process, and part of the fun comes from wondering how some of the pieces of the incomplete jigsaw puzzle fit together ...'

My father worked on the research well into the 1990s as his health started to deteriorate. He had been there, on Ruweisat, on 2 July 1942 and in fact remained there until November that year, but was aware that his own view of the events was only one view. He developed and maintained an extensive correspondence with many others who had been there. He made copious notes, read extensively on the subject and talked with those high and low who could contribute. He made a series of undated working drafts, but, due to ill health was never able to complete the work.

His concern was not to glorify war. It was to provide missing knowledge about the day when Rommel was finally stopped and the tide of the Second World War started to turn in the Allies' favour. Even more importantly, it was to provide some better recognition to the men of the very diverse small force that came together as Robcol that day and which was described a few days later by the commander, Brigadier Rob Waller as 'being nobody's child'. His ambition was to trace as many as possible of those who had been there. In the event, there remain some gaps, but I hope you will agree that he came close.

Although my father took responsibility for the accuracy of this history at the time that he was writing the drafts, ultimately, the errors and omissions in editing the papers that make up this book must be mine alone.

Chris Jephson
Copenhagen, Denmark
February 2017

Abbreviations

ACV	Armoured Command Vehicle
AGPO	Assistant Gun Position Officer
ATS	Auxiliary Territorial Service
'Auk'	General Sir Claude Auchinleck
BGS	Brigadier General Staff
BRA	Brigadier Royal Artillery
BSM	Battalion Sergeant Major
BTE	British Troops in Egypt
CB	Order of the Bath
CBE	Commander British Empire
CO	Commanding Officer
Cols	Columns
CPO	Command Post Officer
CRA	Commander Royal Artillery
CRE	Commander Royal Engineers
CSI	Order of the Star of India
DAK	Deutsche Afrika Korps
DCM	Distinguished Conduct Medal
Div	Division
DL	Doctor of Letters
DSO	Distinguished Service Order
FDL	Forward Defensive or Defended Locality
GCB	Order of the Bath, Grand Cross

GCIE	Order of the Indian Empire, Grand Cross
GCMG	Order of St Michael and St George
GOC	General Officer Commanding
GPO	Gun Position Officer
HAC	Honourable Artillery Company
HMSO	Her Majesty's Stationary Office
KBE	Knight Commander British Empire
KCB	Knight Commander of the Order of the Bath
KCIE	Knight Commander Order of the Indian Empire
KT	Knight Bachelor
LAD	Light Aid Detachment
LO	Liaison Officer
MC	Military Cross
MM	Military Medal
MT	Motorized Transport
NCO	Non-Commissioned Officer
OBE	Order of the British Empire
OP	Observation Post
POW	Prisoner of War
RA	Royal Artillery
RHA	Royal Horse Artillery
RQMS	Regimental Quartermaster Sergeant
TD	Territorial Decoration
VC	Victoria Cross

Main Protagonists

AUCHINLECK, General Sir Claude: Commander in Chief, Middle East, later Field Marshal, GCB, GCIE, CSI, DSO, OBE. Known as 'The Auk'.

FREYBERG, General Bernard: Commander of 2nd New Zealand Expeditionary Force, later 1st Baron Freyberg, VC, GCMG, KCB, DSO and 3 Bars.

GOTT, General William 'Strafer': Commander XIII Corps, later Lt. General CB, CBE, DSO and Bar, MC.

HOLMES, General William: Commander British Troops in Egypt, later Lieutenant General Sir William Holmes, KBE, CB, DSO and Bar.

KESSELRING, Albert: Overall German Commander in the Mediterranean theatre.

KIPPENBERGER, Brigadier Howard: 5th New Zealand Brigade, later Major General Sir Howard Kippenberger, KBE, CB, DSO, ED.

LUMSDEN, General Herbert: Commander 1st Armoured Division, later Lieutenant General, CB, DSO and Bar, MC.

MELLENTHIN, General Friedrich von: Staff Officer in the Afrika Korps.

MONTGOMERY, Lieutenant General Bernard Law: later Field Marshal, 1st Viscount Montgomery of Alamein, KG, GCB, DSO, PC.

NICHOLS, General John 'Crasher': later Major General, DSO and Bar, MC and Bar, Commander 50th (Northumbrian) Infantry Division.

NOBLE, Colonel Arthur: Commander, 1st/4th Essex, later Sir Arthur Noble, KBE, CB, DSO, TD, DL.

NORRIE, General Charles Willoughby: later Lieutenant General, 1st Baron Norrie, GCMG, GCVO, CB, DSO, MC and Bar.

O'CONNOR, Lieutenant General Richard: Commander Western Desert Force, later Lieutenant General Sir Richard O'Connor, KT, GCB, GBE, DSO and Bar, MC.

O'GOWAN, Major General Eric Dorman: The Auk's Acting Chief of the General Staff.

PIENAAR, General Dan: Commander South African Forces, later Major General, CB, DSO and 2 Bars.

RAMSDEN, General William: later Major General, CB, CBE, DSO, MC, Commander XXX Corps.

RINTELEN, General Enno von: German Infantry Commander.

ROMMEL, Erwin: General, later Field Marshal.

RUSSEL 'Pasha': Commander of 5th Indian Infantry Brigade, later General Sir Dudley Russel, KBE, CB, DSO, MC.

STANTON, Major Anthony: Battery Commander, later Major General Anthony Stanton, OBE.

TUKER, General 'Gertie': Commander 4th Indian Division, later Lieutenant General Sir Francis Tuker, KCIE, CB, DSO, OBE.

WALLER, Brigadier Rob: DSO, MC, DL, CRA, 10th Indian Division and Commander of Robcol.

WIDDUP, Lt. Malcolm: Provided the brief description of 3rd RHA's part in the battle. We lived opposite one another in a private road in Surrey and would never have known how close we passed at this time if it had not been for the kindness of his wife in typing some of the early drafts of these pages.

Dedication

A battle is many things to many men. To some it is final and total, to others it is a sustained and terrible ordeal leaving them lacerated with grievous wounds. To all it is an immersion in elemental violence testing body, mind and spirit to the limits. Within the vortex of battle, individuals by their endurance and courage, and by rare deeds of extraordinary valour, will have contributed to victory, or to survival. Those who have remained steadfast will have helped to maintain the subtle links of morale, contributing to the steadfastness of all. Their names will never be known, and their reward will be that they have discovered resources in themselves of which they might otherwise have remained forever unaware. No man who has endured the ordeal of battle is ever quite the same again. He is usually better equipped to face whatever life may hold for him, including death.

There are many unrecorded battles on a small scale, involving perhaps no more than a company of men, a squadron of armour, in which the experience of those involved is total. A major battle is made up of numerous such encounters. The horizons of the ordinary soldier are not wide.[1]

This passage from *The Montgomery Legend* was chosen as a dedication because it explains so clearly what this book is about – an unrecorded encounter on a small scale in which a few men who remained steadfast helped to maintain the steadiness of all. Robcol's horizon was bounded by Ruweisat Ridge. On that ridge – the key point to Alamein – the leading players displayed resources of which they were probably unaware and suffered wounds which, many years later, still bled. They were indeed never quite the same again.

This dedication is addressed to my sons, Christopher and Nicholas. In painting for them a picture of a few men who 'kept their head when all about them' they know that I do not wish to glorify war.

It is, however, a typical paradox of life that this waste of every resource calls forth life's highest virtues. The leadership of two or three great men and the steadfastness of the few who followed them, are examples which they have tried to emulate in what has been at least for them, a more peaceful struggle.

I did not need to dedicate this book to my wife. Although, on volunteering in Leamington for more active service overseas she had had to give up the stripe of a lance corporal, when I married W/212412 Pte Poole, D. M. at the Church of St Michael and All Angels at Heliopolis on 16 March 1945 she was already wearing an Africa Star.

'Jeph' Jephson
Guildford

Captain F. R. 'Jeph' Jephson, MC, TD, in 1942. (Author's collection)

July 1942

'The month that was ignored by the historians and writers of memoirs'[1]

Today, the word Alamein, if it has any meaning to the reader, refers to a battle which started on 23 October 1942 at 2140 hours and ended on 2 November with the breakthrough of the Eighth Army under Montgomery. It is, rightly, associated with great gallantry by the 51st Highland Division and the 9th Australian Division. If you have ever watched one of the occasional replays of the film *Desert Victory* on TV, this is the picture you will have in your mind, lit by the flashes of a thousand guns. If you were particularly quick-sighted, you may even have seen the author of this history shout 'Fire!' into a megaphone at the start of the barrage which was the prelude to those ten historic days.

There is only one thing wrong with this view of history. It is not true. Neither the Highlanders not the Australians were present when the battle of Alamein commenced. Nor was Montgomery – and the view of your author crying havoc and letting slip the dogs of war, though a pleasant conceit, is not true either. The film from which this still is taken was shot nearly four months earlier, on 4 or 5 July to be precise. And, by that date, the events of this history had already taken place. Those who were there know them as First Alamein, a battle which took place in the first four days of July 1942. The facts are these:

At dusk on Wednesday 1 July 1942, Rommel broke through the centre of our defences at Alamein. His tanks overwhelmed the gallant defence of the 18th Indian Infantry Brigade in the Deir el Shein at the foot of

Ruweisat Ridge, the ridge which commands the whole area between the high ground around Alamein station and the Qattara Depression. At that moment, and for the next 12 hours, there was no further organized defence between the spearhead of the Afrika Korps and Alexandria, which they expected to enter in a few hours. Throughout the next day, only a handful of men and guns stood between him and his prize. In Cairo, clouds of smoke from burning files showed that many people believed Rommel would not stop short of the Suez Canal, his stated objective.

But, on Friday 3 July at 2256 hours, only 48 hours after his original breakthrough, Rommel called off his attack and ordered his troops to dig in where they stood. The Delta was saved – and who knows what else besides?

This story is concerned with the interval between these two events – Thursday 2 July 1942 – the day we stopped losing the war.

As Winston Churchill wrote of the year 1942: 'For the first six months all went ill: for the last six months all went well. And this agreeable change continued to the end of the struggle.'

King George VI's biographer, Sir John Wheeler-Bennett, is even more explicit: 'The actual turning of the tide in the 2nd World War may be accurately determined as the first week of July 1942.' We can be yet more exact: the tide turned at about 2100 hours on 2 July 1942 when Rommel's tanks withdrew for the first time since the fall of Tobruk on 20 June or even earlier, since the opening of the German offensive on 26 May.

But, this was unknown in London where Churchill, in the last 48 hours had been facing a bitter Vote of Censure which was defeated on the afternoon of 2 July, at the very climax of the events in the desert. After the vote, Churchill dined with Eden. They will have talked of the danger which Convoy PQ 17 was at that moment facing in northern waters. They may have talked of the danger which Malta was facing from the Luftwaffe and the Italian Fleet. They probably worried about the safety of the Mediterranean Fleet in Alexandria. They almost certainly knew that the fall of Sebastopol was imminent. They did not know of the events on Ruweisat and it seems likely that they discussed the Auk's replacement at the very moment that his personal leadership in the field in the last days of June and his courageous decision earlier in the month to strip his northern flank was about to pay off.

For the 18th Indian Infantry Brigade which took the brunt of the initial attack on 1 July, and the guns of the small column known as Robcol which stopped Rommel on 2 and 3 July, were, in mid-June, in northern Iraq. The Auk's desperate measure of pulling them 1,500 miles from Iraq into the Western Desert just succeeded, but it greatly increased the price of failure. If Robcol had failed, it is doubtful if Rommel would have stopped at the Canal and it does not require much imagination to see his forces threatening to link up with Barbarossa in the Ukraine.

There were many troops, it is true, in the Middle East and the battle maps show the flags of many units, but by now, these were largely bereft of their armour and their guns. Without these, the bravest bodies can, in desert conditions, present little resistance to even a small force of determined armour.

Be that as it may, it is certain that, on 2 July 1942, Rommel's expectation of entering Alexandria within hours and Mussolini's hope of shortly riding through the streets of Cairo on a white charger which was already waiting in Derna, were both dashed on Ruweisat Ridge. It is also certain that the survivors of that small force have no doubt about the fact that this was the turn of the tide that might have overwhelmed the whole Middle East.

There are other reasons, perhaps even more compelling. When you read of the gallantry of Bombardier Johnson you will recognize one of them – particularly as he never received the Victoria Cross which he undoubtedly earned. Brigadier Waller, too, received no honour for his great achievement. Indeed, shortly after the battle, he too was removed from command and his last years were reminiscent of the tragedy of King Lear. Finally, 11th Field, the proud Royal Artillery regiment which provided the guns of Robcol, was 'placed in suspended animation', a fate which it might have avoided at the time had it received the battle honour 'Ruweisat' which it surely won.

Before we get into the story of the guns, this failure to win recognition deserves a moment's thought. We shall see that these events did not pass totally unrecorded – or even totally unacknowledged. Were they swamped by the massive public relations exercise which, as Corelli Barnett and R. W. Thompson have pointed out, was mounted when Montgomery took over in August? To a degree, yes. But, this is not enough reason.

Did the writers of memoirs, the lack of which Connell so eloquently deplores, fail to keep them up to date in the turbulence of retreat – or even destroy them facing the possibility of capture by the enemy? Again, yes. Some records were destroyed and even some official war diaries were clearly written after the battle and show discrepancies of 24 hours or omissions of important detail, which does not make the search for truth any easier.

One reason for this is that units were spread over enormous areas and that headquarters did not know even their own order of battle. Even in Robcol, 11th Field had lost its B Echelon, its supply vehicles, and some guns in Mersa Matruh, while the infantry had sent some of its men back to Cairo.

Back with them had gone all non-combatants. The record of Alamein owes much to its articulate war correspondents, such as Alan Moorehead, Fred Majdalany, Alexander Clifford and Denis Johnston. On 2 July, they were not there: they were reliant on their conducting officers for their opportunity to see history as it was made and, before this battle, all war correspondents had been withdrawn to the Delta where at least one of them was wisely putting his wife and baby on a train to Palestine.

Perhaps these are some of the reasons why one volume of *The Official History of the Second World War* ends with a clear description of events to the end of June and the next picks up the thread about 5 July.

In the missing four days, a small force called Robcol came together from distant parts, as if carried before the wind of the desert. They suffered heavy losses and were dispersed as they had come. This is the story of what they achieved on one of the days they were together.

June 1967–October 1968

As the 25th anniversary of Ruweisat drew near, the memory of the action and the realization of its significance grew sharper in the minds of the small band of survivors. In the years immediately after the war, the need to earn a living, often to start a second or third career and to provide for young families, had pushed this memory from the forefront of their minds. But now it became a little harder each September to watch the annual celebration of the Battle of Britain when the nation's debt to an even smaller band of men had not once been acknowledged. Even the annual remembrance of Alamein every 23 October caused some pain because it totally ignored the events of early July.

True, there had been a short article in *The Royal Artillery Commemoration Book 1939–1945* entitled 'Who Stopped Rommel?' but it was incomplete and in some important details incorrect. Lieutenant General Martin had reviewed the book in 1950 in the *Daily Telegraph* but the review had failed to capture sufficient attention for any definitive answer to the question in its title.

None the less, occasional references to Robcol (sometimes under the guise of '50 Div. Cols.') and to the critical nature of the fighting in the first days of July in books by Sir Arthur Bryant, Sir Brian Horrocks, Sir John Kennedy, Sir David Hunt, Lord Tedder and Lord Alexander, to name a few, held a promise that the facts would some day emerge.

By 1967, the men of Robcol were already full in years. Rob Waller himself was in his seventies, many of those who figure in this history were around fifty. It is an age at which men, while not without hope of future victories, begin to reflect on past achievements.

Early in 1967, an issue of the weekly magazine *History of the Second World War* was devoted to First Alamein by Major General Eric Dorman O'Gowan, the Auk's Acting Chief of the General Staff. It made reference to a 'British 25-pounder field gun which was in action at Ruweisat Ridge on 2nd July 1942' in the Imperial War Museum:

> This gun served with the 11th Field Regiment, Royal Artillery. It was in action at Ruweisat Ridge on 2nd July 1942, when the Regiment played an important part in halting the German advance on Cairo after Rommel had broken through the Alamein line. The 11th Field Regiment together with a company of the Essex Regiment, held the ridge all day, beating off repeated tank and infantry attacks.
>
> Out of about 300 officers and men actively engaged, 87 were killed or wounded. Some 20 German tanks were disabled or destroyed.

The desert sand prickled my eyes, blowing cold across the hall of the Imperial War Museum. My gun, one of *my* guns in this place! It must have been March 1946 when I had last seen this gun, in Salonika ... and must have first seen its smooth lines in Meerut in 1941. On 2 July 1942 – as the Imperial War Museum stood witness – this gun found its place in history.

In a few days, it would be 2 July 1967. Just 25 years before, this was one of nine guns which gave teeth to an 'insignificant little force' which was effectively all that stood between Rommel and the Delta and – as the museum here testified – the Alamein line was broken. It is ironic to think that tens of thousands of visitors have stared at that symbol of the regiment with no realization of the full significance of its message.

At the time, one was sadly aware of the approaching 25th anniversary of that critical day. Some casual remark of my eldest son had made me anxious to get it down on paper – it seemed odd that he would never know the miracle that was a jerry can. Stranger still, to look at him and his brother and realize that they could feel neither the anguish nor the ecstasy of those events which, before I met their mother, had built so much of my character for good and for evil. It suddenly seemed important to make some record for them, however inadequate, of that critical time. In so doing, too, it would quieten in some measure those feelings of guilt towards the friends who fell that day without recognition – perhaps even without the customary, difficult letter to their next-of-kin.

With two fingers on a battered old portable, notes were started of references to 2 July 1942 from many books. Many contained brief mentions of this little battle. All pointed to the fact that in those few hours of daylight the war reached its climax – in the desert and in London.

In London, Churchill faced a House of Commons highly critical of the government's conduct of the war and beat off a Vote of Censure by all but 25 votes. In the desert, on Ruweisat Ridge – at almost the same hour – the last of the nine guns faced the last few tanks of the Deutsches Afrika Korps (DAK). By nightfall, help had arrived and the panzer strength was reduced to 26 runners. In both places it had been a close thing, but the importance of the political battle had obscured the climax of the fighting on land. Nowhere had the nine guns received their full recognition.

And then, in the weekly publication *History of the Second World War* Volume III, Number 5, a reference to a display of weapons, uniforms and equipment used by both sides in the Battle of Gazala caught my eye. The mention of a British 25-pounder field gun which was in action at Ruweisat Ridge on 2 July 1942 brought me across the Geraldine Mary Harmsworth Park, Lord Rothermere's memorial to his mother. There were other guns at Ruweisat Ridge that day, but the one chosen to represent this action had to be from the 83rd/85th Field Battery, Royal Artillery. The '3s and 5s' would remember 2 July and Ruweisat, as our sister Battery, 78th/84th Field Battery RA, would remember 3 July, at the same place and as other gunners would remember other rendezvous with fate at Bir Aslagh, Sidi Rezegh and other names by which, in 1942, we knew one patch of desert from another.

Despite growing certainty as I entered the museum, the shock when it came, drew forth a shudder and a choked 'That's one of *my* guns!' The phlegmatic attendant was not visibly impressed. Undoubtedly other, more famous, soldiers had met their past in his presence. The 2nd of July was a date with little obvious meaning for him. Why should it thrill him? Few Englishmen would recognize it. All the books I had read in recent months pointed to it as a critical date, but none gave a clear picture of its events as they actually happened. Some even forced me to question the beliefs which had led me to adopt the unaccustomed mantle of Clio, the muse of history.

E Troop, 11th Field Regiment RA's 25-pounder Quick Firing Gun, Mark II on display at the Imperial War Museum. (© IWM-1989-50-31)

Of course, on 2 July 1942, this wasn't really my gun. That day I was some distance behind the guns in a scrabbled shallow trench as Battery Command Post Officer. But it was almost certainly mine a few days later when, with both troop commanders wounded, I was promoted to command the surviving members as a troop of the 11th HAC and later, in Italy and Greece, when I took over the battery – the 83rd/85th Field Battery RA, the '3s and 5s'.

The museum attendant, thought outwardly sceptical, was helpful. He directed my steps into a creaking lift and up a spiral staircase into the dome of the building which housed the reference library. An amateur historian, without such help, could remain forever ignorant of this mine of warlike information. My phlegmatic friend's advice and that which I subsequently received in the library from Mr Rigby and his colleagues were vital links in the chain of events which, after so many years, have made this history possible. If this is the appropriate place to record my gratitude, I do so with the greatest pleasure. Without their support this would never have been written.

The library quickly yielded a document, written some time after the war as the reference to new battery numbers showed. Although I originally thought this had been written by officers of 11th Field, later research strongly suggested it had been written as an attempt by Lieutenant Colonel E. H. Colville, DSO, the commanding officer in 1951, to gain the battle honour 'Ruweisat' for the regiment. This failed as the evidence of several key figures whose testimony is included here were not available to Colonel Colville. Entitled 'Ruweisat Ridge – 2nd July 1942', it briefly described the action in terms which left no doubt that the author shared my view on the importance of this date:

> [T]he situation was critical. Tobruk, with its garrison, had been lost on the 20th June. On 1st July pm, the German Panzers in an all-out attack, had overwhelmed the 18th Indian Infantry Brigade in their box at Deir el Shein, and only a handful of men and guns separated Rommel from Alexandria and the Nile Delta. Perhaps not many of these men realised their high destiny. The Alamein line was broken, the road to Cairo and Alexandria lay open, and the fate of the Eighth Army, of Egypt even, and who can tell what besides, was in their hands.

The final sentence of this document runs: 'For the period during which the Eighth Army held the Alamein Line, the FDL's ran through the position occupied by 11th Field Regiment R.A. on 2nd July 42.'

The line, which was broken, had been held.

My doubts in the beliefs which I had held for so many years faded once more. They finally vanished – for good – at the discovery of a document dated 28 February 1946 and addressed to Deputy Assistant Adjutant (DAA), The War Office. It was signed by the BRA, Scottish Command – Brigadier R. P. Waller, the commander of Robcol. No one could speak of that day's fighting with more authority than he and he wrote:

> [On] the evening of 1st July '42 ... the Alamein Line was broken. The only troops available to stop the gap was [sic] a Battle Group forming a few miles to the East, the core of which was 11th Field Regiment RA and a battalion of the Essex Regiment (5th Indian Infantry Brigade). But for their determined stand, it is extremely probable that his [Rommel's] troops would have been in Alexandria next day. There was nothing else to stop him. In effect, it was decisive despite the small number of troops engaged on our side.

My memory of events was stimulated by the recorded facts. This confirmed the need for the story of 2 July to be told, not in a family diary, but for all to read. The anniversary of this date must be celebrated. Its main players must receive the honours which we were too ignorant, too shaken, or too busy to accord them at the time.

And then doubt returned – for the last time. No longer directed at the basis of my story but at my own ability to tell it. Could an amateur view of history, and of necessity a personal one, interest a wider audience? Could this achieve the circulation necessary to make publication possible and worthwhile?

At this stage, it would have been so easy to give up if the *Daily Mail* had not carried the 'Last Word', the sporting article on its back page written by J. L. 'Jim' Manning, son of L. V. Manning, famous sports commentator of my childhood. Jim, too, served in the 11th Field Regiment RA – not on 2 July 1942, but a year later when we were joined by a third battery under a later establishment. His advice would be interested, but unbiased, and professional. It was quickly given and enthusiastic. This story must be written, but first we had to commemorate the anniversary of the battle fought 25 years before.

Through his help, *The Times* of Saturday 1 July 1967 carried this short passage in its 'Diary Column':

EL ALAMEIN'S GALLANT GUNNERS

Nine guns against Rommel
Did nine guns thwart Rommel's advance on Alexandria and deal the deciding blow for the Allies in the battle of El Alamein? The question, so far unanswered by chroniclers of the Western Desert battles, has now come under scrutiny from one of the surviving members of the scratch Robcol brigade whose 25 pounders entrenched in Ruweisat Ridge crippled the vanguard of the two advancing Panzer Divisions.

'It seems to me that little or nothing has been said about the stand which I feel was the deciding factor in the desert battle,' says Mr F. R. Jephson, who has been delving into the history of his old brigade's stand on July 2nd, 25 years ago. 'If the ridge had gone, the Alamein line would have been broken before it began to exist.'

Robcol, led by Brigadier Rob Waller of 10th Indian Division, was in existence for only a few hours. Its guns were brought to the ridge by a 1,500-mile forced march. 'The insignificance of the force probably explains why so little has been said about it,' says Mr Jephson. 'So far my probing has produced a convincing file on the stand. I'm out to find out just how important this stand was to the El Alamein victory.'

It is interesting to note what General von Mellenthin, Rommel's chief of staff, wrote of the day following Robcol's stand: 'Everyone realized that the German offensive … had at last come to an end.' Of the nine guns, two were destroyed, six were repairable and one was still firing.

The article was not quite phrased as I had hoped. Casualties would have been fewer if the guns had, indeed, been 'entrenched'. No mention of our infantry. Bombardier Johnson's gallant death not mentioned, but up and down England a handful of survivors knew that the memory of 2 July 1942 and Ruweisat still held meaning for someone.

Within a week, letters from Colonel Arthur Noble, CO of the 1st/4th Essex Regiment and Brigadier R. P. Waller, commander of Robcol, were my reward. My account of 2 July 1942 no longer rested on my own failing memory and inadequate research. Authoritative voices were raised to support my story of the 'day we stopped losing the war'.

An amateur historian has so much to learn! In the preceding pages, I had wondered about the name of the action which I had been trying to unravel and had opted initially for 'The Guns of Robcol'. On Friday 6 October 1968, I learned in the library of the RA Institution, Woolwich that my labours have been – to a degree at least – in vain: the battle was already named.

It had been a peculiar journey to Woolwich. Sacrificing a day's holiday to travel into London, arriving at the Waterloo so clearly inscribed with words about the abandonment of hope. Crossing, against the taxis, from the familiar daily sorting point to an unknown Waterloo, a Waterloo of strange Kentish names. And then suddenly the realization that the unfamiliar train ran along tracks to which I was not a total stranger. Along this railway line, a young subaltern had travelled from the RA Base Depot to the fleshpots in December 1940. God, was it so long ago! So little seemed to have changed, but me.

To a gunner, Woolwich is home and as I marched, as nearly as middle age allowed, in a 'smart and soldierly fashion' across the square, I had feelings akin to those which I would today experience crossing the Market Place in Ripley, Derbyshire, where I was born. In Woolwich a gunner should not need to ask the way to the nearest toilets! After all, even at the age of 50, my gunner service represented almost one quarter of my adult life. But, in seven and a half years of soldiering, Woolwich claimed only a few days – around Christmas 1940. The parade ground reminded me of the red sky over the docks that December night when Goering first went for the river front with fire bombs. That night, indeed, one could read a newspaper with ease outside the mess at midnight.

A few days later I woke up in a train as a clock struck midnight. Midnight 31 December 1940. The train would end its journey at Gourock in Scotland and, for me, the next staging post would be with 11th Field in Meerut, India. The clock had a familiar ring and a familiar face. It was the clock of the Refuge Assurance Company, seen from Oxford Road station, Manchester. Fate had chosen a surprising New Year's Eve resting place for one who had worked for four years as an actuarial student in the Refuge! Only a few hundred yards on the other side was Ardwick Green and the mess of the Manchester Artillery (52nd Field Regiment RA, TA) in which I had spent much of the last summer of peace and all the first days of the war.

In the Woolwich mess itself, the ante-rooms and the bar had an air of modernity which defeated sentimentality, but the dining room led to a flood of nostalgia. The long, polished tables welcomed me back as an old friend – and waited for friends who would not return. The older diners had faces which I did not remember, but the younger officers looked vaguely familiar. At the head of the table a line of ATS waitresses made memory complete; but now of course, they were called WRACS. Never mind the name. They looked just like those who served before them. There was a further difference at the far end. The portrait of George VI had moved to a side wall, giving place to his daughter and Prince Philip.

The privilege of sitting once more at this table overwhelmed me and I made a mental note to record the kindness of my host. Lieutenant Colonel Peter Coats offered hospitality to a virtual stranger; Brigadier Donald Tarr whom I met for the first time; Brigadier Peter Mead, Secretary of the RA Institution; even Major General Hughes, Colonel Commandant, who showed interest as I walked around the display of RA mess silver. The sight of this stimulated the memory without awakening it, but, as I left the building, I looked up at the ceiling for the marks of the fire bomb and remembered drinking my coffee so many years ago in an air raid and wondering whether the replastered ceiling would hold. My host followed my eyes and confirmed a memory which was too vivid to need confirmation. Through the years it had been kept alive by the Royal Artillery String Band playing, as they played that night, the regimental slow march, 'The Duchess of Kent'. That beautiful princess, too, had died while these chapters have had their slow birth.

My memory strayed to Wimbledon occasions and another martial event 150 years after 18 June 1815, when another lady to bear the name of Kent showed similar graciousness at a cricket match in Brussels and a ball re-enacting the Eve of Waterloo. One would like to think that 2 July 1942 would be so remembered.

At least, now I could give that date a name independent of my own desires. Brigadier Mead had opened the door to the RA library, Woolwich. One of its first yields was a book entitled *The Official Names of the Battles, Actions and Engagements fought by the Land Forces of the Commonwealth during the Second World War 1939–1945* (HMSO). With the authority of Brigadier H. B. Latham, Historical Section, Cabinet Office, I could now state that in 'The Defence of the Alamein Line' (1–27 July), the 'Enemy Offensive [was] Halted' and that between Deir el Shein (1 July) and Ruweisat Ridge (14–16 July), the 'Action on Ruweisat' took place from 2–4 July.[1]

CHAPTER I

Prelude

The story of Robcol is a story of a small mixed force – infantry and other arms centred round a small number of guns. It is a story which is always worth the telling, but it is one which was repeated many times during the desert days. The gallantry of 11th Field on Ruweisat Ridge was, in itself, no greater than that of many similar regiments in similar actions. '*L'histoire se renouvelle éternellement*' even if it differs in its points of detail.

I would not like it to be thought that my pride in Robcol and the 11th Field Regiment RA had made me any less conscious of the gallantry of those other 25-pounder regiments which fought to the death in many theatres of war – but above all in the desert because of the terrain and because of the wretched little 2-pounder guns with which our tanks and our anti-tank units were equipped. Gunners are ubiquitous and, in war, gallantry is commonplace. The significance of 2 July 1942 is that on that day we stopped losing the war.

It should be a significant date to Britons yet few readers are likely to ever have seen it in print before. Already doubt may be creeping across your faces and my sanity impugned. However, if this is so, I am not alone in my folly! It is a fact which has never been much publicized, but which scores of commentators have acknowledged. So many indeed, that the bulk of their testimony must be relegated to addendum 3 if we are ever to get into the events of the actual fighting.

But, let us start by firing a big gun again. The biographer of King George VI, Sir John Wheeler-Bennett, in his book of that name as we have seen, wrote: 'The actual turning of the tide in the Second World War may be accurately determined as the first week of July 1942,' He added, 'After Rommel was repulsed at El Alamein on July 2nd and turned away in deference to British resistance, the Germans never again mounted a major offensive in North Africa.'

Winston Churchill too, had pinpointed this point of the war, but unfortunately in words which are capable of misinterpretation. To most people, Alamein means 23 October 1942. In his book *The Second World War* Volume IV, he wrote: 'Before Alamein we never had a victory. After Alamein we never had a defeat.'

This change took place in the desert, for this was where British land forces were in contact with the enemy, but before we come to this theatre of war, let us take a quick look at the overall scene at the end of June 1942.

The Allied cause had reached its nadir. Anthony Eden described the situation:

> [M]any blows fell, during the early months of 1942, on the three countries which now had to fight together. In the Far East a succession of disasters overwhelmed Malaya, the Philippines, Singapore, the Dutch East Indies and Burma, exposing the whole Pacific and Indian Oceans to the enemy. In the Middle East we once again lost the ground gained by Auchinleck's winter offensive and at midsummer Rommel stood near the gates of Alexandria and the Nile Delta. In Russia the German summer offensive penetrated farther than in the previous year, deep into the Caucasus and to the Volga at Stalingrad.[1]

Let us for a minute review this 'succession of disasters' in the Far East. In addition to the major disasters he mentions Hong Kong had gone, our battleships *Prince of Wales* and *Repulse* had been sunk, Ceylon and Burma were threatened and thus the Indian mainland where the Indian political leaders were in any case agitating for their independence. Nearer at home Malta was starving, and in danger of imminent attack, Greece was lost, also Crete, Turkish Anatolia threatened. Almost the whole coast of North Africa was under Axis control. Rommel was at the gates of Cairo. If it fell Abadan and the Persian Gulf were in jeopardy.

Thompson adds: 'The loss of Abadan and Bahrain would be "calamitous", a loss of thirteen and a half million tons of oil a year to be found elsewhere, and demanding an estimated tanker fleet of 270 vessels to carry it' He continues: 'It was the Auk who really saved us all. The British have never contemplated the abyss which yawned before the Allies in June/July 1942, and so do not appreciate the man who hauled everyone else back to safety. But nobody likes to think that such a situation had ever arisen.'

But, this is to anticipate the story of the 2 July! Let us now leave 'our' war, and turn to the fighting of those who were at that time our strongest ally. Again, we find that these days had a special significance:

> After the winter battles for Moscow, Leningrad, and Kharkov, the Wehrmacht High Command drew up its plans for the second German attempt to crush the USSR. Hitler was utterly confident that the coming campaign would end the war in Russia – but the new plan was very different from the three-pronged, frontal assault of 'Barbarossa' in the previous year. The weight of the Wehrmacht was now directed against the south: two Panzer armies, and the strengthened [Sixth] Army under Paulus, were to smash through to the Volga and conquer the oilfields of Georgia to the line of the Caucasus, with the long-term sequel of a huge flanking move up the Volga to take Moscow from the east.
>
> The immediate targets were the Don and Volga crossings at Voronezh and Stalingrad – and the oil, Hitler's chief obsession. This plan was, in terms of grand strategy, as breath-taking as the original aims of 'Barbarossa' and the new German offensive in Russia was to coincide with Rommel's triumphant career in North Africa. The summer of 1942 marked the nadir of Allied fortunes in the Middle East; the Axis strategists began hopefully to think in terms of vast advances from Egypt, the Caucasus, and the Balkan bases to conquer the other oil regions of the Middle East.
>
> On June 30, the 24th day of the offensive, the Germans succeeded in breaking through to Sebastopol, and that evening the Soviet evacuation began. It lasted until July 3rd.
>
> On July 3rd Sebastopol fell: one of the world's strongest fortresses had at last been overwhelmed. Two Soviet armies had been crushed in the battle, some 90,000 prisoners had been taken by the Germans.[2]

To aid our Russian allies enormous sacrifices were being made – oddly enough the First Protocol defining this aid ran until 30 June 1942. The Americans were sending large quantities of supplies via Iran and, despite shipping losses running into millions of tons, the Murmansk convoys were sailing from British ports. At 2 p.m. on 3 July the battleship *Tirpitz* and the heavy cruiser *Admiral Hipper* left Trondheim and a few hours later, convoy PQ 17 met disaster mainly from Luftwaffe and U-boat attacks, losing 24 out of 35 merchant ships.

Wherever one looks, it was a scene of calamity. But in all this hopelessness there were two points where great victories were being won. The first was in London, in the Houses of Parliament, the second in the desert, some 60 miles outside Alexandria. If either had been lost, it is difficult to guess what course the war might have run.

Let us deal with the battle in the Commons first.

Here Churchill, tired after his second visit to America, where with Roosevelt, he had heard of the fall of Tobruk, was fighting for his political life as a result of a heavy swing against the government in a by-election in Maldon. As in the desert, the first shots were fired on 1 July.

Gerald Pawle tells how the British government under Churchill was described as 'the greatest friends Hitler ever had' in the debate on a Vote of Censure. Lord Winterton and Emmanuel Shinwell spoke against the Government, as did Mr Silverman.

While this was happening, to quote Pawle again, 'On the day the Censure debate opened, Rommel's Afrika Korps reached El Alamein, the last position which offered any real defensive advantage before the Nile Delta.'[3]

On the second day, among others, Hore-Belisha spoke against the government, but according to the writer, the only really effective opposition speech was made by Aneurin Bevan. By 4 p.m. the political battle was over. Churchill had spoken, announcing among other things that the Auk had taken over direct command of the Eighth Army from 25 June, and the Vote of Censure was finally defeated by 475 votes to 25 with Winterton and Shinwell abstaining. According to Eden: 'July 2nd: Winston wound up with one of his most effective speeches, beautifully adjusted to the temper of the House. Work at the Office. Then dined with him alone except for his brother. Much discussion of war situation.'[4]

Commander C. R Thompson, Churchill's aide, speaking of this vote said: 'In its way this was a turning-point in the war, both politically and militarily. Churchill had won his mandate. Soon it was to be reinforced and proudly sustained by a dramatic change in Allied fortunes.'[5]

And R. W. Thompson wrote later of this day: 'Few, if any, in high places harboured doubts that they were living in the decisive hours of the war.' And a few lines further on, quoting Churchill: 'It seemed that we should reach a climax on the Parliamentary and Desert fronts at the same moment.'[6]

In fact, the climax in the desert came a few hours after the climax in London. When Churchill sat down in Westminster, the last small force which divided Rommel from Cairo and Alexandria had suffered grievous casualties. As he sat down to dinner with his brother and Eden, the battle could still have been lost. After dinner Brendan Bracken arrived. Eden describes how Churchill said repeatedly that we had not done as well as we should: 'I am ashamed,' he said. Perhaps as he spoke, the German armour and infantry on Ruweisat Ridge turned and withdrew to the west for the first time since Tobruk.

But Churchill did not know. To Brendan Bracken he suggested a visit to the Middle East. His first resolve was taken to sack Auchinleck, the man who had just won the first round at Alamein. Although persuaded not to go by Brendan Bracken and Alan Brooke, he went a month later and the Auk was replaced on 8 August 1942.

CHAPTER 2

No Eighth Army Clasp

'In deserts where no men abide, thou must have uncommended died'[1]

In some respects, it is strange that no one has yet detailed the many happenings of that day, because there is so much to record. In London, Churchill fought his personal battle in the House of Commons. At the Admiralty, Sir Dudley Pound was taking decisions about a convoy in the Baltic which would give rise to controversial correspondence in *The Times* 25 years later when the Russian ambassador published his memoirs. In Sebastopol the defenders were living through the last hours of their agony.

In Cairo, an hotelkeeper lost an important customer. In the Rue des Soeurs, later so happily renamed Montgomery Street by a whimsical King Farouk, the girls were primping themselves in readiness for their new clients or tearfully preparing to bid adieu to their former protectors. Waiters at Shepheard's Hotel were furtively thumbing their German grammars. One wonders if the keeper of the Garden Bar had found a suitable German synonym for his great invention 'the Suffering Bastard' (more than three ... and it's you). From the Semiramis Hotel, clouds of smoke told of confidential files burning. Pride and lust were in the air the Axis forces breathed, as fear was in the dust of Cairo.

And yet, in those hours, in Derna a white charger lost his moment of glory. Lawrence Boyd gained his Military Cross. Bombardier Johnson earned a Victoria Cross – which he never got. 'Clem' Clements's grandchildren were only a fraction of an inch from never being. Regimental

Sergeant Major Nobby Clark received a lesson on the new telescopic sight. Bill Slight blew himself up. The Africa Korps advanced to within 300 yards of a handful of guns ... and withdrew. The British forces stopped losing the war on land. In silence.

The reasons for this silence are not far to seek. Those who were there had other preoccupations. They were lost, tired, hungry, frightened. Few of them were literate men. Many were dead. None realized at the time quite what they had done. No runner sped to Cairo to tell of the new Leonidas. This Thermopylae was 40 miles wide. Many looked on, but few could see. As *The Royal Artillery Commemoration Book* says, 'good soldiers are not invariably as gifted with the pen as with the sword'.

This point is as quickly proven as made. Although this official gunner record carries a brief description of 2 July 1942 under the title 'Who Stopped Rommel', in its very full chronology of the Second World War there is no detailed entry for July 1942. When a handful of airmen fought a similar battle only two years before, all England could see. They were fighting for their own homes. Newshawks scavenged the battle-field. Film cameras recorded their vapour trails. Radio commentators described their fight as it was happening. The free world rightly thrilled at their names, but who has heard of Bombardier Johnson today?

There were, of course, literate and articulate men in the desert. In addendum 3 we quote the great war correspondents – Moorehead, Clifford, Johnston, Majdalany – but, on 2 July, they were all for good reasons in Cairo. A wandering film cameraman and an editor who cut us in to the film *Desert Victory* are the only incontrovertible proof that 11th Field was even there. That and the desert flowers which grow a little thicker over certain portions of Ruweisat Ridge when it rains in the desert.

Despite my cynicism, the main reasons for this silence are, after all, not so difficult to find. Perhaps the most meaningful is that, in desert conditions, the 'fog of war' implies a 'pea-souper' of the kind that modern smokeless zones seldom suffer.

The second reason lies in the army's dependence on its lines of command. When the chain of command breaks, the battlefield is scattered with the broken links. Our chain of command was shattered.

The Auk was combining the responsibility of Eighth Army Commander with the far more important post of Commander-in-Chief, Middle East. He was away from his base and his communications, having one week ago taken over command of his army in the field. While laying the foundations for final victory in the desert he was losing his personal battle and, at just about the very moment that Rommel was stopped, his political chief had decided to replace him by another. It is not surprising that 2 July meant less to him than 8 August and that, at the time, he could not write of either.

As Thompson illustrates: 'In the political and military crises of June and July, Churchill and Auchinleck faced their challenges with success. Between July 1st and 4th both men emerged triumphant from their personal ordeals.'

Our own immediate commanders were in an equally 'discontinuous' line of succession. Robcol fought under the splendid and firm command of Brigadier Rob Waller – CRA, 10th Indian Division. Only a few hours before, he had been in Mersa Matruh fighting a 'proper' war. Then, after breaking out at dead of night – driving through and with the German columns advancing on Alamein – he found himself in command of a very mixed bag and exercising this responsibility by virtue of orders delegated through a chain of command which can only be described as 'most peculiar'.

The CRA 10th Indian Division, as his diary shows, expected to get orders at 0700 hours on 1 July 1942 from General Nichols, his divisional commander. He can hardly have known General Nichols by sight because this officer had only taken over the division a few days earlier in the full course of the 'Gazala Gallop'. This earlier British defensive line had been penetrated by Rommel's forces on 16 June, leading to the eponymously named general retreat.

General Nichols did not arrive until 1600 hours that day and shortly afterwards left for the Delta, which was in no way surprising since this was where all other troops of the 10th Indian Division were concentrating. Before he arrived, the contemporary diary indicates that Brigadier Waller had received orders from General Ramsden, commanding the 50th Tyne Tees Division. Next day he led his force, Robcol, to the support of the 18th Indian Infantry Brigade in the Deir el Shein. This brigade belonged to the 8th Indian Division, but having hurried day and night from Iraq, it found itself flung into action under command of the 1st South African Division.

Robcol then spent the next 17 days in close contact with the enemy in the key sector of the Alamein Line, for much of the time under command of the 1st Armoured Division. After some days, Robcol became Wall Motor Group and took over units with the unlikely names of Ackcol, Sackcol and Squeakcol. It has not been easy even to identify the jumble of units which these forces represent!

When starting to write this story, I learned of this chain of command for the first time. It was known that on 2 July 1942, 11th Field was in Robcol. That it had at this time formed part of the 50th Division and 1st Armoured Division came as a complete surprise.

Attacks – sometimes successful – were made across the front of this group by South Africans, New Zealanders, the 5th Indian Division and a variety of armoured units. In between actions, and heated conferences in which Brigadier Waller was one of the few voices crying for positive action, General Lumsden said to him, again quoting from the contemporary diary for 11 July: 'They're trying to get you away from this. What formation do you really belong to?'

What formation? The brigadier might well have found it difficult to answer! Whatever his reply, he quoted General Lumsden as saying: 'You'd better come to me. We seem to agree on most things.' Which drew the natural answer: 'I'd like to.'

Despite the protection of this powerful patron, the force which had saved Alexandria started to break up on 15 July. At 1600 on 17 July, General Lumsden, who, according to Auchinleck's despatch had left the battlefield wounded on 15 July, and General Gott met Brigadier Waller at Russel Pasha's HQ and thanked him for the work of the group. On 18 July Brigadier Waller went to the races in Alexandria, unemployed, and 'backed a loser every race'.

Wall Motor Group was succeeded on Ruweisat Ridge by the 5th Indian Division. The history of this division states, '... and brigades came and went from one Division to another. During one period of four weeks the 5th Indian Division had no less than twenty-three changes in brigades, and these involved eleven different brigades, attached for a few hours, for a night, for a week.'[2]

An army reports through its next higher echelon and this state of affairs is an obvious reason for a lack of continuity in reporting. It also made it difficult to reconstruct the events of early July from records. Perhaps as a result, Connell could write with some truth that 'July became the month that was ignored by the historians and the writers of memoirs'.[3]

A third reason can be found on some of the maps of the time. Each of the HQs referred to existed as a living organization – be it only in the shape of one wireless truck or an armoured command vehicle. Each therefore merited its own little flag on the battle maps. When you see the flag '1st Armd Div' it is natural to conjure up a picture of massed armour, guns and lorried infantry. The reality in these days would have been a deception. And so, when you look at a battle map for early July 1942, look beyond the little symbols '1st Armd Div', '22nd Armd Bde', '5th Indian Div' and '50th Div Cols', all of which suggest a desert populated by more than the handful of troops which was actually deployed to face the enemy.

As Thompson wrote, 'The galaxies of headquarters flags dotting the immense areas of the Middle East spoke to Churchill of a power that was not there.' Lesser historians have been misled in a similar way.

At the next level of command, continuity was not much more strongly in evidence. Lieutenant Colonel McCarthy, commanding 11th Field Regiment RA, the main unit in Robcol, might have ensured a reasonable succession. 11th Field Regiment HQ was, after all, situated within a few hundred yards of its gun positions on 2 July until after Montgomery's Alamein. But, in mid-July, Colonel McCarthy was wounded. About this time, Pat Waterfield, the second in command, left to command a regiment. The battery commanders, John Ashton and Duggie Douglas remained in command of their batteries – but both battery captains were to go 'into the bag' at Mersa Matruh.

In the 83rd/85th Battery, both troop commanders were wounded on 2 July. We who remained, were tired … and ignorant. Furthermore, we remained on the ridge from 2 July until the tide of war receded from us in November. On 15 July, the 5th Indian Division took over from Robcol. The guns of 11th Field Regiment RA remained. On 8 September, the 4th Indian Division took over from the 5th Indian Division. By the time rest came, the name of Alamein had a new, and different, meaning.

This new meaning was associated with a new team. Auchinleck, Gott, Norrie, Ramsden and Lumsden now read Alexander, Montgomery, Leese and Horrocks. How often in business does one see that a new management team has no eyes for the achievements of its predecessor? Some people have imputed ill-will to this blindness. I prefer to attribute it solely to ignorance. In The Taste of Courage Montgomery could write with good faith, and with perfect truth: 'Crisis: 25 October: I have always thought that this was when the real crisis in the battle occurred.'[4] He was oblivious to the crisis at Alamein in July.

To quote Thompson again: 'There had been no certainty in the desert war until Auchinleck had saved Egypt at Alamein. These things are swiftly and easily forgotten … It was difficult to believe in September that this was the battlefield of July.'

Let us examine this at work. A little book, Men of Alamein, appeared in September 1943, published by R. Schindler of Cairo. One would think that nothing could be closer to actual history as it was made. It was written by Colonel C. P. S. Denholm-Young, OBE, who played a distinguished role in the 51st Highland Division's successes. Denholm-Young was, like Brutus, an honourable man. He writes of recapturing 'something of the spirit of adventure which penetrated the whole of that wonderful body of fighting men whom the world knows as the Eighth Army. The author had the honour to fight with that Army all the long way from El Alamein across the sands of the Libyan Desert to Tripoli.'

Admirable sentiment, truly expressed, but the 51st Highland Division, in which Colonel Denholm-Young served, was on a ship on 2 July 1942. The Eighth Army suffered more casualties before he arrived than were incurred 'all the way from Alamein across the sands of the Libyan Desert to Tripoli'.

Sir Compton Mackenzie, in his official account of the Indian forces in the Second World War takes a less charitable view of such unintentional distortions of history: 'A legend has grown up that the Eighth Army started its career at the second battle of Alamein, and this legend has been preposterously turned into bad history by those who were responsible for denying to all those who served in it before October 23rd 1942 the numerical "8" on the ribbon of the Africa Star.'[5] Yes, those who died on 2 July 1942 were not even granted the Eighth Army Clasp on their posthumous Africa Star.

Sir John Wheeler-Bennett grows as angry as Sir Compton Mackenzie: 'By what strange and ugly combination of factors were Auchinleck, and officers and men of the Eighth Army who served under him, not merely deprived of the full credit of this victory [he is referring to 2 July] but told to their faces by lesser men that they had not even achieved it, that they had gone down in defeat and retreat, from which miraculously they were retrieved a month later.'[6]

Thompson sees this as a wicked plot: 'Officially, "the turn of the tide" would be held back for nearly four months. To achieve this, it would be necessary to deny the battle of El Alamein, discredit the Commander-in-Chief, and the Eighth Army, and resurrect the myth of the sick and defeated Rommel as an almost invincible demon figure.'

I prefer to see the cause as less Machiavellian. History is a subject easier to get wrong than right. Consider the two following statements:

Carver in *Tobruk* states: 'Tuker's 4th Indian Division, which had no major part to play apart from holding Ruweisat Ridge, was stripped of its transport and told to carry out individual training as best it could.'

Union Jack British Forces Greece edition of Wednesday 12 July 1945, in an article apparently reprinted from the *Illustrated London News* and designed to flatter the 4th Indian Division: 'The division did not take part in the first stage of Montgomery's famous attack, which it watched from height of Ruweisat Ridge.'

Neither statement is, in any way, unfair or incorrect. No infantry from the 4th Indian Division took part in the initial main attack in October. But these two statements take little account of the fact that the 11th Field Regiment RA was in action at Alamein (except for, maybe, three days when 'individual training as best we could' was carried out just behind the line) from 2 July to November and that from 8 September to the end of the war it was part of the 4th Indian Division.

Long before 23 October, we could call fire on to any particle of sand near Ruweisat, giving the coordinates for the target from memory and without a map! And this occupation was carried out in full view of a large part of the Eighth Army, and the enemy. If you had been there, you would remember that OP tower which went up on the Barrel Track, perhaps 2,000 yards north of Pt 64. It was my grandstand for the big event – and had been for lesser events for some time.

Come with me. Let us travel for about 2500 yards west, through the break in the old British minefields, till we get to the edge of the enemy wire. Many years ago – on a still night – you would probably have heard Italian in your left ear and German in your right. The whispering behind you is more difficult to identify. You hope it is an Indian dialect. On the mound in front of you is what we are seeking. It must still be there on Popple's Pimple – that bottle of VAT 69 which Popple of the 4th/16th Punjabis and I (with the help of Gunner Rowland-Jones, signaller, and Gunner Marino, driver) emptied on that hilarious patrol a few nights before the balloon went up. It would be a pity if someone has removed this evidence that the 4th Indian Division were present at Alamein.

However, this is a self-centred view. Although it is in the sense in which it was written, true to say that the division 'had no major part to play', the impression which this and many similar statements leaves, ignores one simple, and rather significant fact. The final breakthrough in Montgomery's Alamein battle was made by a brigade of the 4th Indian Division.

Sir David Hunt: 'It was on the night of the 3rd November that the 5th Indian Brigade, part of 4th Indian Division, was produced out of the hat for the attack which finally loosened the log jam. In a brilliantly successful attack, mounted after a confusing night march, they turned the flank of the enemy's new position, forcing it back so that it covered only the coast road.'[7] As a result of this attack, our armour was through.

These facts are known – and repeated in many books and yet the legend lives on: the 4th Indian Division did not play a big role at

Alamein. Some writers believe that neither Churchill, nor Montgomery, were charitably inclined to Indians and the Indian Army, and whether Thompson is correct in writing the following paragraph, one does not know. If it is true, Montgomery certainly revised his views after the battle of Wadi Akarit in Tunisia in early April 1943:

> The worst was his treatment of the 4th Indian Division, never to be forgiven or forgotten by the Division or its Commander.[8] Montgomery's gratuitous insult to General Auchinleck immediately upon taking over his command, and his inability to acknowledge his inheritance, reflected his dislike of the Indian Army … it seemed to Montgomery that any praise or acknowledgment given to those who had preceded him must detract from his own fame and achievement … Thus he insulted not only some of the finest troops under his command, but denied his army their fighting services.[9]

If he is right, Thompson's introduction to *The Montgomery Legend* would in itself be sufficient explanation for those who died uncommended in the desert on 2 July 1942. But, as has already been said, I prefer to regard the lack of acknowledgement to a natural short-sightedness from which we all suffer rather than to intentional rudeness. This is why in order to make my point about the 4th Indian Division's contribution at Alamein, I cite rather than our own divisional commander, the words of David Hunt, a man who served both the Auk and Montgomery, of whom he wrote: 'In fact it must be clear by now that I am one of those who believe that General Montgomery owed his success not to wearing twice as many cap badges as General Auchinleck, but to having twice as many resources.'

This quote also contains the final explanation of the silence which has puzzled me: the paucity of the Auk's resources during those critical hours. It is perhaps natural egotism to concentrate on one's own part in a play and to be only dimly aware of the other actors. Nevertheless, on the day the Eighth Army finally turned back the Afrika Korps, one might expect to find a star-studded cast and many supporting players. The realization that, for the hours that mattered, one was alone in the spotlights and that the action was largely confined to a dialogue between nine guns and the last few German tanks came slowly and is not easily accepted. Nevertheless, it is true.

CHAPTER 3

The Line That Wasn't

The thought which ends the last chapter may be difficult to accept. In the intervening years many have become used to talking of the Alamein Line to describe that which Connell called 'the ultimate rampart of Alamein' and which Sir Arthur Bryant has described as 'the last ditch in which the tide of war turned'. When the guns roared the prelude to final victory on 23 October, it was indeed a 'line' – a line of wire and minefields covered by fire – but in June 1942 the line was as real as a politician's promise. Many historians have commented on this evident truth but today we still obscure the issue by repeating this comfortable word 'line' as R. H. W. S. Hastings comments:

> It is nonsense to talk of the Alamein 'Line'. When the Riflemen heard the suave voice of the BBC announcer reporting that the Eighth Army had reached the Alamein 'Line' they looked around at the empty desert … and commented as only Riflemen can.
>
> Here in the days of comparative success the Higher Command had ordered a defensive position to be dug. The preparations were far from complete. Astride the coast road a strong position was almost ready for occupation. In other areas, defences had been begun, rations had been dumped and some minefields had been laid.
>
> In fact, the Battalions of the Regiment arrived in a bare desert, like any other, dominated in the south by a gaunt, conical hill called Himeimat and level enough in the centre for such inconsiderable features as the Ruweisat Ridge to be important.
>
> It was clear to them that the Alamein line, on which the uninitiated, the listeners and the general public had perforce to place reliance, since Tobruk,

Sollum and Mersa Matruh, the better-known fortresses, had failed, was a flimsy foundation on which to base their hopes for the defence of the Nile Valley. At Alamein there was no Maginot Line; but it is to the credit of the authorities, who had twice seen the Army at Agheila, that they should have built anything at all within a few miles of the Delta.[1]

Nevertheless, there was a fine defensive position at El Alamein and when Auchinleck took over as Commander-in-Chief in May/June 1941, one of his first steps was to have fortifications prepared there. Sir David Hunt gives a description of this position which this writer cannot hope to equal:

El Alamein was only a name to us then though a very well-known one. It had long been regarded as the best position possible for the defence of Egypt. The name itself means 'the twin cairns'. In the desert it means a waymark and its usual form is a pile of stones. There are a fair number of Alameins as well. With a very small change in the first vowel, of a sort almost impossible for European throats to manage, Alamein would mean 'the two worlds'. This seems a most appropriate name for the place that marked, at one of the crucial moments of the war, the boundary between the two worlds of the Western Allies and the totalitarian powers.

El Alamein itself is nothing but a halt on the desert railway with no more than a short platform and a little hut. It marks the northern end of the shortest distance between the Mediterranean Sea and the Qattara Depression. The Qattara Depression is a miracle of nature. It is plainly the bed of a former sea, sunk below the level of the desert to the north and south. Its bottom is treacherous with quick-sands and is everywhere impassable for motor transport and, at least according to our maps, even for a loaded camel. In many places it is dangerous to attempt on foot. At the north edge it is bounded by sheer cliffs which become steeper as they approach the eastern end. At this eastern end the depression is within 40 miles of the coast which, very conveniently, here bends southwards. The result is that here at last the desert offers a position, both flanks of which are secure.

It is a longish position for the sort of numbers that both sides disposed of, but it is much the shortest such position anywhere between Alexandria in Egypt and Agheila in Libya. This advantage had been naturally enough observed long before and Alamein was always reckoned as the last and strongest position of defence in front of the Delta. Since 1940 work had at intervals been undertaken to fortify this line. The defences were based on four strong points known in desert language as boxes. In the north was the Alamein box, southwest of the railway station. Next came Deir el Shein, based on a small square-shaped depression. The third was Qaret el Abd. This resembles nothing so much as a hill which has been hollowed out with one side removed; as its name means the hill of the slaves, Trigh el Abd, it was natural to suppose that it had in the past served the purpose of a corral for holding slaves. The fourth post was on the Taqa plateau, a high flat-topped hill which reared its head immediately above the cliffs of the depression. Other minor works were built in between these four, tracks were improved, pipe-lines prepared and so on. We were anything but Maginot-minded in the Western Desert but we did have a fairly cheerful confidence in the strength of the Alamein line.[2]

Immediately we come across one of those confusions which make an amateur historian's task both difficult and interesting. Hunt's 'cheerful confidence' rests on the existence – in a gap of 40 miles – of four boxes – at Alamein, Deir el Shein, Qaret el Abd and Taqa. Michael Carver, a soldier of equal stature, writes of three boxes – Alamein, Qaret el Abd and Naqb abu Dweis – and views their defensive value much less enthusiastically:

> One of the new commander's first steps was to order General Sir James Marshall-Cornwall, commanding British Troops in Egypt (BTE), to press on with the construction of a defensive position at El Alamein. Work on this proceeded slowly throughout the rest of the year. It took the classic form of all defensive positions in the Western Desert, to which Rommel's position on the frontier, which he had just successfully held against two British attacks, was no exception. The principal position, destined for the bulk of an infantry position, lay on the coast, covering the road and protected on its north flank by the sea. The main feature of this position was the observation gained from the ridge of Tel el Alamein over the flat and open ground to the south-west.
>
> The next position, in the centre of the line, was to be fifteen miles to the south-west. It was to include the peak of Qaret el Abd, from which good observation was to be had particularly to the north. The area around it was broken up into escarpments and depressions, which made movement difficult. Between El Alamein and Qaret el Abd the ground was generally flat. About halfway between the two the Ruweisat Ridge ran eastwards from just south of a small depression called Deir el Shein. The ridge was no real obstacle to movement. North of it, the ground was flat, with patches of soft sand and tufty bumps. South of it lay a plateau-like area of good hard going, the southern edge of which was later known as Bare Ridge. It followed roughly a line running east for about 12 miles from Qaret el Abd, turning north-east through Alam el Halfa until it finally converged towards the eastern end of Ruweisat Ridge south of El Ruweisat station.
>
> The southern-most position was sited to cover the pass down the escarpment to the Qattara Depression at Naqb abu Dweis. This was almost twice the height of Qaret el Abd. Magnificent and awe-inspiring views spread in every direction, but the place itself was inaccessible and troops there could have little

effect on anything but a direct assault against themselves. Between Qaret el Abd and Naqb abu Dweis lay steep escarpments and imposing heights. Much of the area presented great difficulties of movement to a force travelling west to east. However, once through the narrow neck of smooth ground just north of Gebel Kalakh, a flat smooth plain of firm going ran between, on the north, a series of depressions running south-east from near Qaret el Abd for nearly 20 miles to Deir el Raqil and, on the south, a high escarpment as far as Qaret el Himeimat and then a low ridge running east to Samaket Gaballa. South of this ridge the ground became softer and sloped down until it came to the steep edge of the great depression above the salty, mosquito ridden oasis of El Maghra.[3]

Playfair speaks of 'three defended localities, about fifteen miles apart, at El Alamein, Bab el Qattara (also known as Qaret el Abd) and Naqb abu Dweis'.[4] This version is correct. Confirmation of this fact, important to our central theme, came in 1980 from Major General Douglas Brown. In his career, he served Brigadier Waller in every rank from second lieutenant to lieutenant colonel, and on the brigadier's death, as his executor. In 1941, under the shade of an enormous double-terai hat, he arrived in the Middle East from East Africa to become the G2 Operations in BTE.

Here, the GOC, General Sir James Marshall-Cornwall, had just received orders from the Auk to prepare a fall-back position running from the little railway halt at Alamein to Qattara. Playfair credits General Norrie with wishing to create other localities in the gaps, one of them to be sited at Deir el Shein but at the beginning of July 'no work had yet been done on any of these'.[5] This may explain Rommel's surprise at finding the 18th Indian Infantry Brigade barring his way on 1 July! Douglas Brown is quite categoric: the first plan only envisaged three boxes and, in his view, the strategic importance of Ruweisat was, at that time, not even realized.

A mechanized enemy approaching the Alamein line from the west would find itself naturally funnelled into three possible avenues: the northern, between the railway and Ruweisat Ridge; the centre, just north of Qaret el Abd and then eastward to the south of Ruweisat Ridge and north of Alam el Halfa; the southern, north of Gebel Kalakh, Himeimat and Samaket Gaballa. These avenues would follow the best going and also generally bypass the defensive positions, which would have taken about two infantry divisions to hold.

Such a mobile enemy could not be stopped from passing between and then isolating these 'boxes', as they were sometimes called, which could then be starved or hammered into submission one by one. All their garrisons could do was to shell the enemy they could see with the limited amount of artillery that could be fitted within the perimeter. Any extension of the perimeter, which had to be defended from every direction, greatly increased the number of troops needed to hold it, and particularly the number of anti-tank guns required. The troops within them could not be made mobile without cramming the 'boxes' full of vulnerable trucks. An essential part of the defence was therefore the existence of at least two armoured divisions to operate in the gaps between the defensive positions and deal with any enemy which might penetrate between them or concentrate against one of them.

Without provision for reserves, therefore, the El Alamein line, as planned in 1941, needed a minimum of two infantry and two armoured divisions. As outlined by Lucas Phillips:

> The defence works were of an exiguous nature, being composed of a series of unfinished defence localities or 'boxes', separated from one another by wide spaces, which it was intended should be watched by mobile formations or columns … Frowning immediately above the Deir el Shein was the most pronounced feature yet encountered, running east and west across the front like a long and bony hog's back. This was Ruweisat Ridge, of evil memory. Rocky, austere, 200 feet above sea level, it became the scene of some of the bloodiest and most ill-directed fighting in the days immediately to follow, which formed the concluding phase of the Battle of Gazala.[6]

Corelli Barnett agrees with Carver about the three boxes – but names the middle one as Bab el Qattara.[7] Neither the 1:250,000 map El Daba nor the 1:50,000 map El Diyura shows a Bab el Qattara (Gateway to Qattara) in the centre of the line, though both show Deir el Qattara (Deir is a depression) to the south-west of Pt 100 Qaret el Abd. However, Brigadier Waller's battle map shows Bab el Qattara 3,000 yards east-south-east of Qaret el Abd (now shown as Pt 101).

The unreliability of our maps, added to the descriptive nature of most Arabic place names, is another difficulty for an historian. It is not helped by the fact that the battle area fell onto two different survey grids – purple grid, based on longitude 27E and red grid, based on longitude 31E: the headquarters of Robcol for much of the battle of Ruweisat was very close to longitude 29E.

Whether they believed in three boxes or four, all who described the 'line' are agreed that, on 1 July, it was very lightly held. All also agree that on that date the line was broken in the centre.

In the north, the 1st South African Division was then very thin on the ground but they were in a true defended locality with their 3rd Brigade inside the wire. Their positions would be difficult to describe as 'prepared', but attention had been given to their siting and some work had been done on them. Protected by the sea on their right flank, they were in good ground. Their left flank was covered by the 1st and 2nd South African brigades who were in a more mobile role to the south of the wired perimeter. On 1 July, with the help of the 4th Armoured Brigade who arrived just ahead of the German 90th Light Division, they were able to hold off the thrust towards Alexandria to the extent that the Germans retired 'in panic'.

Dan Pienaar, at the time commander of the 1st South African Division, was however far from happy with the state of preparedness which he found when the South Africans arrived. Denis Johnston vividly describes an interview with him shortly before the battle at:

> a small railway station set in the midst of some hundreds of miles of nothing whatsoever – that is all there is at Alamein.
>
> Pienaar: '… and judging by what they tell me Churchill has been saying in America, he must be very misinformed too … I've got no artillery and no armour … They're doing their best … what there are of them. There are my South Africans, of course. Then there are the Indians, poor fellows, God help them. And the New Zealanders … if they get back this far. Oh … and there's supposed to be some Free French, only I haven't seen them yet.'
>
> 'But, er, General … this line. That must be fairly strong. I understand that it was prepared some time ago, for the final defence of Egypt.'
>
> 'I've been looking over the line,' he continued, 'there are some very good stores and underground shelters, but as far as I can see there aren't any surface defences. They were to come later on, probably.
>
> 'I was scared of the Alamein Box and of what was likely to happen there at any moment, and that annoying fact was plain for all to see.'[8]

In the south, the 2nd New Zealand and the remains of the 5th Indian Division were – on 1 July – in positions at Qaret el Abd, Taqa and

Naqb abu Dweis i.e. on the originally chosen southern defensive line, with some units west of this line. They were too far south to influence the battle which was about to develop in the centre. Neither were they under any enemy pressure. But later Auchinleck, and subsequently Montgomery, decided that this left flank was not worth serious defence. Both, at appropriate moments allowed the enemy free access to the southern channel. As the battle of Alam el Halfa showed in September, this flank was of little value to the enemy provided the centre was firm.

But by nightfall on 1 July the centre was pierced and the way to the Delta lay open. That day, between dawn and dusk, the Afrika Korps destroyed the centre box in the Deir el Shein and removed its gallant defenders – the 18th Indian Infantry Brigade – from the Eighth Army order of battle. This desperate action will be described at greater length in a later chapter, but it is good to quote here Compton Mackenzie: 'The 18th Indian (Infantry) Brigade was never reformed, but during its brief life the resistance it made at Deir el Shein may have saved the Line by the time it gained for the organisation of the defence under Auchinleck's unruffled direction.'[9]

To the south of the Deir el Shein rose 'Beachy Head', a bluff escarpment some 200 feet high and visible for miles around. From it runs Ruweisat Ridge rising gently for 15 miles in an easterly direction and continuing north-eastwards in the direction of Alexandria. Mackenzie again: 'If the enemy could sweep up to the crest of the Ruweisat Ridge, that was the end of the Alamein position.'

David Hunt confirms this view: 'This ridge had always been recognized as one of the keys of the position. It is not high, but high enough in that flat country to command large areas … not only does it give first class observation and fine command but also affords an avenue of good going which led directly through our position and on in the direction of Alexandria.'[10]

It was towards the eastern end of this ridge that Auchinleck had opened his battle headquarters only two days before on 29 June 1942. In his opinion too, Corelli Barnett believed that Ruweisat was the key to the coming battle.

South African historians Turner and Agar-Hamilton describe how General Norrie, after handing over Mersa Matruh on 23 June, took over preparation of this defensive position consisting of three defensive boxes at Alamein, Bab el Qattara and Naqb abu Dweiss. They also describe the arrival of the 18th Indian Infantry Brigade on 28 June to establish a new position at Deir el Shein under command of the 1st South African Division.

It is made clear that in the first critical stages of the Alamein battle, the southern area was never seriously held. In the north, the 1st South African Division consisted of the 3rd South African Brigade with about 1,100 men, the 1st South African Field Regiment and the 7th Medium Regiment RA. They were just strong enough to man the western and south-western faces of the perimeter, leaving the eastern half of the box undefended. To cover the gap of ten miles between the wire and the 18th Indian Infantry Brigade in the Deir el Shein, they organized, at the Auk's insistence during his visit on 29 June, two mobile columns each based on two batteries of artillery and one battalion of infantry. All other troops were sent back to Alexandria.[11]

Below the box in the Deir el Shein we find, over some 30 miles of front, the New Zealand Division and the 9th Indian Brigade of the 5th Indian Division – joined next day, 1 July, by the 7th Motor Brigade of the 7th Armoured Division. This thin khaki line militarily was to have little significance at this stage.

Closing on the Alamein box at noon on 30 June is the German 90th Light Division and the Italian XXI Corps. In the centre is the DAK with the 21st and 15th Panzer Divisions. Behind them, the Allied 1st Armoured Division, what is left of the 4th and 22nd Armoured Brigades, shamble back into the line. The map shows the enormous gaps between the formations, but already the recital of unit headquarters has deceived us. Both the panzer divisions and 90th Light were down to perhaps 1,000 men each and a handful of tanks (Turner and Agar-Hamilton say 41 tanks) while the 1st Armoured Division had perhaps more men, but were down to only a nominal strength in armour.

On the first three days of July, Rommel's main attacks were carried out by the 90th Light Division against the Alamein box and the two panzer divisions in a two-pronged attack through the Deir el Shein and along Ruweisat Ridge. Despite the comparative weakness of the 3rd

South African Brigade, they were in prepared positions and, apart from occupying the sandy midriff left by the thinly padded positions, the 90th Light made little headway.

On 1 July, Rommel recorded: '[L]ate in the afternoon I decided to put everything I could into supporting the southern flank of 90th Light Division's breakthrough attempt'.

This is the day which the South African historians describe as 'the crucial day in the whole desert campaign',[12] but, as Rommel's attack in the centre was, at first, successful, I may be forgiven for christening 2 July not the 1st, as 'the day we stopped losing the war'.

We can now leave the 90th Light, trying in vain to get to the sea between the 2nd South African Brigade Group at Alam el Onsol and the more or less fortified box occupied by the 3rd South African Brigade around El Alamein station. They seem to have chased the 40-odd tanks of the 4th Armoured Brigade of the 1st Armoured Division through the gap, and the afternoon of 1 July finds them bogged down, in a blinding sandstorm, trying to find a weakness in this fairly solid position. The 4th Armoured Brigade are at this time equally ineffective as they spent most of the day getting out of sand.

Farther south however, the combined might of the 15th Panzer and 21st Panzer overcame the raw Indian infantry brigade in the Deir el Shein with only about 55 tanks between them, as the only available British armour, the 22nd Armoured Brigade, had, since dawn when it arrived in the area, withdrawn beyond Ruweisat and failed to return to support the Indian brigade box. Divisional HQ 1st Armoured was some way to the south east and apparently out of touch with the battle. The 22nd Armoured Brigade arrived at Ruweisat with only 28 tanks, of which ten were on tow.

I have tried, to aid comprehension, to reduce the battle to its simplest form but the actual reports of 1 July are far less clear. Rommel thought the 50th Division was where the South Africans were, and placed the 18th Indian Infantry Brigade box as in the Deir el Abyad – two or three miles farther west and peopled it with the 10th Indian Infantry Brigade. Even the Germans record, 'No small disorder reigns.' The fairly well-documented story is a vivid explanation of the difficulties of giving a blow-by-blow account of the more critical and less well-documented story of 2 July.

But, early on 2 July, the DAK swarmed into this gap from the Deir el Shein. In the north, the 90th Light was still bogged down in a sandstorm against the more or less prepared defences of the South Africans, but it was in Rommel's nature to concentrate his last remaining tanks – all that was left of the 15th and 21st Panzer Divisions – to exploit this success. At first it must have seemed to them that they were through.

Most battle maps show the 22nd Armoured Brigade somewhere on the ridge to the east and the headquarters flag of the 1st Armoured Division in the valley south of them, but they were known to be weak. Despite desperate calls for help they had been unable to come to the aid of the 18th Indian Infantry Brigade defending the Deir el Shein the previous day. At least on Ruweisat Ridge, they remained impassive spectators and with gallant but minor exceptions were unable to make any positive contribution to the battle on 2 July.

Some battle maps too, show columns from the 50th Division towards the eastern end of the ridge. But by now this brave division was little more than a headquarters. It was this HQ which, collecting the last battleworthy survivors of Mersa Matruh, launched Robcol into some form of counter-activity – one would not flatter our move forward with the name of counter-attack.

The western end of the Ruweisat Ridge has three slight features of the same height – all shown on most maps as Pt 63. Western Pt 63 rose out of the Deir el Shein and was now in German hands. As the leading units of the DAK approached Middle Pt 63 (later known as Pt 64) an open Ford armoured observation vehicle showed over the ridge on the other side. Robcol had arrived with seventeen 25 pounders, 250 infantry and a few anti-tank guns. Before nightfall some 20 tanks would be knocked out and the leading battery would lose eight of its nine guns – but the gap in the Alamein line had been plugged.

CHAPTER 4

The Will of the Commander

It would be impertinent for a 'weekend' soldier to quote Clausewitz, but the will of the commander as the decisive element in battle can seldom have been demonstrated more clearly than on 2 July 1942. There were so few distracting factors – and the number of troops effectively engaged was so small. Rommel, with a handful of tanks, guns and motorized infantry, found Auchinleck with – at the critical point – an even smaller force of similar composition.

Rommel, on 1 July, had every expectation of reaching Alexandria on 3 July. By the night of 3 July his will to cross the last 60 miles which separated him from Alexandria had evaporated under physical exhaustion, bombing, shelling and the unexpectedly stiff resistance organized by his opponent. In a later chapter, we shall see the Auk – confident amidst calamity, on 29 June, directing the moves which brought this resistance to the right place just in time. In the strategic battle, his will had conquered.

Only three times have I stood face to face with the Auk, but for 25 years he has been one of my heroes. The last time I saw him was in September 1965. After six years in Belgium I had returned to England and, house-hunting, stayed for a few days in an XL Club flat in Whitehall Court. This building also housed the Junior Army and Navy Club. Standing at the bar one evening, the unmistakeable figure of The Chief caught my eye across the room. Accompanied by his sister, this very senior officer was staying at the JANC while attending some function in town. I was fortunate enough to be in the small group which he joined for his nightcap. Perhaps this book owes something to that chance encounter, because, even in retirement, his bearing had lost nothing of the presence which had made such an impression on me 25 years before. The character, so well described by Connell, still shone through with quiet authority and Irish charm. I itched to tell him of our first two encounters, but a crowded bar was not the place for such personal reminiscence.

Since that meeting I have read much of the events which took place under his command. The moments of chaos – revealed by part of this reading – resulting from poor communications and lack of understanding between armies, led by subordinate commanders who on occasion displayed human frailties, and which cannot be ignored even by his most devoted supporter. As Commander-in-Chief he would have been the first to accept responsibility for our mistakes. On the two occasions when he took over direct command of Eighth Army he suffered from the errors which he, as Commander-in-Chief, had allowed others to commit. And yet, by these interventions, on two occasions he saved Eighth Army and saved the Delta … and he did it by his personal strength of character.

The personal magnetism which inspired me so strongly is the more remarkable when you consider that on our first meeting he committed the unforgivable. He was late, and as a result the 11th Field Regiment RA was kept out in the heat of the Iraqi sun for over an hour awaiting his inspection. But we must forgive him for this is most unlike the man we knew him to be. It is small wonder if among his many cares one cropped up to hold him back an hour. For the Auk carried the burdens not of a Montgomery but of an Alexander – and of an Alexander the Great. His presence in Iraq was proof of his continuing pre-occupation with his Northern Command.

A few months later, perhaps as a result of this inspection, the Auk was to strip his northern frontier and, in one of the most far-sighted strategic strokes, rush reinforcements across 1,500 miles of desert to save the Eighth Army and the Delta. They arrived in the nick of time.

In this stream of reinforcements was the 11th Field Regiment RA. In the regiment's advance party, Lieutenant F. R. Jephson. I was heading towards my second meeting with the Auk, and the one which ever since has remained etched in my memory. On my 24th birthday – 29 June 1942 – lost in the desert with one 15-cwt truck and one 3-tonner, perhaps four or five men and seven or eight German prisoners, tired and bewildered, with no map and no information, few arms, but plenty of food (the 3-tonner was the cookhouse vehicle), I eventually hit the coast road. I had no idea where I was. No idea where the enemy was. No traffic on the road. Silence. Suddenly over the eastern ridge appeared a British staff car, followed by one armoured car. Just time to shake myself into a slightly more soldierly posture and to check that the 3-tonner was at a correct distance and I had passed my Commander-in Chief heading towards the enemy with a broad grin of confidence! Years later I read Connell's description of him, standing by the roadside at about the same place and time and knew I had not been dreaming.

The Auk was the first of three key commanders:

Field Marshal Sir Claude J. E. Auchinleck, GCB, GCIE, CSI, DSO, OBE (1884–1981)

Connell's description is vivid and therefore quoted at some length:

> In this sliding, melting world of rout and defeatism Auchinleck stood a lonely and defiant figure and the troops rallied to him. Perhaps the most disconcerting factor for Auchinleck was his continued ignorance of the state of his retreating army, for the Eighth Army HQ could tell him nothing.
>
> Therefore, while the race to El Alamein was still going hard, he left his headquarters – now at Ommayid – and drove back towards the enemy, against the current of retreat, to Daba on the coast road. First, he superintended the destruction of the immense stores at Daba. Then he went out on to the coast road, because 'I wanted to see what the general state of morale and discipline was among the troops coming back'.[1]

The road stretched away from him through the flat, scrubby desert, a black and shimmering tape, two vehicles wide:

> Auchinleck stood in the sand by the roadside, bare-headed, and watched his beaten army stream past him towards El Alamein. It came radiator to tailboard; tanks on transporters; supply trucks; troop carriers; towed bombers without wings, like monstrous maimed insects; trucks loaded with mess and NAAFI

stores and furniture, guns. A yellow-painted travelling fun-fair on the move to the next ground. As a scene of disastrous retreat, it was incongruous: instead of the starvation and frostbite that Corunna, Moscow and Valley Forge have made traditional trappings, there was the travel agents sunshine, the Mediterranean's copper sulphate blue between the white dunes. Their faces dried and brown as biscuit, the men passed by him in trucks powdered thickly with dust and hung about with bed-rolls and billy-cans.[2]

A little later, Connell adds:

> He resolved to strip the army down to what it needed for battle; and he would set an example in his headquarters. His vigil on the roadside has served another purpose: 'I also wanted to show myself a bit, and to talk to one or two of the chaps.' Either there, or while standing up hatless in his car, he chatted to as many as he could, and from as many different formations as possible – to British, Indians, to Commonwealth soldiers. If his men impressed Auchinleck, the Auk equally impressed his men. He looked a fighter, big and burly, with a fighter's pugnacious chin and mouth; and they could tell by the way he talked to them that he was a real chap – no tricks, none of 'the old flannel', the 'bull' through which the British soldier can instantly see.
>
> 'The troops were bewildered,' Auchinleck recollected later, 'but completely unconcerned. There was no sign of panic, such as people trying to pass each other. The spectacle was encouraging from the point of view of morale, but there was terrible disorganization, and I could see the army would need refitting.'[3]

From the open desert, the last British stragglers were coming in. Among these was the 1st Armoured Division, which had hoped for a peaceful journey but which had instead bumped into two Italian divisions once and into the Afrika Korps twice. During the morning of 30 June, X Corps was still streaming east along the coast road past El Alamein and through 1st South African Division, which held the coastal flank. But the stream of vehicles at last dried up; the road stretched empty into the haze before the eyes of the Eighth Army gunners, and somewhere beyond was Rommel.

Auchinleck had now moved from his temporary headquarters at Ommayid to the place behind the Ruweisat Ridge from which he was to direct the battle. To his soldiers he issued a calm and characteristically untheatrical order of the day: 'The enemy is stretching to his limit and thinks we are a broken army .... He hopes to take Egypt by bluff. Show him where he gets off.'

General Sir Claude Auchinleck, Commander-in-Chief, Middle East, June 1941 to August 1942. (© IWM E4559)

When we come to the 11th HAC we shall find that he had a similar effect on their commander, Geoff Armstrong. Countless others would have been able to testify to the electric effect which his bearing had on them. By his handling of his strategic reserve, by his readiness to accept responsibility and to take over the Eighth Army in its critical hour, by his personal example, the Auk was about to impose his will on the enemy commander.

Brigadier R. P. Waller, DSO, MC, DL

But, although Auchinleck's headquarters at the eastern end of Ruweisat Ridge were, on 2 July, sited at the critical point of the battle, when the fight is joined the Commander-in-Chief can no longer greatly influence the tactical battle which his strategy has brought into effect. The dominant will in the tactical battle was that of Brigadier 'Rob' Waller, DSO, MC. How he imposed that will is a story for another chapter, but it is right at this stage to take a look at the commander of Robcol. Since regimental subalterns do not mix with brigadier commanders in battle, my knowledge of him dates from July 1967 – except perhaps for a brief encounter at the height of the Ruweisat battle.

'Come and stay a few days,' said the letter, headed Wyastone Leys, Monmouth, which I received as a result of the short notice in 'The Times Diary'. The chance to meet another of my heroes was too good to refuse, even though I accepted with some trepidation. After all, the Brigadier must have been in his 50s when I was 24, twenty-five years ago. My guess was not far out.

> Waller, Brigadier, Robert Peel, born 1895, educated at Bradfield & the Royal Military Academy, married 1921 to Olave, daughter of the 5th Baron de Robeck.

Kelly's Handbook informed me.

But, as I addressed an envelope to Brigadier R. P. Waller, DSO, MC, my resolve to write this book hardened. The Distinguished Service Order and Military Cross are ribbons which any soldier may wear with pride. They are won by regimental officers for their conduct in battle – but one would expect distinction in a higher order for the commander of the force which finally stopped Rommel. In fact, the same handbook showed that Robcol's brigadier went entirely unhonoured, the MC dated from 1918, and the DSO from 1941. Indeed, as he left the desert in mid-July, there would not even be an '8' on his Africa Star. Brigadier Waller's other decorations were given as Chevalier Legion d'Honneur and Croix de Guerre (France) and Order of the White Lion, 3rd Class and Military Cross (Czechoslovakia), but these were unlikely rewards for the action with which we are concerned. A later edition of *Kelly's* showed the initials D. L.

On arrival at Wyastone Leys these thoughts were gradually confirmed. It may be strange to start researching the story about war in the Western Desert in a large country house set in woodlands above the beautiful valley of the Wye. And yet the memory of such places filled the minds of many of the young men on Ruweisat.

The battle of Ruweisat had not gone entirely unrecognized, for the Auk had sent a telegram of congratulations – but the Auk was gone. Not entirely unrecognized – by General C. C. Harvey, commander of the 8th Indian Division whom he met on an exercise in Iraq on 10 December 1942, for he asked the Brigadier how many guns Robcol started with and was surprised at their small number.

'You were the first to stand and stop him,' said General Harvey. But, his lips were sealed for he served on the court of inquiry into the Gazala Gallop.

News of General Harvey's opinion reached the Brigadier's wife Olave, via a mutual friend, Dick Archer-Houblon, in Somerset early in February 1943. In an airletter dated 11 February she expressed her great pride in her 'famous husband' because General Harvey had said how 'it was you and only you who had stopped Rommel'. Such private acknowledgements were the Brigadier's only reward.

Being human, it would be suprising if he had not occasionally hankered after some more public acknowledgement of Robcol's existence. Indeed, his diary shows that this was so. An entry for 15 February 1943 was written just after he had read GHQ Middle East Forces Summary dated 3 February 1943 and quotes from this document a passage concerning Rommel's daring and luck: 'His luck still never deserted him till the day, 2nd July 1942, when he announced to the world that he had broken through the defences of Alamein and was advancing with two columns on Alexandria and Cairo.'

'And so he had and so he was,' runs the diary,

> but on that day he was stopped by Robcol; and on 3rd and 4th July by Robcol and 22nd Armoured Brigade – and the danger passed. 2nd July 1942 was indeed the critical day. There is no doubt. I feel that Robcol did save Alexandria and most of the credit must go to the 11th Field Regiment R.A. There hasn't been any very public recognition of it, though 11th Field did get a few decorations, certainly, I suppose being nobody's child.

When his wife's airletter arrived in Iraq on 12 March 1943 his diary returns to this theme:

> Being no-one's child we were forgotten. We were under Ramsden (50th Division) at the time but a day or two later came under Lumsden (1st Armoured Division) and then Ramsden was promoted to XXX Corps and then the Auk

left soon after. I feel sometimes that I might have had a mention; but the great thing is that we did stop him – and only just in time. In the Iraq Times, a reprint from the Egyptian Mail rather gives the credit to the South Africans. Actually, on 2nd July they were scarcely engaged being rather behind Robcol. However, they held him up finally some days later. Anyway the fellows who really did the work got a few decorations to show what they'd done.

The thoughts in his diary continually revert to 2 July and, even when he is thinking of himself, those who fell there are much in his mind. Four months later, on 2 November 1942 he is at GHQ PAIForce (Persia and Iraq Command):

> How lucky I am. Walking to the office this morning, the air just cold enough to make one step out, and feeling so fit and well, it came upon me so strongly. How lucky I am to be here, in comfort fit and well. Oh, the contrast to those corrupting, smelling things we left in the no-man's land on Ruweisat Ridge.
>
> The bright clear day somehow made me see the scene or our battlefield of 2nd July as I saw it with Geoff Armstrong on our recce two days later. The one abandoned broken gun, the wrecks of vehicles, the bodies with their stiff hard limbs and grey or blackened faces – after two days' sun. Am I getting too introspective for a good solder?

On the first anniversary, 2 July 1943, the Brigadier was in Shepheard's Hotel in Cairo and wrote, 'The contrast between today and 2nd July 1942 is so extreme that I cannot help thinking about it.'

These paragraphs in the Brigadier's diary illuminate what was, for me, the essential and interesting paradox of the man who stopped Rommel. The picture of the Brigadier, stepping out feeling so fit and well, is what one would expect of the young man, splendid in dress uniform of a captain of Royal Horse Artillery, whose portrait by Denis Fildes (son of Sir Luke Fildes) shone over the central fireplace at Wyastone Leys.

One was not surprised to see his father's portrait by the same artist across the room. This was the son of an aristocrat, a line which goes back to names famous in Cromwell's day. Perhaps a little unfeeling of others' problems, perhaps a Philistine. But, as the above passage shows, the man who also slew Goliath, belied his outward mould. The men who died for him on Ruweisat haunted him all his life. As they haunted others who were there.

Flanking the Fildes portrait were two supporters which, on the second day of my visit, I learned had been made by his wife, Olave, in what must have been one of his happier years, 1958, when he became High Sheriff of Herefordshire at the age of sixty-three.

These supporters reflect the coat of arms of the Waller family: 'three walnut leaves or in a bend sable and argent'. More significant for our purpose, the crest is composed of the same armorial features with – as motto – the one word 'Ruweisat'. In this word, the Brigadier's heart is laid bare and men's ingratitude is tempered by the approval of the Earl Marshal of England and the endorsement of Field Marshal Sir Claude Auchinleck to his undying association with this patch of sandy rock.

As he explained, 'A number of years ago, Garter King of Arms, Sir George Bellow, told me that he thought I should have something in my coat of arms in memory of my actions in the desert. He suggested the word "Ruweisat" under my crest. I felt it would be presumptuous of me to accept this without reference to my old commander, Sir Claude Auchinleck, who replied that I was fully entitled to Ruweisat and that our actions that day had stopped the rot and prevented withdrawal towards Alexandria.'

Having discovered that our giant was no Philistine, it was less of a shock when his diary revealed him in that other role of David. His observation of the battlefield had been, like Wavell, not only that of a soldier, but also of a poet.

Ruweisat Ridge 13th July 1942

('All day the dust blew. It was particularly thick about noon')
The fog of dawn is not more dense;
Dust fills the air,
With aching strain my eyeballs sense
The white heat's glare,
As mid-day sun beats thro' the haze
And shimmers there.
The sand lifts to the swirling breeze
Our cracked lips share;
The hot wind sears the blistered skin
To fresh wounds tear;
The Desert north to Alamein
Is drifting there.

The contrast between the pride of the dashing horseman, the extrovert commander and the sorrow of a sensitive poet are the very warp and woof of this story and of the Brigadier's character. Indeed, such a contrast sets a mirror to war itself – the utter waste of every resource yet calling forth at the same time, life's highest virtues.

The contrasts illuminated the character of this man who was the rock on which Rommel foundered. The Brigadier's strength was not that of an unfeeling man. On 13 July the insignificant little force with which he started on the 2nd had increased to nearly divisional strength – Wall Motor Group consisted of three battle groups such as three brigades might have furnished. Despite the burden of this command he could observe nature and record it in words which many years later ring like the Khamsin itself.

If you had been on the Ridge on that 13 July, the Brigadier's pen picture would make your knuckles itch from the desert sores that were the proud badge of the fighting soldier. We wore our tatty rags to keep the flies out with a modest ostentation like that with which – in pre-war days – we had limped happily into the office on a Monday morning, flaunting a black eye as proof of our weekend's prowess on the rugger field. As a gunner OP officer, of course, you were certain of the biggest and best 'desert knuckles' because your days were spent with hands to eyes observing the enemy. Hands which were holding binoculars were easy prey for the desert flies which swarmed over the gradually mounting corpses decorating the Ruweisat Ridge.

Perhaps this memory is stimulated by the surroundings in which I copied the Brigadier's lines. In the library of Wyastone Leys all was silent, silent as the desert, until across the beautiful Wye valley work restarted on the A40. At least, when I looked up I could see heavy earthmoving equipment cutting a scar across the hillside but, as I wrote, this noise blended with the silence. The clanking did not disturb my thoughts – the low mumble, the whirr of the motor and the squeak of the tracks blended naturally into the Brigadier's description of a day when the 1st Armoured Division rolled in a duststorm along the flanks of Ruweisat.

If this poem touches a chord with you as it did with me, you will not be surprised to learn, as I did, that the Brigadier was descended from that Edmund Waller (1606–87) whose poetry graces *The Golden Treasury* which was often studied at school and from which I quoted at the beginning of chapter 2. If you are left unmoved by the verses of a soldier, I can only quote to you from Sir Walter Scott's 'The Field of Waterloo': 'Forgive, brave Dead, the imperfect lay' which is prefaced by 'It may be some apology for the imperfections of this poem, that it was composed hastily, and … when the Author's labours were liable to frequent interruption …'

Nor to find a further extract in the private papers which showed how moved the Brigadier had been by 'Portrait in a Mirror", Charles Langbridge Morgan's great study of Mental Absolution, Singleness of Mind, Concentration and Acceptance.

In another of his poems written years earlier, the Brigadier looked to home in words which were almost clairvoyant. He saw his fireside, by it was a 'blind, black spaniel'. My last memory of Wyastone Leys was of looking out of the breakfast room across the park. Underneath the window the grass bank fell sharply for 40 feet. It had been steep enough the day before to persuade me to follow the path around. From the staff, I know that the Brigadier had had at least one severe heart attack. He was walking with a mountain pole to help him, but, as I watched, his head appeared over the grassy bank. For him the straightest line up; he was followed by Prince, a black spaniel. The dog was blind.

On 8 April 1978, the Brigadier wrote with the help of his devoted nurse:

> I have gone blind and find dealing with letters rather difficult. A friend has been reading to me John Connell's book on Auchinleck. It brought back, very vividly, our action at Ruweisat, on 2nd and 3rd July 1942, by Robcol, which consisted of 11th Field, and various attached troops. Connell gives the credit for stopping Rommel to 22nd Armoured Brigade, but my memory is that the armour remained behind our left flank all day, until the evening, when prodded by Robert Loder-Symonds of 1st RHA, The Bays sent forward a Honey Squadron, under the ridge on your right, to keep back the German infantry. I do not want to revive old controversies, but I hardly think the armour was at its best just then. I think the German tanks were stopped entirely by the guns of 11th Field, aided by Geoffrey Armstrong's battery of the HAC.

The Brigadier died on 16 December 1978.

Lieutenant Colonel A. O. McCarthy MC

A third commander's will must also have been critical that day – the commander of the guns. Both individually and collectively, in the final analysis, the men who fought the guns determined the fate of Egypt. We shall meet the battery commanders, the troop commanders and the gun commanders more intimately later. They will, I know, forgive me if here I praise Colonel McCarthy to praise them all.

It will be a shorter section than those on the Auk and the brigadier. It was none the less a great pleasure that this section could be written at all. For years I had thought that I would never see Colonel Mac again: even the brigadier thought he was no longer with us. To find him, looking as fit and perky as ever less than 20 miles from the house I had bought on returning to England and to visit him in his house on Armistice Sunday 1967, was therefore doubly rewarding.

Like the brigadier, Colonel Mac kept a diary and allowed me access to it. This time the diary was, at first sight, unrevealing – but perhaps the laconic style is in itself indicative of Colonel Mac's character. For clearly he was a man of action – a happy man, doing a job he liked and without need to record the thoughts which trouble us all in the dark. He was also a busy man and yet the only entries in the diary occur at a time when he was busiest. The first entry is on 9 June and they continue daily until 5 July when there is a break. But these daily entries are limited to brief signposts of our trek from Iraq to the Desert, e.g. 'Thursday 11 June: Left Mosul; Monday 15 June: Left Baghdad; Friday 26 June: Left Cairo.'

This dated itinerary has however been invaluable in fixing details of our approach to battle. No day received more than one line until the breakout from Mersa Matruh on Saturday 27 June when the loss of one 25 pounder and one 2-pounder troop merited four lines. Ruweisat, in comparison, got royal treatment:

> Thursday 2nd July: Went out with Robcol. Had a lot of casualties. Did very well. Battle of Ruweisat ridge.
> Friday 3rd July: Another battle of the same ridge.
> Saturday 4th July: Another artillery battle. Successful.
> Sunday 5th July: I command Robcol

And then a break of 14 days. Dare one read some human frailty in those three words 'Did very well'? Some relief that his Regiment had stood its first test? There was not much to go on. The final entries were similarly informative only by their terseness. They were written with 'hospital' ink and a 'school' pen:

> Sunday 19th July: Wounded, went to No. 64 Alex.
> Monday 20th July: Operated on eye and hand. Other wounds dressed.
> Wednesday 22nd July: Operated on hand.
> Sunday 26th July: Plaster removed without anaesthetic.
> Thursday 28th July: Operated on hand.
> Tuesday 11th August: Operated on hand.

That was all. After 18 days commanding a regiment in action (14 of which were spent commanding the equivalent of a brigade group) the Colonel's active service was finished – or appeared to be – and few would have hoped to have found him in 1967 just about to fly off to Barbados to get to know his first grandchild.

Despite the wounds which forced a long convalescence, by the end of the war, Colonel Mac was doing a significant job at Royal Artillery Base Depot and about this time he flew off to America on an even more important mission.

It was to a man who accompanied him on another flight – also about that time – that I was indebted for a final view of this fighting colonel. The author of the manuscript headed 'Business and Pleasure: A Journey by Jeep and Auster' was unidentifiable and I do not know if this account of a trip to Sinai and TransJordan, including Petra, on reconnaissance for an artillery range has ever been published. If it has, I hope his publishers will allow me to steal the following paragraph:

> You have heard me speak a lot about 'Mac'. He is a living Peter Pan who confounds all the doctors. He has lived and played all his life at a gallop and in 1942 was terribly wounded. A lesser man with less élan would have given up and died, and the doctors clucked and said that he must be very careful and go terribly slow. Mac just galloped the faster and can outlast anyone either at a party or at a gruelling day's activity. I think he does it by a form of lion-hearted bravado. He sets out to beat everyone and the more he does and the more people wonder how he does it, the more his nerves come to his aid and the more he can do. The process is seemingly endless.

The Colonel's iron will carried him through many gallant years as they carried him through the day of 2 July 1942. In doing so he exemplified in every way the words which I chose to quote in the dedication to this book. Since Ruweisat he had faced life knowing that the bullet in his temple was too near the brain for surgery. At the end of the war he flew to USA and to Petra to 'see', today he flies to Barbados to 'get to know' his grandchild. Colonel Mac, like Brigadier Waller and his dog, Prince, is blind.

Colonel Mac died in 1975, aged eighty-one.

CHAPTER 5

Approach to Battle, June 1942[1]

The story of 2 July is a story of nine guns. At least they catch one's eye in the foreground of the picture, a picture which is now dimly lit by the fading lamp of time. The canvas is incomplete, but it has not been retouched in any detail unless it be with the brush of memory.

The nine guns form 83rd/85th Battery RA of the 11th Field Regiment, though four of them would be difficult to recognize as such from the markings they bear. If the canvas were complete, or better lit, it would show eight more guns of 11th Field slightly to the left and rear of our nine guns. These are the guns of the 78th/84th Field Battery RA, sister battery to the 3s and 5s. They are also heavily engaged and it is fortunate that the four guns of B Troop have not completely escaped the artist's attention. The detail at this point is difficult to decipher but it is clear that the composition without them would suffer from over-simplification.

Between the nine guns and the enemy one should be able to spot the anti-tank guns of the 265th Anti-tank Battery RA and the infantry of the 1st/4th Essex. To the left rear, smoke betrays the presence of the 2nd RHA; to the right rear, dust shows the 11th HAC 'marching to the sound of gun-fire'. Vague shapes suggest the presence of armour near at hand but always one's eye returns to the nine guns caught by the artist in the spotlight of history.

A bigger canvas would include the 1st South African Division dug in near the coast, the 2nd New Zealand Division joining briefly in the fight south of the ridge which shelters our nine guns; to the far south a brigade of 5th Indian Division parched of petrol and water on the edge of the great sand wilderness. But again, the eye returns to nine guns for they were all which stood in a direct line between the remains of two panzer divisions and Cairo.

Before the wind obliterates all traces of their tracks in the desert let us retrace the steps which led these nine guns onto a collision course with the DAK not far from the battered tar barrel known as Pt 63, at the end of Ruweisat Ridge.

The obvious starting point for what must inevitably be an account built largely on personal memory, would be up in the northern mountains of Kurdistan where the message arrived on or about 11 June 1942 which led directly, and almost without stopping, to the desert battle. It would be a pleasant starting point for there are few lovelier places on earth than the Ruwandiz Gorge after a year in the deserts of Iraq.

I cannot remember the names of my companions in the 15-cwt truck which crawled up the mountain pass that June day with orders to prepare a regimental rest camp away from the heat of the Kirkuk plains, but I can see the faces as we rounded the corner shutting off the last view of sandy wastes. On green outcrops, Kurdish shepherds sat smoking their long pipes and fondling their beloved rifles. We hoped they understood the peaceful nature of our mission! Suddenly across the valley drifted the smoke of some charcoal fire. It was a clean smell. Seven out of our party of eight turned to each other and as one man said the one word 'England!' Next morning, we had found our camp and cut down a tree to start damming the mountain stream which was to be our regimental swimming pool, when a driver arrived with the message of recall.

This would be an attractive place in which to begin our journey. But, only a lazy historian would ignore the fact that, like King Wenceslas's page, we trod in footsteps boldly printed by other men.

The 11th Field Regiment RA was, as its low number indicated, a regular unit and Colonel McCarthy's attic in Godalming, on Remembrance Sunday 1967, revealed a document. Written, as the text showed, in Salonika in 1946 and refered to hereafter as *The Salonika History*,[2] it enabled me to start my story in an earlier generation. Brown with age and brittle as the bones of an octogenarian this *History of XI Field Regiment 1939–1946* shows the proud past which supported our gunners in 1942. According to this document, 85th Battery can trace its succession back to 1799, 83rd and 84th batteries to 1855 and 78th Battery to 1871. The logic of military numbering seems to have been as Einsteinian then as it is today! It showed that 83rd and 84th batteries' service with Indian troops dated back to the days of the Mutiny:

> 83rd Field Battery RA: 1857–1857: Bareilly, Lucknow, Ramguagd, Shahjehampore, Capture of Ranpoor, Kursiah, Passage of the Gogra, Machleegaon.
> 84th Field Battery RA: 1857–1858: Cawnpore, Kali Naddi, Futterjurh, Oudh, Kanker, Fort Sandia.

If real historians should quarrel with my history or my spelling, let them remember the source of information – a document written in Salonika in March 1946, after five years away from India, away from all sources of information other than Regimental Sergeant Major 'Nobby' Clark's splendid sense of history.

The 83rd and 84th batteries had served together since 1855 and in 1900 they were joined by the 85th Battery to form the 11th Brigade RFA the forerunner of the 11th Field Regiment RA. All the batteries were in the South African War and can quote names like Driefontein, Johannesburg, Relief of Ladysmith, Diamond Hill in their records. All were also in France in 1914 or 1915 and the regiment's name in that war was linked with that of the 3rd Lahore Division. In view of the debt which this history owes to J. L. Manning, reference must also be made to 187th Battery, formed in 1941 which joined us in July 1943 – one year after the events of this story. Because of their pallor they were known as 'Moon Men', but they quickly forgave our brown-kneed snobbery and turned the tables on us by painting a sickly moon on their vehicles as their battery sign. As the original batteries called themselves the '3s and 5s' and the '8s and 4s', the battery commander of the 187th Battery suggested that his men should be called the '6s and 7s'.

When I joined the regiment in Meerut, India, early in 1941, it was still on a peacetime basis of horse-drawn 4.5-inch howitzers and Mark II 18 pounders. In fact, Colonel McCarthy's short history shows that only a year before they had been practising at Tughlakabad, near Delhi, with 15 pounders of Boer War vintage borrowed from Delhi Fort! The first events recorded in this war history are of a sporting nature and the Imperial Delhi Horse Show rates a full paragraph. As one who later commanded the '3s and 5s' it is nice to read that 'almost all the mounted events were won by the 83rd Battery" while the 85th Battery won the Old Comrades Cup for the best all-round battery. In view of later events, we can also take pride in BSM J. Clark of 83rd Battery who came second in the open jumping at Delhi on Rozul Mulluk and in the Handy Hunters on Richard. The equestrian BSM can only be the gallant regimental sergeant major whom we see again on 2 July.

As I wrote this, I could see him in Salonika at the end of hostilities. He stood in the medical officer's dugout before a mirror, unaware that he was observed, and poured out the philosophy of a simple, good, brave, dedicated man in one euphoric sentence: 'The World will march past in Columns of Nations, United Kingdom Leading, His Majesty's Royal Eleventh Field Regiment, WALK MARCH!' With such men at your side, you may lose every battle but the last.[3]

However, the days of saddle soap and gymkhanas were drawing to a close. When the SS *Ormonde* docked in Bombay at the end of February 1941, it carried a stiffening of battle-hardened (three weeks' retreat in France) 'Terriers', the Territorial Army, to leaven the Regular Army in India. The regiment had six six-wheeled Morris 30 cwts plus eight 15-cwt Chevrolet trucks and 13 Norton motorcycles per battery. Some towing lorries appear to have arrived before the end of 1940, but half the guns were still horse-drawn.

As a Terrier, at least I could appear in mess in blue patrols – even though my box spurs may have produced a somewhat hollow clank. In this, we 'foreigners' were one up on the locally engaged Calcutta jute-wallahs. A nice rivalry developed between the 'box-wallahs', the weekend soldiers and the regulars. On balance, I suppose the box-wallahs won, for they had the most money. But this did not matter to the regulars for they did not accept as living anyone who had not been to the Royal Military Academy. 'When I was at the Shop ...' became a cry which scared the souls of Terrier and box-wallah alike until the day when the then battery captain, Jimmy Breakell, put his famous question, 'Excuse me, sir, which shop? ... knocking, bucket or the?' When Matruh fell, Jimmy's brief military career ended before it had really begun, but I would not have been the only one to remember his impact on The British Army in India.

I suppose that training took up a good deal of this time and certainly I remember being savagely punished for my night blindness. But, my last memories of India are of sport – of Colonel 'Friz' Fowler (later commander of 1st Armoured Division Support Group) giving sex education to the young ladies of Meerut on the polo ground and of the 64 inelegant, but useful, runs (equal to my highest ever) I scraped against the Sergeants' XI. A glimpse of Rhanikhet and Nainital (Indian hill stations) where, after the heat of the plains, one could not walk the few hundred yards to the club without having to pop behind a tree – the Himalayas in the moonlight – a brief rustle of petticoats – the cough of some too-large cat in the rest-house garden – the ignominy of a mountain pony which the British Raj demanded I should mount (at 23, one feels these things) – and we were embarking in Bombay for Basra.

From Basra on the coast of Iraq to Rawandiz in Iraqi Kurdistan, need not delay us long – though it filled more than ten months of a young man's life. Shu'arba Camp, where the dry desert heat laid low large numbers of a regiment that had already soldiered for years in India, until we started salt-drinking parades to replace the minerals our pores were losing. The air-conditioned Airport Hotel at Basra where a number of officers lost their lives for returning to the midday sun after taking on a few cold beers in the invigorating air-conditioned bar. The regiment preparing for the invasion of Iran ... and going to Ahwaz in Iran without me because a gunner who doesn't care about his guns swinging dangerously over the Shatt al-Arab is a sick gunner.

Sand-fly fever and a temperature chart beyond understanding. Malignant malaria and relapsing Malta fever, jaundice. Specialists flying all around the Middle East (these were early days for tropical fevers) to gloat over a patient whose chart was sustained in absurdity under the influence of three conflicting temperature cycles. Learning Arabic script to keep a sanity threatened when neighbouring beds were filled on the same day by sufferers from frostbite (from Mosul) and heat exhaustion.

Convalescence in Beirut, vermouth cassis on the verandah of the Hotel St Georges, the taverne in a cave near the Hotel Normandie where Madame delighted in teaching young English subalterns 'Chevalier de la Table Ronde' and others. She taught so well that in Belgium 23 years later – the next time one had the opportunity for such student madness – the words came unprompted. Madame frowning at the soulful accordionist when he broke into his native Viennese waltzes.

Ba'albek in Lebanon – in great slabs of orange stone – a wonder of architecture and engineering that did not for once disappoint a taste now dulled by wonders. The cedars of Lebanon, black against the melting snow. Return to Mosul by the Nairn bus service whose articulated, air-conditioned coaches had, since 1923, run across desert roads which none but the drivers could distinguish and along which we were to return so soon.

The winged bulls uncovered in a Gurkha slit-trench at Nineveh, Iraq. Two hundred miles each way with Clem (D Troop commander, wounded on 2 July after some magnificent observed shooting) to attend a Coptic wedding in a territory reputedly inhabited by Yazidi devil propitiators. Walking across the burning sands from Altun Kupri on the river so melodiously known as the Lesser Zab, to the mound of Erbil, the Iraqi city raised on the eternal refuse of the old Arbela, to win a bottle of whisky.

Memories flood back to colour a canvas which only a few minutes ago seemed dull and uninteresting. But this is a good point to return to Ruwandiz.

Perhaps my trip into the hills was a reward for making good my stupid boast, perhaps an unspoken apology for the fact that when I finally panted up the ziggurat which leads to the centre of Erbil, it was discovered that my promised whisky had been left in camp 35 miles away.

Perhaps, on the other hand, this trip had a military significance of which I could not know. *The Salonika History* states that the regiment moved on 15 June, but the Colonel's diary is equally specific. He was called to Baghdad on 11 June. The trip to Ruwandiz had taken place after our warning order to move. J. L. Scoullar comments: 'Auchinleck emphasized that "it is of paramount importance that we avoid disclosing our weakness or our intentions to the enemy, to Turkey, or to the local populations". Troop movements in the northern frontier area were to be maintained on the same scale as in the past to avoid giving an impression of a change in plans.'[4]

Our regimental rest camp fits neatly into the deception plan!

The battle of Gazala and getting to Ruweisat

The battle of Gazala is the subject of other histories and we shall only linger on two dates which are vital to our narrative.

The first is 5 June 1942. On this day the Eighth Army, which had already lost the 150th Infantry Division and much of the 1st Army Tank Brigade, counter-attacked and lost most of its remaining armour and its guns. Just how heavy the losses were was hidden in reports which were often ill-informed and occasionally, one suspects, ill-inspired. But it is clear that tank losses were probably well over a hundred and that four regiments of artillery, supporting the 10th Indian Brigade, and the support group of the 22nd Armoured Brigade with yet another field regiment, had virtually disappeared from the Eighth Army order of battle. Perhaps the realization of this was the starting point for our march from Iraq. As General Ritchie's communique at midnight of 6/7 June said: 'Gunners look like being a bottleneck.'

The second vital date is that of 'Black Saturday', 13 June 1942. Turner and Agar-Hamilton show that the fighting actually took place on 12 June, but, presumably the appreciation of disaster came the next day.

Liddell Hart has described, speaking of 14 June, how 'The 1st British Armoured Division was no longer in a fit state for action and left the battle-field during the night', its remaining tanks being transferred to 4th Armoured Brigade of 7th Armoured Division, bringing this brigade up to 60 tanks.

Whatever the exact timing, it is clear that between 10 and 15 June, great movements were afoot. Movements that made Ruweisat necessary. Movements which made Ruweisat possible.

In the Western Desert the battle of Gazala, which had begun on 26 May, after swinging pendulum-like in favour first of one side and then of the other, was being lost. It is a convenient point to join the fighting there because the battle which we prefer to call Ruweisat, and others have named First Alamein, is not incorrectly described by others as the end of the Gazala battle. It will also serve to introduce us to the units of Eighth Army and to the third vital date.

That date was 20 June 1942. The main units of the Eighth Army in action over this period, XIII Corps and XXX Corps comprised the 1st South African Division, 2nd South African Division, 50th Tyne-Tees Division, 1st Armoured Division, 7th Armoured Division, 5th Indian Division and the 10th Indian Division and a number of independent brigades among which we must name 1st Free French Brigade in Bir Hackeim. On this day – according to Churchill – our tank strength dropped from 300 to 70 without corresponding loss to the enemy. Again, too, the guns suffered.

While I suggested earlier that Black Saturday might have been the spur to our transfer, it is now clear that 5 June led to the Auk's decision to denude his Middle Eastern northern frontier. Black Saturday merely confirmed the wisdom of that decision. It did not make it any less courageous. Within days, X Corps HQ and two of the finest divisions in the world – the 2nd New Zealand and 9th Australian were on the move to the Eighth Army's aid. They were followed by a less experienced force drawn from 8th Indian Division. Among these untried reinforcements was 18th Indian Infantry Brigade, oblivious of the fate which awaited it on 1 July in the Deir el Shein. Somewhere in the columns also marched the 1st/4th Essex and 11th Field Regiment RA who were to provide the nucleus of the insignificant little force, Robcol.

The urgent concentration of this new corps about 1,500 miles from its starting points is one of the greatest marching stories of all time and, seen from a modern satellite would also have provided one of the most dramatic pictures of all time. The signal for the 'off' reached the starters, scattered throughout the vast area controlled by Ninth and Tenth armies, in many different circumstances. Lieutenant Colonel Scoullar relates how, on 10 June, General Freyberg, commander of the 2nd New Zealand

Expeditionary Force heard of the fall of Bir Hackeim on 11 June while he was on reconnaissance in the mountains of South West Persia. In such a crisis, his Kiwis could not be left in Syria out of the battle and by the evening of 13 June, he had flown to Cairo where the Auk ordered him to concentrate his division by the frontier.[5]

In 11th Field, Colonel McCarthy's diary shows that he was in the officers' mess of 40 Rest Camp on an exercise with the Devons and Dorsets, to be followed a few days later by the Essex Regiment. The dates are crossed out on the entry for Thursday 11 June which now reads 'Left Mosul'. On 13 June, as Freyberg arrived in Cairo and the battle for Gazala reached its moment of decision, Colonel Mac arrived in Baghdad.

In the Lebanon, Freyberg's HQ received the order to move on 14 June and left Ba'albek at 0600 hours on 16 June to reopen west of Mersa Matruh, 900 miles away at 2100 hours on 20 June. Two New Zealand field regiments left the same day as the HQ and got to Mersa Matruh on 21 June.

Brigadier Kippenberger of the 5th New Zealand Brigade had just left hospital at Zahla after a bout of shingles and chickenpox. After

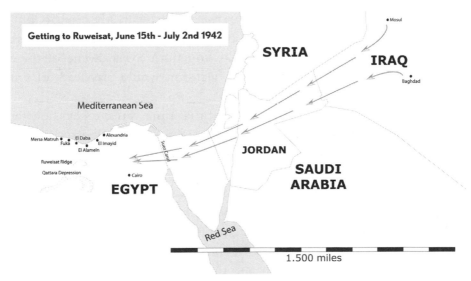

Getting to Ruweisat, 15 June–2 July 1942. (Courtesy of Graphic Performance)

convalescence at Haifa, he resumed command of his brigade and immediately went off to do training in the desert 60 miles south-east of Aleppo.

The 5th New Zealand Brigade moved on 18 June, following 4th Brigade who travelled one day ahead of them. The last New Zealand units reached El Amiriya, south of Alexandria, on 25 June. Since leaving Cairo, they must have felt like someone trying to enter a football ground just after the referee has blown 'no side'.

On 20 June, all New Zealand brigade and unit commanders were 'put in the picture', a grim one, by General Freyberg. As Tobruk fell, the 5th New Zealand Brigade were approaching Alexandria on the strategic road. Brigadier Kippenberger reached Mersa Matruh on 21 June at 1100 hours and attended a divisional conference in the underground Fortress HQ. Here he learned that 1st Armoured had been reduced to about a hundred runners, many of them light Stuart tanks; that the 1st South African Division was in 'fair order', that the 50th and 5th Indian divisions were down to 'little more than weak brigade groups' and that there was not much else to the west.

Across a quarter of a century, the picture is clear. As the western defences crumbled, the desert to the east thickened with dust. The 10th Indian Division had started to arrive, part was already near Sollum. The New Zealand division would be complete in a 'couple of days'. The 9th Australian Division was following from Syria. Some of these troops, like the 9th Australian and the armour, would play lead roles at Montgomery's Alamein.

To Brigadier Kippenberger, it seemed that time was the key: he later acknowledged the vital day bought by the 18th Indian Infantry Brigade on 1 July; it is unlikely that he knew much of the final 24 hours won by Robcol.

The 5th New Zealand Brigade received orders at this conference to hold the eastern sector of Mersa Matruh. We can leave them here, enjoying occasional bathes in Smuggler's Cove, working hard at preparing a position, being bombed, until 25 June. This was the day that 11th Field arrived in Cairo and the day that the Auk faced up to what Corelli Barnett calls 'the reality of command'. With his Deputy Commander General Staff (DCGS) General Dorman O'Gowan, he flew to O'Connor's operations room in Baggush in Egypt.

Lieutenant General O'Connor, commander of the Western Desert Force, was actually a POW at the time. Gott's XIII Corps on the frontier had been overrun. The enemy was already at Sidi Barrani. Norrie's XXX Corps had handed over two days earlier to the new arrivals from Syria and gone off to start the defences at Alamein. General Holmes, Commander British Troops in Egypt, was certain that Rommel would attack X Corps in Mersa Matruh the next day.

Auchinleck had to buy time – time for the help that was on the way, to arrive. He took over direct command of Eighth Army and changed the plan; Mersa Matruh would not be held. If the enemy threatened to bottle them up in the fortress, they must break out to El Alamein, the final position. Churchill did not understand, but now the Auk was in the desert. He was committed and away from the burdens imposed by communications at that time.

The 10th Indian, on arrival, would relieve the Kiwis in Mersa Matruh. The 2nd New Zealand Division would move south into the desert and meet the invading force head on. On 26 June, the New Zealand division took up positions on the cliffs of Minquar Qain, 25 miles south of Mersa Matruh, with the 21st Brigade 20 miles farther south at Bir Khaldar. The 1st Armoured Division 'said still to have 100 tanks' was in the neighbourhood and an Indian brigade was some miles to the east at Minquar Sidi Hamza. There were gaps of several miles between the defended localities, mobile battle groups were to operate in these gaps. There was much dissension among some of the commanders about this plan. One of them described a 'battle group' as a 'brigade which has been twice overrun by tanks'.

Five hundred miles east of the New Zealanders from the valleys of the Tigris and the Euphrates and from the oilfields of Kirkuk where the 'burning fiery furnace' of Shadrach, Meshach and Abednego still lit the night sky, came another column. In this column we find the units that wrote 'Mene, Mene, Tekel, Upharsin' in the annals of Rommel's Afrika Korps.

To those new to the desert, one grain of sand looks much like its neighbour. If one could stop and discover there would be much to learn, but 150 miles a day is a fair stretch for laden gun-towers across a scorching desert. The names remind us that this is the cradle of history, but we cannot remember which chapter – Mosul, Quayara, Baghdad, Habbabiya – this is less difficult, for the history of the siege was then more recent and one recalled how, only a few months before, Gloster Gladiator biplanes had been shooting down Messerschmitts too fast and modern to fly in tight circles at 80 mph.

On to numbers LG5, H3 and H4 – a landing ground and two pumping stations on the oil pipeline to Homs – and then Mafraq in Jordan, surely a name known to T. E. Lawrence. In my case, this journey was made at speed and alone – without the comforting presence of the column of guns and without the disciplined pace which their presence would have dictated. As Officer Commanding Advance Party, it was my duty to prepare the desert staging posts for occupation when the regimental column arrived. As the journey progressed, so the advance party's pace increased, quickened by rumours of a thousand Polish ATS girls travelling the same route just ahead of us. Every day we seemed to get nearer but like Achilles and the tortoise, never quite closed the gap.

Finally, we crossed the Jordan and camped for 24 hours near the Mediterranean at Giv'at Olga, near Hadera in today's Israel. As we tasted briefly the fruits of a civilization we had not known for months, Tobruk fell and the leading troops of the 2nd New Zealanders reached Mersa Matruh. From them to us stretched a thin line of tarmac with one column going west and flanked by many columns heading east.

Just one month earlier, HQ 10th Indian Division had made the same journey. The Brigade Major, B. A. G. Jones, later described his thoughts on the journey in verse:

Convoy, Iraq to Egypt

Over the desert the thin wind whips,
Slowly the convoy moves along,
A driver mutters through broken lips
Some stupid oath or some stupid song.

No nice exact road lies ahead
With milestones white to prove our pace,
A thousand tracks here cross and spread
Upon the desert's burning face.

The noonday sun strikes down to slow
The turnings of my wandering mind,
Who cares now whither we shall go,
Or, having gone, what we shall find?

Here black burnt stones replace the sand
And heat the wind whose horrid breath
Flies sterile, dry across a land
That wears the rusted pall of death.

The energy of thought is spent
Dead is the remnant of our wills,
We follow where another went
To fate that lies behind dark hills.

At last the sun to crimson turns,
The wind has gone into the west,
The blasted rock no longer burns;
Our convoy slowly comes to rest.

Swift night descends and with it rise
A multitude of small bright fires.
To days of peace the wind soon flies
With memories of lost desires.

As one by one those fires die out
Beside the lorries, line on line,
A sentry stamps and turns about.
The silence of the night is mine.

From Hadera south, through the plains of Charon, past Beersheba into the desert of Sinai – now surely we were in the land of Lawrence and Allenby and without knowing it the forerunners of Dayan. Then Asluj, the Canal and finally Cairo. Vague memory speaks of the pyramids. Mena House and a camp called Cowley close to Cairo. I cannot remember visiting the fleshpots of Cairo at this time nor can I recall any urge to do so. We had, in any case, much to keep us occupied in preparing for the action which was now inevitable.

26 June 1942

On the day that the Auk assumed personal command of the Eighth Army, the 11th Field Regiment marched from Cowley Camp, Cairo. Moving along the narrow tarmac strip leading past the Coptic monasteries of the Wadi Natrun, past the salt lakes which flank Alexandria, the Regiment turned left at El Amiriya along the coastal road and into the Western Desert. On the way we passed, without any hint of what they would mean to us, little halts on the railway running beside the road, halts called El Hammam, El Ruweisat and El Imayid. A short distance ahead of us we ran off the 1:500,000 map Cairo based on red grid (longitude 31E) and hit a further railway halt marked El Alamein.

Down in the desert to our left, the skyline shimmered in the morning sun over a low ridge ending in a sharp bluff. We did not then know its name – most of us had not been issued with maps. If we had, we should, in all probability, have been little the wiser. I was now looking at Geoff Armstrong's map, sheet 14 of the 1:250,000 map of Egypt and Cyrenaica headed El Daba. Approaching longitude 29E the stations I have mentioned are clearly shown. From El Ruweisat station running just west–south-west, are the contour lines of 50 metres, 60 metres and sometimes 70 and 80 metres. They mark a steep escarpment which rises from near Ruweisat station at 80 metres to 90 metres, drops to 79 and up sharply again to 101 metres. Thence it descends gradually through 95, 93 and 87 towards 79 metres at Alam Baoshaza just inside the area of purple grid, based on longitude 27E. From here a nameless ridge runs slightly north-west for 15 kilometres to Pt 64. This was the ridge which we were to know as Ruweisat and Pt 64, the battered tar barrel which became to us the left hand of Pt 63. On this map, the ridge bears no name though it clearly ends in the rough depressions of Deir el Abyad and El Mreir. Just north of Pt 64 is a squiggle like a jelly-baby or a tooth extracted with infected roots. This marks the Deir el Shein.

But, even if we had had maps that day and even if the maps showed the ground in greater detail, it is unlikely that we would have paid more than passing interest to the cliff which the troops later knew as Beachy Head. This was the observation post that was as bitterly fought for as any other OP in the war – the goal which was to haunt me for four long, fly-struck months. As we passed, we knew nothing of the digging started here in 1940 nor of the decision which the Auk would shortly take to provide Montgomery with a suitable field for victory here. Our eyes were fixed forward, looking for we knew not what – past Sidi Abd el Rahman without being conscious of the saint's tomb, the White Mosque – to halt finally at El Daba. Here our column halted for the night of 26 June – our first night in the Western Desert.

Above, came a *thrump-thrump* of desynchronized engines, which to those who had spent the war in India was just an aeroplane, but to the few who had come out from wartime England, could only mean trouble. Trouble, fortunately not for us, but for the RAF at Daba aerodrome nearby. Green rookies though we were, the noise could not keep us, tired by the long journey and the mounting nervous strain, awake long. It did though speed the digging of our first 'serious' slit-trenches. By now, little holes in the ground marked our passage for many hundreds of miles but this time our digging was in earnest. Throughout the following months, I had the great fortune to travel with two men who were not only regular soldiers, but also Durham miners. Perhaps this book would not have been written but for their skill with a pick and a spade.

27 June 1942

On again after our first real desert breakfast. Was it 'burgoo' of biscuits boiled with jam or a 'rill-mill' of soya-links and bacon, perhaps a feast of 'fried bully and peas' or even 'sardines on hard tack' – for we were still rich after our brief stay in Cairo. Certainly, it was washed down with a 'piyala' of hot, sweet 'char'. Only one day in the war did I fail to get a 'piyala of char'. That day is remembered with a bleak horror which would surprise my sons who associate their father with harder stuff. With the char must have come a heavenly 'Camel to Consumer' – heavenly, despite the pejorative name, for this was real luxury from the city of sin. In a few days we would be back on 'Vs', those tubes of faintly rotting hay. Not many weeks would pass before one Victory V puffed in turn by the four members of an OP truck would be a pleasure to remember.

As the column started, one was still conscious of traffic flowing eastward, but as the column advanced farther west, the flood weakened and dried to a trickle. Past Fuka, there was little movement and by Sidi Haneish, none. Suddenly the desert seemed very quiet. As the kilometre posts indicated the approaching nearness of Mersa Matruh, the silence seemed to drown the noise of the vehicles. At Sidi Haneish, the escarpment came close to the road like a low cloud. After flowing through this channel the convoy was alone, swamped by silence which was only made more intense by distant thunder.

As the column approached Mersa Matruh, the leading vehicle passed the stone marking 15 kilometres from that haven. It bore a sign which read '11th Field Stop Here'.

CHAPTER 6

Approach to Battle, 27 June–
1 July 1942

The regiment pulled off the road and halted in the sand dunes in extended order. The CO went forward to reconnoitre and returned with orders from 50th Division. The orders were that B Echelon was to be brigaded with other echelons under the direct command of 50th Division, and the regiment, with other elements of 50th Division, was to break through the encircling Germans and return to Daba.

Rumour had it that the road we had just come along was now closed by the enemy. As the afternoon wore on, the noise of firing from that direction gave force to this rumour and all uncertainty ceased with the arrival of a shell from a gun fired to the east of us. Our long march was over; the regiment was under fire for the first time. Before we could put into practice the skills acquired in long months of training, before the sleek barrels of our burnished guns could speak in anger and fulfil the purpose of their creation, we were 'on the run'.

The 3-ton trucks of B Echelon, loaded with our only possessions and on which we had lavished such care in the dull days of Iraq, were to be left behind with Jimmy Breakell, the battery captain. Shops, whether 'knocking, bucket or The' would in hours be beyond his reach, for Jimmy was heading for 'the bag'. With him would go our service dress, the Sam Browne belts we so carefully polished; the greatest loss of all, a 3-tonner almost full of crates of whisky! Whisky bought by the officers' mess of the '3s and 5s' and brought all the way from India, whisky hoarded from the greed of junior officers by the strong mind of Major Anthony Stanton, our battery commander. Many an evening after hard training in Iraq we had pleaded with him for another 'peg'. For a year, we had been limited to two a night so that when we were called to the desert, as we knew some day we must be, we would not lack for 'comforts'. Now Anthony had left us to go to Staff College.

His place had been taken by Major J. M. Douglas, and 'Duggie' marched to war blessing Anthony's careful housekeeping. But, as we saw Jimmy marshalling his small force of soft-skinned lorries, preparatory to reporting to Captain John Evans-Lawrence, the senior battery captain (of 78th/84th Battery) who was to command the regimental B Echelon, we realized that we had little chance of ever reaping the rewards of our abstinence. Thank God that one or two of us had the presence of mind to call on the mess lorry before it disappeared. Even then, so rooted was the habit of self-denial that we limited our withdrawals to one bottle per man.

As dusk fell, the column formed up in desert formation to the south of the Matruh road and pointing south. In the centre and to the rear the remaining soft-skinned vehicles, flanking them the guns in line astern, outside them, a line of 2-pounder anti-tank guns on portees, ahead, the light-armoured observation vehicles of the CO, the battery commanders and the troop commanders. Mingling with the guns were a company of Royal Northumberland Fusiliers with medium machine guns, and companies of the 1st/4th Essex Regiment. Ahead of the armoured cars, at least for the breakout, was a screen of Honey tanks.

Dusk fell and the column moved off slowly towards a line of tele-graph poles on the escarpment. Orders were to move south through the German leaguers and down into the desert where a New Zealand column was reported to be, then to turn east for 50 miles before heading north to El Daba. In a few weeks, such a night march would be regarded as 'a piece of cake'. Many other units undertook similar operations that night. But, they were already desert-hardened. For the 11th Field this was a baptismal ceremony without benefit of godparents! Few of us knew where we were starting from, fewer where we were going. No one knew what lay between. To the initiated, a tar barrel with a number standing next to a faint hollow in the ground was as a traffic sign reading 'Charing Cross 1m'. To the newcomer, the contours of the desert said nothing and distance could not be measured by eye.

Even as the column moved off, disaster struck E Troop. A direct hit on a tractor left it a blazing witness of the place from which we had come. Somehow its gun and trailer must have been hitched onto a 3-tonner for the four guns of E Troop followed D Troop to the top of the escarpment. By now it was dark, though not pitch black and the skyline was lit by flares and tracer. On the top visibility was not too bad, but in the soft sand of the wadis, darkness was complete. In one of those, a vehicle overturned, revving furiously in the soft, yielding sand, the following gun stuck fast. Behind, occasional shell bursts drove the following vehicles into the shelter of the wadi. E Troop was stuck.

Shortly, the column halted to regain the disciplined formation which the wadis had broken up. In front, Major Douglas, like a good shepherd, sensed his missing sheep. He retraced the column's steps just as the head of E Troop, urged on by the furious oaths of RSM Harvey, broke out of the wadi. One tractor emerged towing its gun and was directed by the major down the telegraph poles towards the disappearing column. A second gun followed, and then a third.

'Follow that quad!' they were ordered. But, No. 4 gun did not emerge. Presumably this was the gun which had lost its quad at the start. Towed by a 3-tonner, it would be deprived of the self-winching gear with which the gun-towing quads had been pulling themselves out. Without this gear, a vehicle, once stuck, cannot escape without help from another truck.

E Troop was reduced to three guns and they were marching behind a leader with only a vague indication of where they should be heading. Having directed three guns of E Troop back towards the column, Major Douglas went on to look for the missing No. 4. By now the column had moved on and Major Douglas was himself 'lost'. Perhaps he did not know it, perhaps he did and saved himself by a superb bit of navigation, perhaps it was just a lucky chance. While the guns of E Troop lumbered off into the desert, the battery commander regained contact with the larger part of his command and resumed his station at the head of the column with the other armoured cars, fussing like corvettes around a naval convoy.

The second in command, Major Pat Waterfield, came up and with suitably nautical expressions, urging the OP cars to greater zigzag efforts. In following a straight line pockets of enemy or patches of bad going could be missed to trap the following guns. The whole frontage of the column had to be covered by the handful of armoured vehicles in the screen. Spurred on by Pat Waterfield's command of English expletives, the armoured screen disappeared into the night, zigzagging furiously. Behind roared Major Waterfield, with a fresh load of invective, just in time to curb the keenness which his first intervention had aroused and to prevent the column breaking up completely.

'Enemy tanks ahead,' came the message from the armoured vehicles, 'D Troop, action!' Out of the quads tumbled sleepy gunners. A well-trained crew can have a round 'up the range' from the travelling position in well under a minute. By night and in one's first action, it took longer before the No. 1 reported 'ready to fire'. By the time D Troop's trails had hit the ground on this occasion, the OPs were fraternizing with the enemy, who turned out to be the armoured cars of a similar 'breakout' column.

But only slightly afterwards, the column halted again. This time, small-arms fire showed that the enemy was far from friendly. 11th Field was once more receiving baptism: bombed for the first time at Daba the night before, shelled for the first time that afternoon, now under small-arms fire for the first time.

Slowly the tracer rose towards the column. The slow track of a tracer bullet aimed at someone else defies logical explanation. But, suddenly it was no longer aimed at someone else, it was aimed at you. No longer was it a Bonfire Night rocket climbing slowly to fall almost lethargically, but a fluorescent mosquito zipping past the ears and demanding to be squashed with a blow of the hand. Now that bottle from the mess truck assumed its real value. Now you blessed the major whose parsimony you have cursed for months. Better to hand a whole convoy of whisky 3-tonners to the Germans than to arrive at this point without some aid to courage. Your driver agreed! Years later one must learn to drive without drinking, but tonight, yellow lines have not been invented.

There were no kerbstones, only sandy hollows and rocky outcrops. Tonight you could run into or over anything without losing your no claims bonus, provided you do not stop!

The firing came from a German leaguer where the weary Afrika Korps was protesting against the disturbance of their sleep. It was heaviest on the right flank where shortly a vehicle was blazing. This time it was one of theirs. Major Paul, commander of our anti-tank battery, had written off an enemy truck and majors Douglas and Waterfield were now the proud possessors of a number of German prisoners.

In the centre of the column, in the peculiar pink box which was the Regimental Signals Centre, 'Pip' Mott's wireless operator was vainly sending the regimental call sign into the night air. No response from 50th Division. They had an urgent message for the column – a message actually recalling the guns to defend Mersa Matruh. It was not delivered, although they heard our signals. Pip's call sign and codes had been picked up on the march when we passed through the base echelons, perhaps in Cairo, or Alex, perhaps at Daba or Fuka. They were unknown to HQ in Mersa Matruh and, despite the signaller's repeated call, the urgent orders were never passed.

Towards the back of the column, Sergeant Hatfield was following the truck in front when it took a direct hit. Gathering up the unhurt driver and a gunner, their next two trucks were also hit and finding a deep ditch they settled in to wait. In the early hours of the morning they walked east in the darkness and were eventually picked up by a XXX Corps signals truck and returned to the unit.

Away on our right, a similar column was less fortunate. Like 11th Field, 11th HAC had also burst through the enemy leaguers. Unlike us, they are desert hardened. Unlike us, they knew where they were and where they have come from. They belonged. Even in the depths of the desert they were in contact. They had had a harder fight to get out than we had, but, just when they were congratulating themselves that the worst was past, the message was received. Having broken out, they must now break in again! Tomorrow night, they would break out yet again!

The desert night slowly gave way to a desert dawn and that clear light of day which precedes the mirages of mid-morning. The column marched on to the south and turned left without meeting a sign of life. Later one remembered the desert as a friendly home, but to a new unit commander, without any opportunity to get his men acclimatized, retreating without any real chance to engage the enemy, with B Echelon and a number of guns already lost, with little knowledge of where the Eighth Army was to be found, the desert must have seemed a vast and lonely place.

But, if Colonel Mac allowed himself time for such introspection, he did not record it. His diary for Saturday 27 June read: 'Joined 50th Division. Attacked 1930 hours, got through. Lost one 25 pounder Troop and one 2 pounder Troop.'

If we had expected to bump into the New Zealanders that night, Brigadier Kippenberger explained why we could not find them: they were no longer there.[1]

Their position at Minqar Qaim, the firm rock towards which our column had been directed, had been attacked by the main force of the DAK as early as 0900 on the morning of 27 June and by midday the enemy was around the right flank of the New Zealand division. It must have been the left flank of this enemy force which within a few hours had turned north and cut the road behind us. But by then the Kiwis had suffered a grievous blow: General Freyberg had been wounded.

Brigadier Inglis took command of a force which was surrounded. He turned to the 1st Armoured Division for help – but this, General Lumsden could not give. Like us, the Kiwis were having difficulties with their wireless and were therefore unable to call up their heavy transport for the breakout. When they did get through, like us, they had no codes and the B Echelon commander, despite recourse to nicknames as proof of identity, regarded an order to march east as a German trick. But, as our E Troop floundered in the wadi, the New Zealand Division moved east through the thin circle of the enemy. Our haven no longer existed.

The Kiwis escaped to fight another day – even though it was some time before they could produce a coherent ration strength. At 1000 hours on 28 June, Brigadier Kippenberger took up position astride the line of retreat and with his Brigade Major, 'Monty' Fairbrother, was – after enjoying a desert breakfast – 'advertising' for a rear-guard. As the last lone Bren-carrier passed, he counted heads in his little force. The 5th New Zealand Brigade counted three staff cars and four 3-tonners.

28 June 1942

At 0800, 28 June, as the New Zealanders were trickling into the Kaponga Box, the name they had given to the box at Qaret el Abd, 11th Field stopped to 'brew up'. Each vehicle lit its petrol sand fire and soon the water was boiling in the cut-off four-sided petrol tins that served as kettles. But, before the water was on the boil, a German reconnaissance vehicle (or a vehicle assumed to be German) was observed on a rise overlooking the position. Amidst much swearing the half-heated cans of precious water were bundled into the backs of trucks. Fingers were cut on the jagged edges of hot tins of soya-links but, in minutes, the column had formed a defensive perimeter with the guns able to fire in any direction. In this state of armed readiness, breakfast was finished, heads were counted, petrol and water redistributed and, amid the shouting and cursing which accompanies even the most good-humoured military operation, the regiment was on the march again.

When the guns' chief concern is the expectation that enemy tanks will appear over the next hill at any moment, the Battery Command Post Officer is a useless appendix. His role in life is concerned with surveying and communication, techniques which are not called for when targets are engaged over open sights. So now I found myself relegated to the position of what, in polite society might be called 'back-stop Charlie'.

Little of this day of marching eastwards remains in my memory, though at some time in the day our guns dropped trails and prepared to engage the 1st Armoured Division. There is a clear impression of the column ahead being Stuka'ed in a wadi, another memory of sweating over sand tracks to free other vehicles stuck in soft sand and then the realization that I was alone in the desert with one 15-cwt truck and one 3-tonner. A 'back-stop' is without the benefit of a long stop.

In the 3-tonner were seven German prisoners wearing the khaki 'cricketing cap' of the Afrika Korps and a couple of British cooks. In the 15 cwt, one or two non-military survey types, myself and a driver.

The Germans seemed decent types, though scruffily dressed. It seemed a pity that we might have to shoot them because night was falling and these fit young men outnumbered my unmilitary force. How seriously I considered this thought I cannot now say. Certainly it was in my mind for some time; however, night passed without resort to such violent measures. Whether the prisoners cooked for us, or we for them, I cannot remember.

Some few miles away in the desert, the regiment also leaguered. As fuel was getting low, a check was made and the resources of each vehicle equalized. In one of the regimental HQ 3-tonners two faces, darker than the rest, betrayed the loyalty of our camp followers. The regimental 'moochi' (North Indian for a cobbler or saddler) and an Indian fitter from the Light Aid Detachment shamefacedly answered the RSM. They had wanted to be with the guns rather than be left with B Echelon.

In Mersa Matruh, Brigadier Waller crossed the railway line at 2200 hours, having destroyed his diary lest it be captured during the breakout.

29 June 1942

As dawn broke on my 24th birthday, the desert was veiled in heavy mist. In this mist two armies lay intertwined, unrecognizable from the air or from the ground as friend or foe – the Germans travelling in English and German vehicles, the British in trucks with similar markings. As Paolo Caccia-Dominioni wrote, '… an uninitiated observer would have stood amazed at the sight of a British Army in flight and turning every so often to snap at a second British Army hard on its heels.'[2] From Mersa Matruh too, the 11th HAC broke out for the second time.

In Mersa Matruh, John Evans-Lawrence and Jimmy Breakell prepared for the end. Some at least of E Troops four lost guns (with their accompanying anti-tank guns) were with them and *The Salonika History* records how E Troop fought most gallantly under RSM Harvey as the 50th Division HQ was overrun. But though John Evans-Lawrence escaped a few days later, to rejoin 11th Field and die in mid-July, Jimmy Breakell also appears here for the last time in this narrative – as does our mess 3-tonner, almost full of whisky.

After that misty breakfast, my little convoy struck out into the unknown. For lack of better direction, I imagine that we travelled towards the rising sun. As this climbed the heavens, the farthest ridges of sand slowly floated upwards, leaving the appearance of a great salt lake in the middle distance. In this mirage, skyscrapers projected themselves into the sandy sky. Around the base of these mammoth buildings little figures of matchstick men scurried, suddenly to shoot to the 14th floor – an apparition that caused us to move forward more slowly and perhaps led our prisoners to dream of freedom. But, the strange shapes were quickly revealed as part of the headquarters of 1st Armoured Division, where we were received with glacial warmth.

When, two years earlier we had come home from Dunkirk in expectation of court-martial, some of us had been surprised to find ourselves heroes. Now one knew that the breakout from Mersa Matruh had been truly heroic, but the attitude of the young staff officer in the 1st Armoured Division HQ showed clearly his distrust of our martial intentions. It seemed hard to march so far through so much trouble only to provide an object of scorn for such a precocious young fellow. At that time, we did not realize how low was the morale of our armour – nor how much they had suffered – and so, after the briefest of encounters, our two trucks drove off and were, once more, lost in the desert.

The memory of this encounter would be of little value to this narrative but for one fact. My mental picture of the 1st Armoured Division shows vehicles as far as the eye can see – 15 cwts, 3-tonners, command vehicles, tank transporters, wireless trucks … but not one tank. Without this memory, the maps of 2 July that showed the 1st Armoured Division would paint a different picture, but, with this memory, one realizes the softness and the great expanse presented by the underbelly of an armoured division on the move.

About the time I was striking out from 1st Armoured Division HQ towards where I reasoned the coast road must be, the advanced elements of 11th Field were running onto El Daba aerodrome. As they arrived, they saw little groups of people in blue-grey uniforms, but closer inspection showed these to be RAF rear parties and not advanced German patrols. Distant explosions explained the nature of the RAF's business, but the column had no difficulty in finding petrol for the thirsty vehicles, though aviation spirit to the gun towers was like serving Château d'Yquem at a hot-pot supper.

Even more important than petrol was the survival of the water point – water for the quads, jerry cans to fill, dusty throats and caked faces to slake almost without guilt. But only just in time; as the column left, a loud explosion showed that the South African sapper officer who had watched their generous ration so tolerantly, had done his work. The next column would not be so fortunate.

When fortune is kind, she can be a generous jade. With full tanks and full water bottles, the column ran past the NAAFI at Daba, just as they were preparing to evacuate. As one who followed too late, I am – even many years later – glad that I cannot describe their loot. But some free beers that day went down throats which within hours would be choked with sand forever.

Soon after midday, the regiment set off once more in an easterly direction. Colonel Mac had given orders that the strictest march discipline was to be maintained. With regulation spacing the column moved off. Over an eastern ridge, miles in front of the reported prepared position to which they now knew they were retiring, appeared an armoured car and a staff car containing the unmistakeable figure of the Auk. I have quoted from Connell elsewhere in these pages, Geoff Armstrong's impressions are also reported, my own feelings when I followed the regiment some distance behind have been shared with you, the gunners were no less surprised and delighted. The General smiled at them, and cheered them up as he did me.

Although one's memory is of an encounter on a lonely road, it is evident that in fact, the traffic was thickening between Fuka and Alamein. Brigadier Waller, still CRA of the 10th Indian Division, recorded that he arrived six miles south of Alamein just after noon. Geoff Armstrong led the six remaining guns of the 11th HAC past a smiling Auchinleck at about the same time. This meeting was registered by some army photographer and appeared the following Monday, 6 July, in *Le Journal d'Alexandrie et La Bourse Egyptienne*.

The same paper carried the news that on the Saturday evening, 4 July, the Duchess of Kent had given birth to a baby boy: '*La Duchesse et le petit*

Prince se portent bien.' It also describes *'aucun changement important dans les conditions de la bataille d'Alamein'*, where *'le combat d'hier a eu lieu presque au meme encroit que précédement'*. A roughly sketched map shows the area of the battle but neither Ruweisat Ridge nor the Deir el Shein were features known to the artist.

In the photo was the Auk in his staff car as I had seen him shortly before. Geoff Armstrong was standing by the road wearing, of all unlikely headdresses, a solar topee of Indian pattern. Geoff later described how he adopted this headgear at first as a joke, and kept it as a symbol. In a similar way, I later adopted a blue and red dress 'fore and aft' forage cap so the Indian troops would recognize the strange officer who was their 'top-khana wallah'.

But though many units had passed this way in the last few hours, the flow was now dying down to a trickle. Few of those who now passed were in a fit condition to take on a determined enemy.

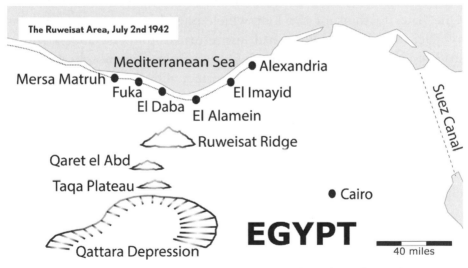

The Ruweisat Area, 2 July 1942. (Courtesy of Graphic Performance)

30 June 1942

11th Field took up positions in support of the South African box about two miles west of El Alamein railway station. 'Strafer' Gott's opinion as quoted by Kippenberger was that, on that day: 'The New Zealand Division was battle-worthy but very few other people were and he feared the worst.'

In this place, the 24 hours which are missing from most accounts must have been spent. I had a clear recollection of pulling into the regimental area late enough to feel like a new boy in a club where everyone else knew his way around, of a night's peaceful sleep and even of a short swim in the sea, a swim which would have been longer if planes had not arrived to emphasize the nakedness which young men did not feel just because they were unclothed. Somewhere here my prisoners must have left but memory does not retain their going. Nor can I remember the move, some time on 1 July, which took us from here first eastward, then southward on to the Gebel Bein Gebir.

But before we left, at about 1630 hours on 30 June, the first shells fell on the Alamein box. They landed in the regiment's gun position without causing casualties, though the RQMS's 3-tonner was destroyed. One hates to think of the loot which must have gone up with this vehicle, though ostensibly it had just returned from Alexandria with a load of small arms ammunition. It is certain that, for months to come, the RQMS was provided with the perfect alibi for any missing item of equipment. It is also clear from the records that this happy accident taught us one of the first lessons in desert warfare, because *The Salonika History* continues that 'all soft skinned vehicles were then moved back 1,000 yards'. It is equally clear from the record that the regiment's first shots 'in anger' were fired from this position: 'The guns continued to engage targets in support of the Box until nightfall.'

One has no recollection of what the targets were – perhaps just harassing fire down the now deserted Fuka road. As the battery still consisted of the four guns of D Troop, there would be little employment for a Command Post Officer whose main duty would be to 'link' their fire to that of a non-existent E Troop. But this sad state of affairs was soon to be rectified.

At night, into the leaguer which the regiment had formed around the guns, trickled the first of the desert nomads from which a new E Troop was to be built. One of these wandering guns was, within

48 hours, to provide the last straw on which Rommel broke the back of his advance. It is more than likely that if these five guns had not stayed to join 11th Field, the 3rd of July would have seen Rommel at the gates of Cairo.

Perhaps they joined with us, in the hours between nightfall 30 June and dawn 2 July, because of some unbroken will to continue the fight. Perhaps they were just tired of being alone and looked to us for comfort – and rations. Perhaps they were bullied into turning about by some irate staff officer at a control point. That day of 30 June, Brigadier Waller moved behind the minefield and we know that his spirit was unbroken. Elsewhere we find Claude Eastman, CRA of 50th Division, with one gun left out of his command of 72 still urging it towards the enemy. It could have been either of these senior officers who turned back the gun that finally decided Ruweisat and, at Ruweisat, Alamein.

We do know that, by dawn on 2 July, E Troop consisted of five guns: one from 32nd Field, one from 121st Field, two from 157th Field and a survivor from the original E Troop, complete now with Gun Position Officer from 32nd Field and under the command of Captain Lawrence Boyd. During the breakout, he had been doing 'corvette' duty to the convoy, and so missed the fate which befell his own guns outside Mersa Matruh.

We also know that our pitiful little 2-pounders had been reinforced by six 6-pounders. The credit for this goes to the Adjutant, Captain Tommy Tomson.

1 July 1942

Wednesday1 July in Colonel Mac's diary does not help us much. It contains two words: 'stayed Elamine' (actually El Imayid). Colonel Mac's spelling of place names supports my belief that maps were in very short supply. As the unknown author of the trip to Petra whom we quoted earlier wrote: 'I like this part of the world as you never need to spell a thing or a place twice the same, even on the same page.' But, it does not help the amateur historian.

The Salonika History recorded that this day, 'Ash Wednesday' – so named because of the burning of documents in Cairo – 1 July 1942, was spent 'cleaning up and preparing for battle'. It continued: 'The CO visited Brigadier Waller who was then forming Robcol.' Rather like a City financier calling on someone floating a new company. But it brings us to the start of this story.

As we leave the regiment, now joined by a company of 1st/4th Essex Regiment, on the night of 1/2 July at the eastern end of Ruweisat Ridge, little parties of men slip past in the shadows. They are survivors of the 18th Indian Infantry Division, the defenders of the Deir el Shein. The Alamein position is broken.

Deir el Shein, 1 July 1942[3]

The story of the 18th Indian Infantry Brigade in the Deir el Shein has also been told elsewhere, but it is clear that without the time bought by them, the outcome of the battle at Ruweisat the following day, 2 July 1942 would likely have been very different.

About eight miles to the south of Alamein railway station, lies a shallow depression known as Deir el Shein. This shallow dip in the ground lay at the western end of Ruweisat ridge, the ridge of hard rock which General Tuker, whose troops were to occupy it for nearly four months, described as 'vital'. This lay between the box held by the 1st South African Division at Alamein and one ten miles farther south held by the remnants of the New Zealand division.

The 18th Indian Infantry Brigade had moved from Iraq to Palestine where its transport was to meet the brigade which consisted of the 2nd/5th Essex Regiment, 2nd/3rd Gurkha Rifles, the 4th/11th Sikh Regiment supported by the 121st Field Regiment RA. They were not equipped for war. They had no carriers and even their training anti-tank 2-pounders had been withdrawn. They did not expect to be put to the test so soon. Indeed, some of them thought they were heading for a pleasant spell in Cyprus. But on 23 June, 121st Field were moving across the Sinai desert, destination Mersa Matruh. The unit's transport had not arrived in time and, as the need for troops was urgent, the brigade travelled to Egypt by road and by rail. The trains were made up of normal peacetime rolling stock, with first-, second-, and third-class carriages.

The Essex account is clear that they arrived at the small station of Galal, just west of El Daba at about 2100 on 26 June. Here they presented an excellent air target to the advancing enemy and were quickly bombed, suffering two killed and four or five wounded. Empty oil drums were set alight and the night was an unpleasant baptism of fire. Near them, the 4th/11th Sikhs also suffered and it was suddenly brought home to me, more than 25 years later, that the burning oil drums may have led the same planes to spare 11th Field who were also hearing desynchronized engines for the first time, only a few miles away.

As 11th Field carried on towards encirclement in Mersa Matruh, the trains carrying the 18th Indian Infantry Brigade turned about and headed back to Alamein. There the 2nd/5th Essex and 4th/11th Sikhs detrained and found that 2nd/3rd Gurkhas had already arrived. As the Field Regiment and Brigade HQ with the motor transport were somewhere on the road between Sinai and Mersa Matruh, Lieutenant Colonel May of 2nd/5th Essex took command of the three battalions and – borrowing a vehicle – went to HQ 1st South African Division. There he was fortunate enough to find Lieutenant General Sir Willoughby Norrie, commander XXX Corps, who was charged with preparing the defences in the Alamein gap.

According to the Essex history, General Norrie did not expect that he would need to use this raw brigade. It had, in any case, no transport, no carriers, no guns, no headquarters – and no commander. The HQ was miles away, the brigade commander had been left in Palestine on the sick list and his temporary replacement, Lieutenant Colonel C. E. Gray, did not arrive to take over from Lieutenant Colonel May until the evening of 28 June.

The 18th Indian Infantry Brigade deserve more attention than can be afforded in this book and yet linger for some moments with them we must because, with them, begins the story of Robcol. There is too, something particularly poignant about their arrival at the Hougoumont of Alamein. They had been swept hundreds of miles, as flotsam, on to the sands of Ruweisat and, with better planning, would have gone into battle well prepared and well armed. And yet, if some strategic genius had not signed the order which spurred them from Erbil on 9 June, Rommel would have bypassed the South African box at Alamein on 1 July. Robcol, not Rommel, would have arrived too late at Pt 63.

On 28 June 1942, they took up position in the Deir el Shein. As some of the battalion transport had at last arrived, they were spared the march to the only battle position they would ever know. With their hockey sticks and rifles, these three battalions took up position at the western end of the Deir el Shein. With the steep crag of Far Pt 63 behind them and the saucer-shaped depression of the Shein in which to hide their echelons, it was a position in which a division, well dug in and wired and with friendly troops on its flanks, could have held out for a long time. When it was lost, the sharp sides of the Deir infuriated British gunners in the months to come.

But, though these three battalions allowed for a second brigade in their plan of defence, no help arrived. The second brigade should have come from the 50th Division, but the Tynesiders by now had little to send even if they ever received the order.

No preparations had been made for the defence of the Shein and it is pitiful to read of their efforts to get wire, mines and water from an Alamein defence which had not yet had any chance to shake itself into any sort of military posture. The South Africans were most helpful in lending bulldozers and pneumatic drills, but the sand in this part of the desert covered a rock of a stubborn hardness which demanded time and time was running out.

Nevertheless, even time relented a little. During the evening of 30 June, 2nd/5th Essex collected four 2-pounder anti-tank guns from El Alamein. 'Two lacked sights, and the accompanying ammunition was very limited. There was not a single Bren carrier with the battalion. However, six 6 pounder anti-tank guns manned by a company of the Buffs pulled in during the night.'

These sentences are from the Essex history and they illustrate how history is written. This scratch force, who arrived at the crossroads of history partly by mistake and partly as the result of a brilliant – and frighteningly bold – strategic decision by the Auk, pick up four pop-guns, two of which had no sights, and six real anti-tank guns wander into their position.

Even better, and even more finely timed, eighteen 25-pounders from the 121st, 124th and 97th Field (Kent Yeomanry) also entered the box during the night, all that was left of the three regiments. The 2nd/5th Essex particularly welcomed the six guns of the 275th Battery under Major W. K. Paul. Twenty-six years later I would spend an evening talking with an Essex soldier who had dug the gun pits, during which occasional enemy planes had visited and hindered progress.

After 48 hours of work, the three battalions had prepared some sort of home, a home which was egg-shaped. The box, approximately 4,000 yards by 2,000 yards, was defended by the 4th/11th Sikhs to the north-west, the Essex to the north-east, the south-west by 66th Field Company, with the south-east being held by the Gurkhas. Wire had been laid around the box on the enemy side of the minefields that they had laid around the box. There was no lack of wire but mines often arrived without fuses. With guns arriving during the night, there had been little time left to dig them in properly and they later suffered accordingly. It had also proven impossible to close the gaps in the perimeter for lack of mines. All this had been achieved on dry rations and three quarters of a gallon of water a day.

On the evening 30 June, enemy troops attacked the South African box on the main coast road, but were driven back. They then turned south and the South Africans warned the 18th Indian Infantry Brigade to expect an attack from the north-west. The South Africans' battle could be clearly heard as it approached their own position.

At 0545 hours, 1 July, patrols reported enemy tanks and infantry approaching and at 0900 hours shells fell on the southern edge followed by more in the Brigade HQ position. By 1000 hours, enemy artillery was concentrating on the Essex, pounding them heavily and from about 1100 hours onwards, while still keeping heavy fire on the Essex, the artillery 'searched' the rest of the box.

About that time two British prisoners approached under a white flag with a message that the defenders were to surrender or suffer attack. They were able to provide some valuable information before returning with the message 'to stick it up and be damned'.

Lucas Phillips's description is illuminating. As CO 121st Field Regiment, after describing how the attempt to get the garrison to surrender had been rejected, he writes:

> [W]hat was left of the garrison stood fast, the Regiments fighting independently in a day of fiery heat, and 121st Field Regiment being left at the end of the day with one gun (which would join 11th Field during the night) and one round of ammunition. The Germans, losing eighteen tanks, were surprisingly shaken. Six of them were knocked out at close range by the 25 pounders of 275th Battery under Major William Paul, and others by boldly handled 6 pounders under Major N. Metcalf, both of 121st Field Regiment under Lieutenant Colonel Edmund Stansfield, and by the guns of the Buffs under Major P. G. Clarke. The advance was blocked until dusk, when what was left of the garrison withdrew, having received no support from any other formation.

At about 1300 hours, aided by a dust storm and the dust raised by their shelling, the Germans lifted mines between the Essex right and Gurkha left. Infantry and machine guns moved forward and were engaged, but the machine guns became established and later caused considerable trouble.

This attack was followed by about 30 to 40 German tanks. A number of these came through the gap in the minefield, behind the Essex and the Gurkhas. The Essex anti-tank guns and 25-pounders engaged the tanks and knocked out two, but eventually most of the guns were knocked out. The German tanks then forced the Essex to surrender. The tanks then turned their attention to the Sikhs and captured most of the battalion.

The brigade had sent out appeals for help at about 1500 hours but it was either too late to ask or the help was too far away to arrive in time. The tanks, both inside and outside, now attacked the Gurkhas. Brigade headquarters was overrun by tanks supported by infantry and at about 1900 hours, the Gurkha battalion commander issued an order to leave immediately, in trucks where possible. Under cover of darkness and dust, the remnants of the Gurkha battalion broke through a gap, most men having to get away on foot.

Compton Mackenzie describes how four of the guns of 121st Field were still in action when the panzers finally overran the position and how 'many of the gunners were able to escape capture because the German tank crews found some beer in the Mess tent and stopped to drink it'.

An Allied aerial bombardment that night created a diversion and enabled others who had been captured to get away. Those who could made for the El Alamein box, while others joined units and small groups moving east. General Auchinleck was later to say of this action: 'Only one infantry battalion survived the attack but the stand made by the brigade certainly gained valuable time for the organization of the El Alamein line generally.'

The 2nd/5th Essex description of the 'action at the Shein' enabled me to follow the course of events fairly closely. There is no doubt that the 18th Indian Infantry Brigade felt they had been let down by the 1st Armoured Division. 'Here the Brigade, all alone ...' is another *cri de coeur* from Lucas Phillips and, elsewhere, he speaks of 'two serious weaknesses ... the complete failure of cooperation between infantry and tanks, and the dispersal of force by the fragmentation of divisions'. As a result, 'before the end of July, a deep distrust of each other had grown up between the infantry and the armour'.

Without an understanding of this most painful symptom, it is also not easy to realize the long silence about Ruweisat. *Crisis in the Desert* gives an explanation of these events which we accept the more readily because the 1st Armoured Division and 22nd Armoured Brigade were desertworthy friends of many other encounters.

Two final features are of particular interest to us: that the remainder of the Gurkha Battalion disengaged and linked up during the night with the main British forces at El Alamein.

What a joy it was to write those words. As I first started making notes on Robcol in 1966, *The Times* reported the Defence Council's view that the Gurkhas were not suitable for use west of Suez. For days I watched the correspondence columns, expecting to find the pen of our great and literate General 'Gertie' Tuker dripping vitriol in their defence. Perhaps those who fought alongside the Gurkhas were stunned into silence, but one saw no word of protest. 'Gertie' Tuker had since died, and it has been left to my blunter nib to refute this ridiculous calumny.

One does not clearly remember these survivors from the Deir el Shein and the Brigadier's diary does not mention them in his order of battle for 2 July. However, the order of battle for Robcol – 2 July – in *The Royal Artillery Commemoration Book* records: 'Detachment of Gurkhas [from 18th Indian Infantry Brigade], one BP and about 100 OR's.' Brigadier Waller himself confirmed that they 'wanted to fight with us – their morale was high'. I would have expected no less from the 2nd/3rd Gurkhas.

Finally, that 'one gun' of 121st Field left at the end of the day. We have devoted so many pages to the 18th Indian Infantry Brigade because the action at Ruweisat demands that due credit be given to the men who defended the Deir el Shein with 'no support from any other formation'. As we became engrossed in the tale of the 121st Field, a new conviction grew. A quick reference to *The Salonika History* and to the document first seen in the Imperial War Museum both confirmed the belief. The surviving gun of 121st Field became, in its own right, one of the guns of Robcol. It pulled out of the Deir el Shein and, within hours, was in action again – the fifth gun of E Troop, 11th Field.

CHAPTER 7

The Brigadier's Battle Map

The Brigadier's AB 119 yielded a special prize – his battle map. This map showed the position of the forward troops during the critical first days of July. It also showed the importance of Ruweisat Ridge, springing out like a lizard's tongue into the jampot of the Deir el Shein.

The threat to the Delta at the beginning of July developed in the centre of the Alamein Line and this book's main interest is with events on Ruweisat Ridge, but military positions do not exist in isolation. To understand the centre, we must understand the position to the north and south of Ruweisat. To the north, we see only the 1st South African Division, but we see them clearly – if through their own eyes – thanks to Agar-Hamilton's and Turner's excellent book. This was not easy to find in England, but we have a ringside seat thanks to the interest of Geoff Armstrong of 11th HAC whose belief in the significance of 2 July led him to help the South African authors as he later helped me. The book carries a crested plate 'With the compliments of the Prime Minister, Union of South Africa' and is accompanied by a charming letter from J. A. Agar-Hamilton, Editor in Chief, Union War Histories, writing from the 'Kantoor van die Eerste Minister' (Office of the Prime Minister).

The preface shows clearly that one purpose of the book is to ease, in some degree, the shame of Tobruk, but pride has also demanded that it continue to Alamein. Jan Christiaan Smuts was aware, perhaps more sharply than Churchill, of events in the desert at the beginning of July. As his son's biography stated,

On 1st July they reached the defensible narrow thirty-mile waist between the impossible Qattara Depression and the sea. Here, at El Alamein, our army turned and stood. It is a matter of pride to South Africans that the first three German attempts to pierce this thin line were made and repulsed on the South African sector. There were in fact, during the first few critical days, little beyond Springboks and a few remnants of battered British units in the line. Axis flags were flown in expectation in Alexandria and Cairo.

Considering the book's political and nationalist motivation, the South African authors are extremely fair and objective. Their interest in the first days of July lies in the German assaults on the South African box. We are here concerned with the same battle, seen from a point some miles to the south. Their heroes are South African; ours are the 'few remnants of battered British units in the line'. Their troops were operating from the one somewhat reasonably secured base at Alamein, ours were launched 'into the blue'. They had a comparatively fresh division of 3 Brigade groups. Robcol started with a total of 17 guns and one half-strength company of infantry. Their maps show Rommel's armour concentrated against Ruweisat Ridge on 2 July, but Robcol stood fast although the 1st South African Brigade was withdrawn. Their withdrawal exposed Robcol's right flank for some vital hours until the 11th HAC arrived, followed by Ackcol and the 3rd RHA who came to plug the gap.

It is clear from a number of accounts, that this withdrawal was to some extent at least a result of poor communication and a misunderstanding between generals Norrie and Pienaar. It is recorded with complete honesty in *Crisis in the Desert* and the South African account unconsciously illustrates the nature of this misunderstanding. The commander of the 1st South African Brigade, after the fall of Deir el Shein, was very conscious of the need for armoured protection on his left flank.

At first he expected the 1st Armoured Division to fill this role, but, about midday, he learnt that they had been ordered to sweep south and west of Ruweisat. 'The Brigade then learned that a column which the War Diary describes as belonging to 50th Division, would come in on its left flank. Communication was established, but the War Diary states that the column was afterwards diverted elsewhere.'[1] There follows an accurate account of Robcol, which received its first orders from 50th

Division, but the authors fail to see the connection. In fact, they later surmise that the column, attributed to the 50th Division, was Steve Weir's force of New Zealand artillery which had moved towards, but never reached, the vital ridge.

I have recorded the withdrawal of the 1st South African Brigade at some length not to belittle the South African soldiers – they acted under orders – but because this withdrawal underlines the vital nature of Robcol's defence. The centre had been pierced, the northern box turned, the south was fluid. If Robcol went all was gone.

Inside the wire, the 3rd South African Brigade manned positions which it would be an exaggeration, as we have seen, to describe as 'prepared' – but at least attention had been given to their siting, and some work had been done on them. Even so, the South African commander, Dan Pienaar, was far from happy with the state of preparedness he found on arrival. As Denis Johnston tells, Pienaar, when he talked to him shortly before the battle, had just been looking over the line – there were some very good stores and underground shelters but hardly any surface defences. None the less, when the South African box was attacked, it was able to hold without too much difficulty. Their other two brigades were in a more mobile role to the south of the wired perimeter and, on 1 July, with the help of 4th Armoured Brigade who arrived just ahead of the German 90th Light Division, were able to hold off the first German thrust towards Alexandria, and the Germans retired 'in panic'.

According to the War Office narrator, the South Africans also repulsed three attacks on 2 July. In the course of these, they sent repeated messages to Robcol that they were under 25-pounder fire. Certainly the guns of 11th Field aiming up at the German tanks on the ridge fired many shells that went whistling into oblivion, but from the map it is difficult to see how guns pointing due west could, except in the very closest encounter, land shells on troops to the north or north-east of their position. At least one of 11th Field's wounded was hit by a 25-pounder shell. The Germans had captured substantial equipment including both guns and ammunition between Gazala and Alamein. According to Lieutenant Colonel J. L. Scoullar, the 90th Light Division alone arrived at Alamein with 19 field guns, including four British 25-pounders.

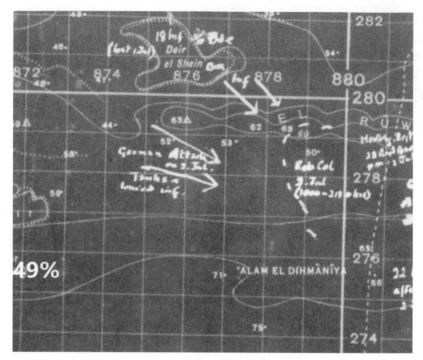

Part of Brigadier Rob Waller's Battle Map, 2 July 1942. (Author's collection)

On the map, the contour numbers on the ridge's northern face drop sharply down to a fairly level, but rough-surfaced, plateau which stretches to an escarpment by the sea. Some eight miles to the north of the ridge lies the railway halt which bears the name by which this whole area and this whole span of four months would shortly become known. A narrow strip of tarmac ran alongside the railway track, between it and the sea which formed a right flank that could not be turned. A semi-circular apron of wire protected the area around the station. Apart from the beach, it was broken ground, affording some cover.

The map's top right corner, in the Brigadier's own hand, showed his estimate of the position of the 1st South African Brigade, the most southerly of the three South African brigades on 2 July. They occupied what is vividly described in *Crisis in the Desert* as The Hotbox.[2] Their brigade commander was very conscious of the need for armoured protection on his left flank. The messages he received about a column 'belonging to

50th Division' appeared to be garbled or only half understood. Some time in the afternoon of 2 July, it was clear from the South African account that the Hotbox was evacuated. The 1st South African Brigade Group had, in the first two days of July lost six killed, 27 wounded and four missing. Nineteen of the casualties came from the 7th South African Field Regiment. It was therefore as a statement of military fact, and not with acrimony, that one notes how their withdrawal exposed the right flank of Robcol.

Some 2,000 yards to the south of the ridge, the cross-hatchings showed where the ground again rises towards the higher, rougher terrain flanking the Qattara Depression. This was the front of XIII Corps. Far to the south, other maps show the flags of the 5th Indian Division and the 7th Armoured Division, but they arrived back this far sadly depleted. Nearest to Ruweisat was the 2nd New Zealand Division. Though not shown on the Brigadier's map, they were on the line 270 which runs across the page about a quarter of the way up at Qaret el Abd and Alam Nayil. From there, on 3 July, they made a most successful sortie against the Italian Ariete Division where, according to Brigadier Howard Kippenberger, they took 350 prisoners and destroyed 44 guns.

But, on the 2 July, they were at extreme range and had little impact on events on Ruweisat and it is against Ruweisat that, as the Brigadier's arrows show, the German tanks and lorried infantry struck. They came from the depression of the Deir el Shein towards the north face of the ridge while an encircling force moved down the funnel of low ground south of the ridge, a funnel which later became known as 'Stuka Valley'.

At the western end of the ridge, three points dominate its last three or four miles of length. They were all known as Pt 63. Western Pt 63, overlooking the steep sides of the Deir el Shein, remained the goal just outside our reach for the next four months. Some 2,600 yards east of Middle Pt 63 (shown on some maps as Pt 64) was the area from which the first DAK attack was observed. Middle Pt 63 changed hands several times in July 1942. Eastern Pt 63 represented the farthest point of the enemy's reconnaissance north of the ridge on 2 July and was, as the Brigadier's markings show, the centre point of our forward boundary for the remaining days of the action at Ruweisat. On 3 and 4 July, Robcol was still the cork in the centre of the funnel but by now, both Robcol and the armoured brigades had received valuable reinforcements. From 5 July, the Brigadier's enlarged command was known as Wall Motor Group and before this scratch force was disbanded, Brigadier Waller was commanding a formidable list of proud but depleted units.

One last feature claims our attention before we leave the Brigadier's map. It is the heavy dotted line which starts at the bottom left-hand corner of the map and goes off the page just to the left of centre. It is the Sidi abd el Rahman track and on it at the end of June, XXX Corps had established four control posts to help reform the army retreating from Mersa Matruh and to sort out combatant troops from non-combatants.

Two of these posts are just off the map to the north: post 1 on the coast road, post 2 some way north-east of Deir el Abyad. Post 3 is at Abar el Mukheisin where the track crosses the 870 easting line, level with the Deir el Shein. Though most of Robcol got back on the coast road, through control post 1, some, including Brigadier Waller and his Brigade Major, came in through the door of control post 3. The fourth post was just above northing line 270, on the track at the level of Qaret el Abd.

The existence of these four control posts may be the reason, as we saw earlier, for some military commentators to have written of four prepared positions between the sea and the Qattara Depression – little enough to be sure to fill a gap of nearly 40 miles. In reality only three had been planned. So, when Robcol advanced along Ruweisat, they marched over virgin desert, though their language when it came to digging in to its rocky surface might have suggested the opposite.

Michael Carver comments that the ridge was no real obstacle to movement. That is true, but it commanded the approaches to the Delta more effectively than isolated craggy pimples which rise in the south to more than twice its height. The fighting of the next four months is proof enough of that.

Many accounts contain descriptions of Ruweisat in the first four days of July and, though short and leaving lacunae which this account aims to fill, are authoritative. On Ruweisat, they often show the flag of the 1st Armoured Division or 22nd Armoured Brigade and the phrase '50 Div Cols'. Indeed, the official War Office narrator has written, 'on 28th

June 50 Div had formed three 8 gun battle groups and was in 30 Corps reserve'.

The arrival of the 22nd Armoured Brigade on Robcol's left rear in the afternoon of 2 July is recorded on the Brigadier's map and their contribution to the action is described in a later chapter, but can the three '50 Div Cols' be identified? And how can the date 28 June be reconciled with the breakout of 50th Division HQ from Mersa Matruh on the nights of 27/28 June and 28/29 June? Even if the dates can be reconciled, it is difficult to see how the 50th Division had 24 of their own guns left by 28 June. The 72nd Field Regiment had been wiped out with the 150th Brigade at Gazala on1 June and both the 74th Field and 124th Field regiments had since suffered heavy losses.

Let us look at the Narrator's statement again: 'meanwhile on 28th June 50 Div had formed 3 × eight gun battle groups and was in 30 Corps reserve'. Then let us remember that there was an army in the field composed of the active divisions, brigades and regiments whose names stud this narrative. Back in the Delta, but closer to the fighting than they had ever been, was the huge chairborne army that the logistics of modern war demands. It was feared that the army in the field would be annihilated before fresh troops and fresh equipment including tanks and guns, could arrive in the Canal Zone. The first was due in about a week's time. 8th Armoured Division arrived in Egypt on 5 July after a voyage of two months and there were others behind them. But these were unseasoned troops, new to the desert. Active units were ordered to send back to base all who can be spared from the immediate task.

Between Mersa Matruh and Alamein the desert tracks were solid with badly battered and scattered fighting units making their way east to reform on their lost headquarters. East of Alamein, the desert was equally populated with non-combatants returning under orders to the Delta against a stream of reinforcements and makeshift units in search of a track leading to a commander they did not know. On arrival, some of them would be ordered to hand over their arms and equipment to an established unit and to return east again. It would be small wonder if the narrator's statement is not simply based on incorrect information. As a first hypothesis 'three 50 Div Cols' may even refer to the columns which, under orders from 50th Division, broke out of Mersa Matruh on the 27/28 June, rather than to those who fought on Ruweisat.

The Narrator continues, 'on 26th June 30 Corps was placed under "EgyptForce" with effect from 12.00 hours with the task of organising the reception of elements which had been thinned out from the Matruh area and allotting them sectors of the Alamein position' and he described how they established the four control posts which we have just discussed. He then went on to state that on 28 June, 50th Division was in XXX Corps reserve. From our knowledge of their strength two days later, it is fortunate that, thanks to the 18th Indian Infantry Brigade, they were not forced to commit that reserve for another 48 hours.

Behind them, other frenzied efforts were being made to bring together an effective army reserve. According to the 1960 HMSO publication *Orders of Battle*, the 10th Armoured Division were charged with organizing the last defences of the Delta. They were in a considerable state of flux, short of equipment and not up to establishment. This divisional HQ acted as HQ Gateforce (under Major General Gatehouse) from 1 to 17 July 1942. Their HQ Royal Artillery became part of Reesforce for the defence of the Cairo bridgehead from 17 June to 20 August 1942; 'during this time 50th Division Royal Artillery was attached to the Division as supporting artillery'.

This can only refer to the period after First Alamein as 50th Division cannot be breaking out of Mersa Matruh, forming columns on Ruweisat and supplying guns to Army Reserve on the same day and from heavily depleted resources. Not at least unless Rear 50th Division HQ commanded resources unknown to Advanced 50th Division HQ.

There are three other possible explanations for '50 Div Cols'.

Firstly, that they did not exist, apart from Robcol, except as the optimistic interpretation of messages conveying intentions as objectives achieved. Brigadier Waller himself, at El Imayid station at 0700 hours on 1 July, received orders to form two columns: 'I was to organize two columns – from the remains of 11th Field RA and any other guns I could get.' But, as we have seen, there were no other guns available.

Secondly, that the phrase is an inaccurate description of guns which did take part in the action:

a. Robcol with its total of 17 guns of which four were recent arrivals from other regiments,
b. Eight guns from 124th Field Regiment, genuine survivors of the 50th Division, which in some accounts arrive to help 18th Indian Infantry Brigade in the Deir el Shein where they were almost certainly wiped out on 1 July,
c. The surviving guns of 11th HAC under Geoff Armstrong who reported to Claude Eastman, CRA 50th Division at Hammam in the late afternoon of 29 June and was offered 'the one remaining 50th Division 25 pounder, a troop of Light Anti-Aircraft and the balance of a 2 pounder troop of Anti-Tank'.

These guns united with 11th Field in Robcol and were not separately identified on the map.

Thirdly, 50th Division Columns may refer to Robcol, Ackcol and Squeakcol, three columns which came together on Ruweisat under Brigadier Waller's command, but not on 2 July.

When this position stabilized Robcol grew into Wall Motor Group. A handwritten Wall Motor Group operation order dated 10 July 1942, for an attack by the New Zealanders on the western end of Ruweisat, with the final and unattained objective of Western Pt 63, shows that the Brigadier's column had been joined by Ackcol and Squeakcol.

Ackcol

Was commanded by Lieutenant Colonel J. Ackroyd-Hunt and was built on the 3rd RHA and three companies of Coldstream and Scots Guards.

Ackcol's arrival on Ruweisat can be fixed from an army message form pasted in the Brigadier's diary, backing on his description of the evening of 2 July. The Brigadier has written on it 'Received about 20.30 hours on July 2 from 50 Div' and it is interesting that 50th Division is still sending messages to Robcol whom, if they had any master at this time one would expect to find in touch with 1st Armoured Division. The message runs, 'latest information enemy tanks concentrating 880280. Assist our armour by bringing all available fire to bear if not already doing so. Ackcol being ordered to close up to friends on your north'.

Leaving aside the somewhat redundant nature of the first two sentences, the last sentence shows that Ackcol was being directed into the gap left by the withdrawal of the 1st South African Brigade from the Hotbox.

The 3rd RHA, the guns of Ackcol, had, like the other RHA units, been in the desert since early in the war and had distinguished themselves in 1941 with the 7th Armoured Division. Early in 1942, they were pulled back to Khatatba, a few miles north-west of Cairo to become part of the 10th Armoured Division which was then being formed. In April 1942, a young wartime officer from England, by name of Malcolm Widdup, joined this hardened formation and his evidence supplements the account of their arrival on Ruweisat, recorded in a somewhat scanty regimental war diary and in *Crisis in the Desert*.

The 3rd RHA received orders at Khatatba at 1130 hours on 30 June to move to Halfway House on the Cairo–Alexandria road. They moved at 1430 hours and leaguered one mile to the north of Halfway House for the night. There they learned that they were to come under 50th Division. At first light on 1 July, as the DAK were closing on the Deir el Shein, they moved off against a stream of traffic. Mid-afternoon brought them to the end of the barrel track short of Amiriya. Left-handed, they turned into the desert. Not the clean empty desert they would end by loving, but the dusty desert track which ran to the south of the metalled road, a track which choked and blinded the drivers. Gradually the oncoming traffic thinned. As night fell the column was somewhere near Burg el Arab and leaguered with, according to the war diary, infantry of the Green Howards, infantry from the 50th Division. It was Malcolm's first night in the desert.

As dusk fell, the world contracted until it was limited by the shadows of one's torch and the feel of the sand in one's first scrambled slit-trench. The truck was a spare gun-tractor with a flat metal top and a winch which Malcolm blessed when they continued at flirst light the next day – 2 July 1942 – in the soft sand parallel to the coast road. Much winching brought the convoy to a turning point and at midday they turned south towards Gebel el Gebir where the Auk and his staff were rallying the last effective guns of the Eighth Army. According to their war diary, they did little 'shooting' that day, though A Troop of D Battery did 'a little long range firing and registration'.

They arrived at the Hotbox just after dawn on 3 July, and found a party of German 90th Light in occupation. They drove them out, taking some 20 prisoners. Half an hour later, however, the shell fire falling on the position became intense and Ackcol fell back to a spot just south of the South African brigade, losing some prisoners in the process.

Ackcol clearly form part of the guns of Robcol. They lost their first OP officer, Lieutenant MacLeod, on Ruweisat on the morning of 3 July. The next day, the red-hatted General Ramsden arrived on the gun position and drew fire, as red-hatted generals tend to do. His car with shattered tyres remained as a memento of his visit.

The next day Malcolm Widdup was wounded, though he, like Ackcol remained on Ruweisat for another fortnight, coming under Brigadier Rob Waller on 5 July as part of Wall Motor Group. In three days of the action on Ruweisat, the 3rd RHA lost half their officers killed or wounded, but, they were not actually on Ruweisat on 2 July. Brigadier Waller was quite explicit: our right rear was exposed late that afternoon or early evening until Ackcol arrived next morning.

Squeakcol

Was commanded by Lieutenant Colonel D. Purdon, MC and was formed from the 339th Battery of the 104th RHA (Essex Yeomanry) and the 9th Rifle Brigade. The 1st Northumberland Fusiliers (Anti-Tank), one platoon of The Buffs (Anti-Tank) and 113th Light Anti-Aircraft Battery were split among the three columns.

The gap on Robcol's right flank might have yawned wider were it not for Squeakcol. The 1st Armoured Division War Diary for 2 July gives a map reference for the position of the 9th Rifle Brigade which would put them in the Hotbox at midday on 2 July. As the Rifle Brigade's war history states, 'The 9th Battalion … were used to plug every gap in the line from Alamein to Himeimat, never remaining long in one place or under one command. They had a stay in all the more important places and yet were never lucky enough to be able to show any substantial concrete results for their efforts.'

In the retreat to Alamein, the 9th Rifle Brigade was supported by the 339th Battery of the 104th RHA and although their war diary shows that the Regimental HQ was sent back to the Delta on 1 July, it seems almost certain that this battery, with the 9th Rifle Brigade, perhaps already known as a column bearing 'Squeak' Purdon's name, was rushed north to help stem the thrust, where Rommel was concentrating everything that he could muster in an attempt to break the Alamein line in the centre, before the defence could be consolidated.

According to *The Royal Artillery Commemoration Book*, 'On the morning of July 2nd, Robcol was joined by a battery of 104th RHA.' If this is true, an utterly exhausted 339th Battery of the 104th RHA – after heavy casualties in men and guns – contributed one six-gun troop to Robcol. They were in support of the 9th Rifle Brigade who, according to the 1st Armoured Division War Diary, were at 1200 hours on 2 July still under command of the 1st Armoured Division in an area just south of the Hotbox to the right rear of 11th Field, some 4,000 yards north of the ridge.

They probably did not stay there long. A 22nd Armoured Brigade report reads, '… the Regiment was ordered to move south at once onto the Ruweisat Ridge and north again at midday to support 1st South African Division who were being attacked by enemy tanks.' They were not there long either as according to the report, they 'were ordered to move south again and then six miles west, this time to support the Indian Brigade'. This could just possibly be a description of the armour's unavailing attempt to come to the support of 18th Indian Infantry Brigade in the Deir el Shein the day before – so many accounts for this period are 24 hours out – but it fits even better with Dan Pienaar's expectation on 2 July that the 1st Armoured Division would protect his southern flank on which he withdrew his flank brigade, leaving a gap which was not filled until Ackcol arrived the next morning.

It would not be right, in this account of 2 July 1942, to exclude any unit which took part in the battle. It seems clear that both the 3rd and 104th RHA were among the guns of Robcol, but it is unlikely that they were directly involved on 2 July itself. Both Brigadier Waller and Douglas Brown were later quite explicit. No other 50th Division column was ready on the morning of 2 July. As shown in an earlier chapter, Brigadier Waller in his letter of 28 February 1946 wrote, '... the only troops available to stop the gap was a Battle Group.'

His map, which reflects the position as he saw it at the time, is proof positive. On the morning of 2 July, when the German infantry attacked out of the Deir el Shein towards the two pimples on the lizard's tongue of Ruweisat and their column of tanks and lorried infantry swung around western Pt 63 heading east into the funnel south of the ridge, they met Robcol and only Robcol, advancing in battle formation on a collision course on the southern flank of Ruweisat. The 83rd/85th Field Battery (the '3s and 5s') was the right-hand battery and the four guns of D Troop were closest to the ridge.

CHAPTER 8

Two Diaries

B. A. G. Jones's diary for 2 July begins: 'I was called at 04.00 hours and continued to organize things.' Since the 'things' he organized were to save Cairo and who knows what besides, let us pause briefly to work out how this tall, young gunner major came to wake up that morning on Pt 97 ridge – the Gebel Bein Gebir.

Although we spent that day and some days to come separated only by a few hundred yards of camel-thorn and sandy rock, it was 25 years beyond Ruweisat before I met him in person for the first time and, for five hours, shared experiences and our mutual opinion of Brigadier Waller's place in history. When we met I somehow expected a younger man, of less striking appearance. Time does not age the memory of our schoolfriends, nor the imagined picture of those whom we have known – unseen – by their nicknames for so long. But although all I knew of this distinguished brigadier, who strode to meet me in London, was his initials – B. A. G. – I felt I knew him better than one shared experience of long ago could ever merit. On Ruweisat, he was also, as Brigade Major, the man closest to Rob Waller.

My article in 'The Times Diary' had produced from him a letter: 'I am quite sure now that his [Brigadier Waller's] determination and leadership did more than anything else to stop Rommel's drive on Alex,' and a diary.

The diary was, like Brigadier Waller's, written on W.D. paper, but, where the Brigadier's was an Army Signalling Scribbling Book (Instructional Purposes Only) AB 119, B. A. G. Jones's was an Army

Book 152 – Correspondence Book (Field Services) – smaller than the Brigadier's with squared pages and a soft back. It is the second of its kind and runs from 16 May to 18 July 1942. It contains 152 pages of handwriting. The inside cover shows that it was written to Mrs Jones in Cape Town and so it was therefore both wonderful, and somewhat disconcerting, to be allowed to read it in 1967. The diarist confessed, 'I begin to wonder if you or anyone else will ever read it. I'm frightened of the "anyone else" as it's meant for you only.'

Twenty-five years later, I am the 'anyone else' to come between man and wife. It is a confidence I will not abuse. But I do not think that B. A. G. Jones had this situation in mind. 'Anyone else' to him at that time almost certainly meant a brother officer making a sad little pile of personal belongings to send home – or some intruding enemy searching a prisoner's papers. Oddly enough, in writing this so many years later, I have the same feelings as B. A. G. Jones when he filled this AB 152 – the desire to record things for those who remain, the need to read and – at the same time – the fear that 'somebody else' will be somebody who cannot, or will not, understand.

From 16 May to 3 June the writing in the diary shows no sign of natural breaks and could have been written at one sitting. It is double spaced and on one side only 'so that I can add bits later'. From 4 June onwards it shows more signs of intermittent addition. Since these dates cover a march from Iraq to beyond Mersa Matruh, along a route very close to that which the 18th Indian Infantry Brigade, 11th Field and others would follow within the month, it is probable that the diary for this period was brought up to date early in June, but it was certainly filled in at frequent intervals during the ensuing battle.

The first entry, 16 May, found B. A. G. Jones at 12 hours' notice to move to the Delta. The 17th May, the divisional commander and his G1 left by air. Their names would soon become well known to desert soldiers for Rees and Holworthy would both command the 4th Indian Division. In the desert of London many years later, few but those who served under them would recognize their names.

After the inevitable 24-hour postponement, he started out across the desert at 0700 hours, 21 May – 145 miles the first day to Landing

Ground 5 (LG5), a 'long dull trip in a foul dust storm'. Next day, 101 miles through Rutbah to H3; 24 May, 96 miles to H4; 25 May, 103 miles past H5 to Mafraq. Does this recital of pumping stations on the Homs pipeline mean anything to a reader today? It was an uncomfortable journey across arid desert and yet that pipeline was one of the strategic objectives for which Rommel was aiming.

B. A. G. Jones at least profited from the passage through Mafraq to admire the interesting old Roman ruins and, snuggling in his bed-roll against the cold desert night, to remember that this had been the granary of the Roman Empire. This thought would be perhaps more meaningful next day, 26 May, as the column drove some 120 miles to Tulkarm through fine cornfields running down fairly steep hills into the valley of the Jordan. The landmarks this day will be significant to a wider audience – Mt Gilboa on our left, the Plain of Esdraelon, up on the hills to the north Nazareth, we crossed the plain to Megiddo. Such names recall the other feet which have left their imprints on this dusty way. B. A. G. Jones suddenly finds it 'hard to write of this trip – after the endless desert, the growing crops, wild poppies, meadowsweet and the wild flowers of Palestine had the same effect as drink on us'.

He was certainly in a contemplative frame of mind. The diary records, and one would hesitate to share such a confidence if one did not know that he would be proud to bear such witness: 'I read the Bible for a bit and so to bed.'

The words illuminated the diary and they gave some explanation of my own suspicions in the mind of the people for whom one writes. This is not a book to the glory of war, but to the memory of those who sacrificed themselves that others may live. And so his Pepysian phrase somehow seemed composed of 'comfortable words'. Here also, for the first time in the diary, we meet the future commander of Robcol: 'Brigadier Waller had fever.'

On 27 May, the day the battle of Gazala began, B. A. G. Jones arrived in Jerusalem from Nablus at about 1130 hours and, after expressing his amazement at the crowd of churches stretched from one hilltop to the other, he visited both the King David Hotel and the Holy Sepulchre.

Whatever he felt about the hotel, the Sepulchre failed to impress. True, there was, as indeed to him in all Palestine, 'a feeling of great age about … but no feeling of sanctity'.

The Virgin with the Diamond Eyes which weep real tears made him conscious of the tourist interest and comfortable ecclesiastical living, 'but of true religion, or indeed belief, there was nothing'.

And so, along the Via Dolorosa to the Mosque of Omar (where he was impressed) and past the Wailing Wall to the Paymaster. On to Tel Aviv. Next day, past Beersheba back into the desert, 120 miles to Asluj. Then a long stage, 160 miles through a 'howling desert' to the Canal. The 30th May an even longer journey, 200 miles past Tel el Kebir, Cairo, Mena, The Pyramids ('such a damn-fool thing to build') to Amiriya. Heavy dew. To Mersa Matruh 31 May, and the tragedy of broken sunglasses. On 1 June, the little HQ went on to Salum and Halfaya Pass.

His diary also records other thoughts that day, which I could not record if I did not know his later esteem for Brigadier Waller. Now, I may quote from his diary because of his admiration for him but, briefly, 1 June, talking to Martin Gregson, another gunner, he found Brigadier Waller 'an imperial little snob'. Even before the proof of battle, however, he adds quickly 'but he does command'.

Now the battle is getting close and it is probably in the long periods of intense boredom which battle engenders that the diary is brought up to date. The 2nd of June at Gambut brings the first rumours that all is not going well. 157th Field and 97th Field cause entries in the diary. Within a few pages, on 7 June, 4th and 25th field regiments have been overrun and by the next day, 157th Field has ceased to exist. '421st Battery had at the end only one gun left in action and it without ammunition.'

In the meantime, he had made a rather aimless trip around the desert 'littered with abandoned German equipment – damn good equipment, too … all the BBC stuff about shoddy and 'ersatz' material is just so much hooey' and found Brigadier Waller 'a maddening back seat driver'.

The losses in the first week of June were more serious than Jones knew. Half a dozen regiments of artillery had by now virtually disappeared from the order of battle. Tank losses too had been heavy, well over 100, with the 2nd Armoured Brigade particularly affected. It will not now be long before 11th Field receive orders to 'follow where another went' in convoy from Iraq to Egypt.

The next entry is dated 13 June:

> [T]here must have been moments of great confidence and optimism, lulls and then again the gravest doubts. There is a tank action going on at this moment 09.00 hours. It's funny how remote one feels. This action may well be the decisive point of this battle, if not of the whole campaign, yet one hears little of it and just gets on with the ordinary things.

As he wrote these lines, he could not have known that 13 June 1942 would be known in desert history as 'Black Saturday'. He also records at length a trip into Tobruk which he made with Brigadier Waller the previous Wednesday, 10 June. He still finds him a difficult travelling companion. The Brigadier took the wheel. 'He is a bad and nervous driver – now I know why he always directs from the back seat!' But worldly jealousies are forgotten in a Tobruk church. The statue of the Virgin in the ruins has a message which the Virgin of the Diamond Eyes in Jerusalem could not convey. A hole in the wall reminded him of soldiers of an earlier war. Through the hole the sight of the High Altar and the cruciform shadow cast by a broken chandelier led to thoughts of religion and the agony of war which may not be shared, though one hopes that something of their spirit will shine from the story of the sacrifice of 2 July.

During the afternoon of 14 June Brigadier Waller tells him that the withdrawal to the Egyptian frontier has been ordered – there are only 50 tanks left – Tobruk will NOT be held. By 14 June, according to Churchill, our tank strength had fallen from 300 to seventy. But, by now the decision had been taken by the Auk to strip the Middle East's northern flank. Meanwhile, the tide of battle continued to run against the Allied Forces.

Between 15 and 18 June, B. A. G. Jones bumps into Arthur Howell, who will later command 11th Field, and Friz Fowler, 11th Field's old CO, now commanding the guns of 1st Armoured Division.

17 June: '11th RHA arrived under Leggatt … somewhat under half strength.'

He also runs into Claude Eastman, CRA 50th Division, who in a few days will send the 11th RHA marching to the sound of the 11th Field's guns. The familiar names make one realize just how small was the body of men who fought Britain's battles in the desert years.

But the most revealing entry is of 17 June when Meade Dennis, CRA XXX Corps, comes to their HQ and, on the phone to the BGS of XXX Corps,

> told him in the most un-telephonic language that unless we get more artillery here we might as well get back to Alex! Friz was in and out too – I've never seen him so angry. Indeed, all gunners are out here – they reckon that the Cavalry won't go in and that time and again, guns are left to hold the baby with no protection. Well, the proof is there with six Field Regiments completely written off – I suppose we have now got about 1/3 of the Artillery we started the battle with.

The diary records feelings which were very common at that time. We shall find them repeated on 2 July.

The next entry is 18 June: 'All my good intentions of recording thoughts and reactions are going, for one has so little time that all I can do is try and write things up every so often – a hell of a lot has happened since I wrote that last paragraph.'

Between 19 and 21 June, remnants of various artillery regiments flit across the diary pages – 1st Field, 3rd Field (3 guns!), 2nd RHA, 11th RHA. The 2nd RHA receives a favourable mention, but the 11th RHA is 'a sight more Honourable than Artillery'. On 2 July, both these regiments will do very well, and 11th HAC under Geoff Armstrong will disprove Jones's view of 21 June that they were a 'slow, stupid indifferent Regiment'.

On 21 June, Brigadier Waller also brought news of the fall of Tobruk while 'Crasher' Nichols, from 50th Division, was appointed by Gott to take over the 10th Indian Division. Three days later they arrived at Mersa Matruh and Brigadier Waller and Jones went off to report to X Corps, newly arrived from Syria to take over the defences. With them came the 121st Field Regiment from Iraq, who will shortly die in the Deir el Shein. That night his most serious enemy comes from an invasion of bedbugs which make him glad next day to trace Cleopatra's steps across the white sands to bathe at Mersa Matruh. 'I believe there are some interesting ruins. I wish I had time to look at them.'

Next day, 26 June, the corps commander arrived with news that the Auk had taken over direct command of the Eighth Army. Mersa Matruh would not be defended. There was a major change of plan. 'A line is also being built … too dangerous to say much of that now. I am delighted as I hate these damn boxes.'

Then 27 June. 'It is a longish time since I last wrote in this … mostly because there's not been the time. I have however kept pencil notes in my working notebook and so can write it up fairly easily.'

A line was being built – at Alamein – but, except for the 1st South African Division and the little 18th Indian Infantry Brigade, the troops to man it were around Mersa Matruh. That day, 27 June, Jones recorded an order from the General: 'Arty of 25 Bde must also engage enemy to SE,' adding the comment, 'Incredible! What could it mean?'

It meant that the Germans had now cut the road and encircled the garrison of Mersa Matruh. Just before the Afrika Korps reached the coast, a column of guns drove into the outskirts of the box'. The 11th Field had arrived – hotfoot from Iraq.

As Jones went to bed on the night of 27 June, he felt 'the situation was still a bit vague'.

He might have found it more worrying if he had known that, in the desert to the south, XIII Corps – acting under orders which will always cause controversy – had withdrawn, leaving the flank open and X Corps in Mersa Matruh encircled and alone. This news reached him the next morning from Brigadier Waller, 28 June, after having had the luxury of washing his hair. The Brigadier also told of various clashes in the night, one of which was 11th Field breaking out and another, of 11th HAC breaking out and then back in again. Shortly afterwards, the CRE came in to Divisional HQ from a trip down the road and reported, 'It looks as if Jerry is across about 5 kilometres of it – all very odd!'

The CRE's recce forms a convenient bridge to another diary, that kept by Brigadier Waller. The first entry in this diary is dated 30 June 1942, because:

> On the evening of 28th June, (the night after the CRE's report), I destroyed my diary lest it be captured during our break-out from Mersa Matruh. Luckily my diary to 26th June had been sent out that day by MacGregor – I trust it has

arrived safely by now. The entries 26th–29th June in this book are therefore filled in from memory.

On 26th June there was a good deal of fighting on our perimeter and our columns were forced inside Mersa Matruh after capturing a few prisoners.

At midnight, just as I was off to bed a report came in that the coast road (the only road) was cut about 30 Kms from Mersa Matruh, between us and Daba. The CRE took out a patrol to investigate.

28th June: The road was cut all night and efforts to open it failed. From accounts given me there was a good deal of confusion and very little control.

The two diaries meet at this point, which was a critical one, not only for the course of the battle, but also for the man who is destined to save Egypt. The Brigadier went to the conference at Corps HQ at 1500 hours on 28 June. When the alternatives were considered – break out to the south, withdraw along the blocked coast road or pull back into Mersa Matruh – he spoke up for a fighting breakthrough. He was sufficiently proud to call this a 'fateful and fatal decision'. His Brigade Major will not disagree, though his Cromwellian rectitude is diverted by a friend who 'won' a lady's foundation garment as the Mersa Matruh NAAFI and Officers' Shop were evacuated!

When the decision to break through was finally taken, Brigadier Waller noted:

Orders were at once issued for each brigade to make its own arrangements for escape. 5th Brigade were to maintain themselves until dark on their existing line, 21st Brigade who were behind 5th Brigade left also. 25th Brigade were to disengage as best they could and get out. They had been heavily engaged all day and the battle increased in noise and din as night drew on. No move beyond the present line was to take place before 21.00, but forming up behind was allowed from 19.00.

B. A. G. Jones describes how the afternoon was spent burning all secret papers. HQ 10th Indian Division was to be escorted by 6th (SAAC) Native Carabineers. As they formed up, Stukas appeared, but, though the raid was heavy, there was no real damage. At about 1700 hours, the HQ left 'The Tombs of the Bulls' and drove out towards 5th Brigade through a certain amount of shelling. 'News is that the Boche has completely surrounded us, but he can't be in strength everywhere.'

Rear Division and the echelons had already gone by 1900 hours when Division HQ, which was to follow 5th Brigade, moved out of Mersa Matruh. Their orders were, after the breakout, to assemble five miles south-west of Fuka on 29 June and to occupy a line to the west.

The breakout force 'Formed up behind 5th Brigade just north of the railway and immediately south of the town and east of Pt 132. There was a certain amount of shell-fire so I [Brigadier Waller] held everyone back a bit. The General arrived at dusk (21.00 hours) and we crossed the railway about 22.00 hours and formed up in 4 parallel columns.'

Twenty-four hours earlier, 11th Field had moved off in a similar form-ation, but our columns contained both guns and infantry. A diagram in Brigadier Waller's diary shows four columns of headquarters troops, with three armoured cars to the front, three to each side and – in the rear – one company of Gurkhas and a troop of the 1st Indian Anti-Tank Regiment.

As they formed up, '5th Brigade reported that the last gap had been closed and that Russell Pasha's intention was to make a get-away in small parties.'

From 2130 hours onwards, they gradually moved off.

There was a full moon and little cloud and all around the south-western, southern and south-eastern horizon showed the German Verey lights and flares.

> Soon after 22.00 we took ground to the west and wheeled near the eastern edge of the minefield and halted. Away to the west and north west, the action with 25 pounder rear parties had become intense. North of us, Mersa Matruh's dumps and works were being blown up and south east, the noise and tracer occasioned by parties of 5th Brigade bumping the Jerry screen flared and died alternately.
>
> Some of the explosions from Mersa Matruh were terrific and the whole northern sky seemed ablaze.
>
> Immediately south of where we stood, there seemed a gap of about 800 metres in the line of Boche flares. This we decided to make for.

After paying a tribute to John Humphreys, the Adjutant, whose navig-ation carried them through, the Brigadier goes on:

> By 22.30 hours the noise to our south east had died down and a few minutes later we moved forward. Our pace in the bright moonlight was about 12–15 mph in

spite of rough going. On the first scarp we passed within a few hundred yards of a Boche leaguer without disturbing them, though they fired on the rear of a column which followed us and who may have gone a shade closer.

We travelled 8 miles on a bearing of 190 degrees and then 7 miles due south. This brought us to the second escarpment and we turned along it and below it intending to make a leg of 20 miles at 100 degrees. This we thought would bring us clear of the enemy and we could then turn due east to our rendez-vous.

Soon after turning east my car, which was already on tow due to a petrol stoppage, stuck in heavy sand, as did the sedan behind us.

By the time we had cleared our three vehicles, the column had gone on.

To give us a better chance of escape, as Sergeant Andrews thought he could rapidly put right my petrol stoppage, we pulled up to do so.

While all this was going on, there was continuous firing to the north and north-east 'only a few hundred yards away' and as Jones relates, 'the distraction of Mersa Matruh was like the eruption of a volcano.'

To quote Jones again: 'It was all very big and our little party of station wagon, sedan and truck felt very small – the sedan's hooter kept sticking and its blare was terrifying.' If you have ever suffered the embarrassment of a stuck horn in a suburban main street, perhaps you can imagine some of the horror of this occasion.

Brigadier Waller and his sedan. (Author's collection)

It took about 20 minutes to put the petrol stoppage right. During this time, part of Divisional HQ with Victor Holland, passed the little party which eventually followed in their tracks – being forced up the escarpment to the south by enemy leaguers and flares.

As Brigadier Waller reports, 'Here the going was very bad and eventually the sedan broke its front axle and had to be destroyed and abandoned ... By now a thick mist had started and we had to keep the windscreen open, the going was bloody and what with the wet mist etc., life was pretty miserable.'

The Brigadier continues,

29th June 04.00 hours ... heavy mist – several times columns passed across going in various directions. We kept quiet and let them go without probing as to which side they were on.

My intention was to get to our assembly area south-west of Fuka before halting. The light was growing, but the mist persisted. We now congratulated ourselves we were clear and I was thinking that we should be able to halt and brew up.

Suddenly out of a bank of mist without warning we ran into an open leaguer. I was shocked to see Boche headgear on the men standing about. Mac, on the towing truck, standing up with his British hat, looked back at me with horror and surprise. A sentry unslung his auto-rifle and shouted 'Halt!' B. A. G. Jones was driving our car without a hat, beside him in the front seat was Robert wearing a topee. I hatless, was standing up in the back seat, head and shoulders outside the roof. Sergeant Andrews, who was driving the towing truck wore a topee too.

I waved to the sentry and shouted 'all right – all right' – almost as much to keep the towing truck from stopping as to reassure the sentry. I suppose he thought it was the Nazi salute.

Apparently my loud cry and wave was good enough and Andrews kept going. The leaguer was endless and contained tanks, troop carriers, lorries and anti-tank guns, both ex-British and Jerry. Andrews was getting faster and faster. We jolted and swung behind him and I feared too great a pace might make them suspicious or that the tow-rope might snap. Men looked up and watched us. A gunner in an anti-tank gun seat idly swung his gun around towards us, but no one seemed very interested. They were getting their breakfasts.

It took 8½ minutes but at last we were through and about 300 yards beyond the last two tanks, the tow-rope snapped. The tower stopped and came back. Mac wanted to abandon the station wagon, but it had all my kit in it and I wasn't going to leave it after getting it so far – it would have given the show away too.

> We mended the break with a reef knot and went on, turning south. B. A. G. Jones did it very quickly!
>
> In two miles we saw a few vehicles waving blue flags and met Purvis and the remains of his Brigade HQ.

Brigadier Purvis of the 21st Brigade, according to B. A. G. Jones who also records these incidents though in less detail, 'produced another rope and so we teamed up until we reached XIII Corps HQ. A most exciting night and exactly like a Point to Point!'

XIII Corps HQ was, according to the Brigadier, about 40 miles south-west of El Alamein. The newcomers were 'well received and given breakfast', as were others who collected here – General Holmes (X Corps commander), 'who made his getaway by the main road, Denis O'Halloran, General Nichols and John Humphreys, who turned up about 11.00 hours and went on soon after'. The Divisional Commander's only orders to the Brigadier, his CRA, at this brief meeting seem to have been 'to collect the division behind (east of) El Alamein by the sea. At 12.15, having collected most of RAHQ, went on.'

According to Jones, who benefitted from the pause to enjoy a record 'wash and brush up … all of our little HQ section got through, though we lost 2 trucks – and so back to the Alamein line where I tried to collect up our scattered units'.

The Brigadier continued, 'Found a division collecting post about 6 miles south of Alamein on the road – outside the minefield – and halted for the night with 21st Brigade – 30 miles north east of XIII Corps. No orders, but Purvis said a recce was underway.'

B. A. G. Jones added, 'We spent the night on the ground there and moved back through the line next day, being the 30th June … We had no orders of any sort and did not know where the General and G1 were. So we stopped on the Alex Road and started collecting.'

The Brigadier's notes for the day show,

> 30th June. No orders. 12th Lancers asked us to move behind the minefield as the Boche were closing. Followed 21st Brigade through the 18th Indian Infantry Brigade box [Deir el Shein]. Saw Tony Stanton and 'A' Battery NH [Northumberland Fusiliers] but could not stop.
>
> Found ourselves behind 2nd South African Brigade. Long delay searching for Division. No word from the General.

> South Africans asked us to move as the enemy were closing and they did not want a mass of soft stuff behind their HQ's. Decided to take the troops present, Divisional HQ and details of 21st Brigade, 25th Brigade on to the main road.
> Still no orders.

As they came into Alamein via the Deir el Shein, neither Brigadier Waller nor B. A. G. Jones had seen the Auk, as we who arrived soon after them did, on the coast road.

The Brigadier continues, 'About 13.00 hours Wallington appeared and gave us a concentration area of about 6 miles square. Moved Division into north part of it. Heavy sand so did not go further in than necessary. Went to XXX Corps and saw Meade Dennis.'

While Jones adds, '... XXX Corps, where we had tea with Meade Dennis, where conversation about the morale of 1st and 7th Armoured Divisions was illuminating and later proved correct. And so, back to our camp where we found that most of the chaps had moved. However, we stayed put – no General or orders.'

I have not attempted to clothe these actions with words of my own, because I could not hope to add to the descriptions which these two literate officers wrote. Their words have a ring of authenticity which no subsequent admirer could equal.

'No orders': throughout this anxious day this small HQ sought orders, orders to turn around and fight the enemy. When they got none, they stayed put. As a result, next day, 1 July, they were there to organize the battle which on 2 July would save Egypt.

1 July 1942

At last orders arrived. They must have come early because at 0700 hours both B. A. G. Jones and Brigadier Waller rendezvoused at El Imayid station, as the Brigadier's diary states, 'there to meet General Nichols'. But, before this, Jones 'nipped across to see "Wee Mac" who with his Regiment [11th Field] had joined us.' It is the first mention of 11th Field in these diaries, though individual officers connected with the regiment have flitted across the pages.

B. A. G. Jones continues, 'We sat at El Imayid for a long time – no one arrived – I chatted to Mac, who showed me photos of his wife and baby. G1 arrived.' The Brigadier: 'I was to organize two columns. From remains of 1st/4th Essex, 2nd/11th Sikhs and 11th Field RA and any other guns I could get – 2nd/11th Sikhs seemed to me to need rest and reorganize and I dismissed them.'

Jones again, 'The whole Division to go back to Mena to reform but the 1st/4th Essex and 11th Field are to form Robcol under our command, and then we are to go under 50th Division. We go and see XXX Corps and General Ramsden of 50th Division and spend the day trying to organize our show – feeling very dirty and tired and hungry.'

The Brigadier, 'The General did not arrive until 16.00, by which time I had formed one column of 1st/4th Essex (less one company), 11th Field RA, Division provided a small HQ.' There is an implied criticism of the General's absence here. However, the Brigadier told me later that 'Crasher' Nichols, who had only arrived to command the 10th Indian Division in June, had gone off to rally his old brigade. He was to leave again to command the 50th Division in July.

The Brigadier again:

> 16.00 hours. Moved to Pt 95 (the Gebel Bein Gebir, at the eastern end of Ruweisat Ridge) with 11th Field's guns and one company Essex of about 250 rifles, remainder not being ready. Contacted General Ramsden and leaguered. Ordered to report to General Ramsden at 07.00 tomorrow. The 18th Indian Infantry Brigade was attacked and overrun this afternoon.

B. A. G. Jones's diary ends in almost similar terms, though he is a little more specific about the fate of Deir el Shein: 'We eventually move up on to Pt 97 ridge where we spend the night. News arrives that the 18th Brigade box in the Alamein line had been evacuated.'

And so, as the sun goes down on the Gebel Bein Gebir, the Brigadier and B. A. G. Jones have 'organized their show' – a small HQ, some guns and one understrength company of infantry. They know that in front of them the Afrika Korps have smashed through a brigade position onto the key ridge of Ruweisat at its western end. The Alamein line is broken. There is no organized resistance in front of the DAK, except for this tiny force of men who are 'feeling very dirty and tired and hungry'.

1st/4th Essex

The small HQ preparing for the night on the Gebel Bein Gebir comprised '11th Field and one company Essex, remainder not being ready'. The one company was C Company under Major L. W. A. Chappell. Twenty-five years later, I was privileged to meet Leonard Chappell again, with Colonel Arthur Noble who commanded 1st/4th Essex that day, but this time, my contacts had kept no diary. However, Colonel Noble was kind enough to present me with a copy of *The Essex Regiment 1929–1950* by Colonel T. A. Martin MBE, to 'an old comrade in arms' and it is from this book that I borrow my quotations concerning this battalion which, in 1945 received Winston Churchill as their Honorary Colonel.

Like the 11th Field, 1st/4th Essex served with the 4th Indian Division from 1942 to the end of the war. During this period, our guns often supported them and therefore the faces of Leonard Chappell and Arthur Noble were less unfamiliar, even after so many years, than Brigadier Waller and B. A. G. Jones. After July, they shared with 11th Field the privilege of 'season tickets' on Ruweisat. General Tuker, commander of the 4th Indian Division in a foreword to their history rightly speaks of 'their endurance, week after week, in the early days of the defence of the Ruweisat Ridge' and describes them as 'one of the greatest infantry battalions of the 2nd World War'. Praise from 'Gertie' Tuker was praise which a soldier valued, for he was one of the truly great divisional commanders.

As Major Chappell reported his company ready for action, a decision was made to add his company to the mobile column forming under Brigadier Waller. Brigadier Waller had decided that, in view of the situation, the column – to be known as Robcol – must move that evening, 1 July. As the first two Essex companies were not yet re-equipped and rationed, Robcol moved off with C Company and 11th Field Regiment RA. Before 1st/4th Essex finally said goodbye to the ridge four months later, they were to lose 26 killed and 83 wounded – but no prisoners.

It has been comparatively easy to fix 1st/4th Essex in time and space. For most units this is all I can hope to do, but for the 1st/4th Essex, it is not enough. Robcol contained many indomitable stragglers but it was built around two units that still existed as cohesive fighting elements, led by two determined lieutenant colonels. Time and again I have asked myself what did 1st/4th Essex do on Ruweisat. The answer is that they did very little, but in doing little they achieved everything. Being there was enough.

This does nothing to diminish my feelings for the men whose presence lent our guns protection. It is not easy to do nothing at any time; it is hell to do nothing when a tank–gun duel is going on over your head. This book would be incomplete without some evidence of the feelings of C Company, 1st/4th Essex as they huddled in their imperfect sand-wombs on 2 July. Above all, 13th Platoon, who protected D Troop's men in moments of great stress. How did they feel?

That I can attempt an answer is due to the continued interest of both Colonel Noble and Leonard Chappell. Colonel Noble wrote to his wife throughout the war, conscious of the need for security but occasional phrases pierce the murk over Ruweisat.

On 5 July, Arthur Noble found time to write for the first time in a month, 'I leave you to guess why.' He had lost all his kit, presumably at Mersa Matruh, and had received no mail himself for a very long time. He is conscious of the part 1st/4th Essex have just played, that 'this battle out here has rather a large significance'. Within the last 48 hours, 1st/4th Essex had received a congratulatory message from the Auk.

On 19 July, he was 'still in the thick of it' as he had been 'for some 6 weeks now'. He was 'very confident of the situation'. He had 'learned what utter exhaustion means'. Later in August he was 'sitting in an unpleasant part of the desert in a mosquito net', complaining of the flies which now had easy rations on Ruweisat. He wrote that he had 'not had a bath since early June' and was proud both that he had 'avoided getting lousy' and that one of his sergeants had received an immediate award of a Distinguished Conduct Medal – the battalion's first decoration.

These contacts also led me to Regimental Quartermaster Sergeant Croucher, who came back to the Alamein position with the Colonel and thus, like him, passed through the the 2nd/5th Essex Regiment in the Deir el Shein. As Robcol was being formed, his duties took him hunting for supplies and water. His description of his journey back was valuable because of his clear memory of an empty desert, with some tracks, but not a strand of wire. To him, the line at Alamein had substance only on a map. Of the action itself, he could say little except for the journeys he made with the wounded, of 'an eminent surgeon' who was working in two lorries, back to back.

And to Sergeant Wynn, one for whom I had been searching. On 2 July, he was commanding 13th Platoon, C Company, ordered by Major Chappell to defend our forward guns, D Troop, against ground attack. Armed with rifles and Bren guns they took up their position around the diamond of the guns. 13th Platoon reached the position on 2 July about midday and tried to dig in. The verb 'tried' showed his lively memory of the rock of Ruweisat, and needed no further explanation. In this position, they were badly shelled and 13th Platoon suffered casualties. Most of the German fire came from tanks above 13th Platoon's position. The closest they got was about 600 to 700 yards.

The picture matches other descriptions of the battle. Its veracity was made final by Sergeant Wynn's answer to my question about what the infantry could do in such a position: 'I spent hours watching two beetles make love!' Though he remembers the German tanks, Sergeant Wynn had no memory of British tanks in his field of vision. At some stage that day, one of the Essex men, Tommy Townsend, passed through the regimental aid post en route to having his wounded arm amputated and was reminded of a butcher's shop. But this is not a 'blood and thunder' story: it is intended as a tribute to the resolution of those men who sat in the sand around our guns while hell passed over their heads.

CHAPTER 9

11th HAC's March to the Sound of Gunfire

'Poor sods,' said Gerry de Boinville. It came over the R/T loud and clear, bringing a deeper flush of anger to Major Armstrong's already fevered cheeks. In the excitement of first contact, Gerry must have instinctively pressed his hand-microphone to report in the same instant that his compassion was aroused by the sight that met his eyes. Geoff Armstrong's temper flared in a short spasm at this breaking of wireless silence. Should he add to the risk of discovery by giving Gerry the rocket he had earned? But no more words came over the crackling of the radio.

What had caused the outburst? Gerry was on the left of the column of six 25-pounders, hull down to the ridge which dominated the landscape. In front of the commander was nothing but drifting sand, though his eardrums felt the shock of heavy detonations, the clanking of the Honey's tracks above the continuing rumble of its engine effectively blotted out any noise of gunfire. The earphones around his neck added a crackle which further reduced the efficiency of his ears as detectors. Pulling left, Geoff Armstrong moved towards de Boinville on the ridge and, dropping his headset, he signalled to his driver to stop as they got into a hull-down position.

The Honey stopped – with its engine running – but now even over the noise of its motor, Geoff could distinctly make out the crack of

25-pounders answering German armour. He would have found it difficult to describe the way in which one noise differed from the other,
but after months in action, his instinct told him where to look for both.
It took him some time to focus on the action which – as he took up
position standing with legs apart on the turret of his tank – was clearly
visible. His binoculars clouded over as they touched his face. The fever
within him made him brim with impatience, adding to the heat of the
desert afternoon.

For a short spell, the mirage was made doubly obscure by a drop of
sweat in the narrow eye-piece. He wiped it away with a filthy handker-
chief which made him think enviously of the clean linen worn by the
Colonel when he got back from his unexpected trip to Alex. But, his
short dream of civilization was swept away by the sight revealed as he
twiddled the micrometre screw of his binoculars. To his left front lay a
troop of 25-pounders – visible only as black specks, but of a rectilinear
shape which stood out from the black blobs of desert vegetation. Behind
them, one, two, three quads of an unusual type and scattered between
them all the signs of a British position. Quite a good position too –
though perhaps a little too close to the crest.

Several hundred yards ahead of them, puffs of smoke betrayed the
handful of other British guns. Geoff could not see them clearly but
it was obvious to his practised eye that they were in the open, too far
from the crest of the ridge behind which they were shooting. As he
looked, a salvo obscured them from his view, but in the sand thrown up
by the shells he could see men scurrying like ants busy at a task which
at a distance made little visible sense. In the murky haze a flash of red
told where a German tank shell had set an ammunition trailer on fire.
'Poor sods' indeed: Gerry was right. When would our side ever learn
the value of proper siting for 25-pounders? But, as he looked, the guns
flashed and, almost at the same instant, red flames on the ridge several
thousand yards ahead of 11th HAC showed that, though poorly sited,
the guns were well served.

Some way back stood an unusual type of armoured observation vehicle
and, behind that, a squat wireless truck. Not far behind that, a second
armoured vehicle with the figure of a man standing erect on its highest

point, glasses glued to his eyes suggested the probable presence of the commander of the force, which the 11th HAC were marching to join.

Before crossing the ridge to confirm his deduction, Armstrong cast a glance behind him and noted with pleasure the excellent march discipline of his small force. Six months in the desert had taught them the use of ground and there was no longer any need to curse at vehicles perched on skylines. In the hollows among the broken desert vegetation, even the big quads were difficult to make out and spaced as they were, would present a poor target to any snooping enemy aircraft. Seeing the OP tanks slow down and halt, the quads automatically and without apparent orders, made a full circle and stopped with their guns in a staggered semi-circle facing the enemy. Armstrong felt pride in the thought that, within seconds and as the result of one simple command, he could put a shell 'down the range' at any enemy who might appear.

His pride died as quickly as it had flared. In imagination, one never loses a ranging round and brackets are quickly split to allow the satisfactory crack of gun fire. A regimental target today would escape the full punishment of 24 guns. Never mind, his surviving six guns would still put up a good show ... No, not six, he could count seven as the column shook itself out in the shallow basin under the ridge. Of course, there was that chap from one of the 50th Division regiments that Claude Eastman, the CRA of 50th Division, had given him when he reported back, was it one or two days ago? Wish one could remember the No. 1's name ... seemed a decent chap ... not a Horse Gunner of course, but well trained ... perhaps Yeomanry ... seem to remember that 50th Division had some Yeomanry regiments ... haven't now ... Claude Eastman seemed to think this one gun was all that was left ... one gun out of seventy-two ... 50th Division always seemed to catch the tough jobs.

Armstrong's mind wandered as a fever wracked his body, exhausted by the events of recent weeks and the strain of the last few days and nights. Must pull one's self together before reporting to this new chap. Make a good show at all costs. It seemed a long way back to Armoury House and yet it was just a year since, on 30 June 1941, that 11th HAC had paraded at Chilton Foliat before the king and queen. In fact, come to think of it, a desert lifetime had been crammed into only just over six months. Funny to think of that carefully posed photograph with their majesties and to realize how many faces would not face the camera again:[1] 'Slogger' Armitage, Hew Thompson, Venning, Leechman, Hopkins, Howard Bourne, McCallum.

All this since 18 January 1942 when 11th HAC first fired their guns in battle across a stretch of sand dunes on the desert south of Benghazi. Christ, what a shambles that had been! Three Jock columns out on a spree near El Agheila, expecting little action and a good deal of boredom; with orders not, repeat not, to allow themselves to be pinned to the ground. But these orders took little account of the deep sand against which 60 horsepower was of so little use.

Let's see, A Battery with Baron Column (under the command of the CO, Lieutenant Colonel 'Baron' Ebbels, had lost all its eight guns, one after another, floundering in that horrible sand. That was where 'Slogger' Armitage died so gallantly and where he himself had been rescued by George Buchanan in a Dodge truck which George had stolen from his German captors. Not a brilliant start. All the same, some of the chaps had shown up damn well and since that blooding had put up a pretty good show. It wasn't in every regiment that the officers could lay or use a telescopic sight against tanks as well as the regular No. 2s – but old Slogger had proved the value of officers' gun drill before he got hit.

B Battery, of James Column had done well too, and though they lost a lot of 'soft' vehicles, they had ended their first engagement with six serviceable guns and no casualties. Not like E Battery who lost 70 men with Charles Column. Hew Thompson was one of those who would not face the camera again. Still, they had some good shooting – even though one of their best shots was against their own B Echelon vehicles captured in a wadi at Sammun. Only lost one gun as far as I can remember and Lieutenant Boys put up a rather good show rescuing the sights, breechblock and firing mechanism of that. B and E then formed a composite battery when we reformed at Charruba. Charruba – where we found real water! Clear water from a stream – at least it was clear except for those little red insects. Could do with a brew of Charruba tea right now.

Come to think of it, am I right about reforming just there? Perhaps it was a bit farther west we reformed. That was where I became 2 I/C.

Must have been nearer Gazala, because for nearly five months we did nothing much but train – A Battery with the Queen's Bays, B with the 10th Hussars and E with the 9th Lancers. Of course, the 9th Lancers went back to Sidi Rezegh for a bit and E Battery lost H Troop with the Free French near Mekila. That was where Lieutenant Venning's face vanished from the photo. Afterwards, we built one serviceable gun from the remains of three and General Koenig put the troop in for a collective Croix de Guerre – if only some fool at HQ hadn't refused to recognize General Koenig as entitled to award honours in the name of France.

It was after that that Rommel attacked at Gazala – let's see, it would be the night of 26/27 May. We don't seem to have had a moment to scratch our bottoms since then – and we were in from the first day, with the Bays, 10th Hussars and 9th Lancers. In fact, it was that first day that Robin Smith did so well and got the MC. Our brigade got four 105s, five 88s, six 50mm, four Mark IVs and one Mark III that day ... and we damn near had him by the short and curlies in the Cauldron (where Geoff Armstrong won his own MC).

It must have been next day when I got mixed up in that bit of a schamozzle at Bir Aslagh and our Anti-Tank chaps (239th Anti-Tank Battery) did so well. Three tanks with four shots ... but they were all knocked out themselves and the battery commander (Major Charlton) was killed sitting in the layer's seat. Young Fish (Ken Fishburn, a neighbour for ten years before the coincidence was discovered) who had joined us, was wounded too, so of course he wouldn't be in the photo.

If only our counter-attack had got moving sooner ... but it was too late (4/5 June) and so four regiments of artillery were wiped out. It was a few days later that Leggatt took over the regiment when Vaughan-Hughes went to be CRA 7th Armoured. About this time too, Leechman was killed in a minefield. My old Bedouin dog, too, or perhaps that was a few days later ... only had her about three weeks but she was a good old girl. But, in the catastrophes of 12/13 June, one could not afford to be sentimental over a dog – 150 tanks lost in one day!

And we had two days shooting at tanks over open sights from every ruddy angle, though by 15 June we were back at Acroma. But, we'd buried Hoppy by then, I think – just been given his own battery too ...

Major J. W. Hopkins, for one day! God knows how we got down the Acroma escarpment that night ... but we did. When did I last sleep? I shall never forget that night at Gambut – the first full night's sleep for 40 days. And, I suppose we had a little rest in those three days digging at Sollum before we were pulled out to Mersa Matruh.

We arrived in an air raid on the night 24/25 June just as Rommel completed the encirclement of the town. After two quiet days, dawn on the 27th found us about ten miles south-east of Mersa Matruh and in full view of two German leaguers. That night we broke out with the 6th Durham Light Infantry ... bloody well broke out ... into the open desert and then got called back again! 11th Field broke out the same way, that night or the next one, they also were called back but never received the message. Next night, we did it again ... with the East Yorks this time, on a bearing of 180 degrees.

That was where the sixth face disappeared from the photo, Major Howard Bourne (a captain when the photo was taken), killed commanding our 239th Anti-Tank Battery. What a firework display.

And then somewhere on the coast road, after Fuka, the column marched slap bang into the Auk himself, grinning like a Cheshire cat and exuding confidence.

'Coming down the road damn well,' said the General. 'Do they look like a broken army to you?' he said to me.

'Of course not.' I said. People may say what they like about the Auk, but there by the side of the road he not only pumped confidence into his retreating army but he also told me exactly what he was going to do to stop Rommel.

But, when we got to the assembly point at Alamein we were damned tired. Tired as if our arms would fall off from the weight of our hands. Tired. Tired. Where's our bloody CO? I asked and no one knew. So, tired, or not, I had to report for the regiment. For the regiment ... for six guns. But I wonder why he stooged off to Alex? Must have had a good reason. But he appointed me 2 I/C and sent me off to attend Claude Eastman's (CRA 50th Division) conference.

'Don't overstate the strength of the regiment,' he warned before he left. So, there I was in front of Claude Eastman – dapper man.

'State your strength.'

'Six guns, 120 odd men, one Honey tank OP, a few shaky trucks, some wireless sets that don't work and one 6-pounder.'

And then, the colonels of the three regiments of the 50th Division reported but Claude wasn't listening. He already knew the score: 'Any survivors from 50th Division regiments will come under command of Major Armstrong.'

And so, 11th HAC was reinforced by a troop of light anti-aircraft, one or two 2-pounder anti-tank guns and one 25-pounder. One 25-pounder! All that was left of the 72 guns of 50th Division. Poor sods.

'I want you to reform and be ready to march at first light,' said the CRA.

'I'm sorry, sir,' I said, the men are worn out, asleep on their feet. I've no petrol, little ammunition and no one's had hot food for days. First light is impossible. But we'll be ready to march by midday.'

As I spoke, I had no idea whether I was guilty of mutiny or of a foolish boast. It seemed absurd to think that some of my sleep-walkers would ever respond to a military order again. Some had fallen off their trucks as we stopped and curled up in the sand. Curled up without a brew-up. When the British soldier forsakes his ritual brew-up he is near the limit of endurance. But as I faced the Brigadier I could see the old sweats crouched over a flickering petrol-filled hole. By now the stronger spirits would have cried 'Char up!' shaking the sleepers as an Islington landlady shakes her lodger the morning after Blackheath versus Wasps. On a cup of char, the gunners could march again.

'We'll be ready to march by mid-day, sir,' I reaffirmed. Maybe the quartermaster would be able to accelerate matters with an issue of rum.

Back at the vehicles proved I was right on both counts. Flickering petrol flames, like minor planets in the falling twilight, told of life-saving brews. The track to the mess truck was littered with blankets hiding bodies which grunted, swore and turned over as one stumbled into them. But around the guns and the vehicles figures were moving. Moving often in a dream, weaving rather than walking, but moving to purpose – topping up radiators, emptying square petrol cans into thirsty tanks, refilling the limbers and hurling 110lb ammo boxes into high

3-tonners under the eye of a strangely quiet sergeant major, no – three sergeant majors: BSMs Butt, Kay and Eldred and BQMS Singleton. Backbone of the army.

What have we got for officers? Captain J. H. McCallum (of the photo, later killed), Captain G. N. P. C. de Boinville, Captain R. N .Smith, Lieutenant J. P. Thomson-Glover, Lieutenant B. H. S. Laskey (also in the photo, killed at El Hammam), Lieutenant Robert Lee Trapnell (Survey Officer), Lieutenant J. A. F. Sewell (Medical Officer), Captain John Martin, the Padre Reverend 'Ken' Oliver and shortly afterwards, Captain K. E. Bolton. A little below regimental strength. But all good men.

Send the Padre off to Alex – go round the hotels – find the CO. Off round the vehicles – check that suspension – look at that recuperator – how are you off for A/P shot – drive – nag – drive. God, I feel bloody!

Never mind, at 1200 hours yesterday, the 1 July, the 11th HAC marched. Marched westward with the East Yorks 'battle group'. We moved along the eastern edge of the ridge to the high point at Pt 101. We started to form a strongpoint with the few remaining troops of 50th Division who had orders to form a back-stop in this area, leaguering for the night some miles west of Hammam. As we slept, the defenders of Deir el Shein streamed back up the ridge running from Pt 63 to Gebel Bein Gebir. The panzers and their lorried infantry streamed behind them. The line was broken.

God, I could sleep forever. But I could focus on Claude Eastman's face as he gave us our orders. 'March to the sound of gunfire,' he said. 'The Boche is breaking through and there's nothing between here and Alex. Take your battery 15 miles due west and report to Brigadier Rob Waller who wants every gun he can get.' No information about the enemy, nothing else about our own troops – just 'march to the sound of guns'.

So we limbered up and marched, left the infantry behind and marched, marched due west along the ridge in our usual desert formation, ready for instant action with OPs out in front. As we marched, the sun came around until it was almost in our eyes. It got more difficult to make out the ridge in front, but the 'sound of gun fire' grew ever louder. We marched for eight miles – into the lower ground north of the ridge with nothing but crackle on the few working radio sets. Once the set in my

Honey was shaken off net and, before my signaller got it back on to frequency, we had a few bars of 'Always'. He was still fine-tuning when Gerry's voice came over, strength 5, loud and clear. 'Poor sods.'

'March to the sound of poor sods ... march to the sodding sound.' Geoff's mind boiled with fever and with that ice-heat which affects all men in the approach to battle. 'Drive straight at that square armoured OP,' came the instinctive command to the driver and the Honey surged over the ridge. As he did so, Armstrong looked right and saw the South Africans weren't there! He was conscious out of the corner of his eye that the dust cloud on his right front had thickened. The dull sound of gunfire was punctuated by sharper notes. Boom became crack and the camel-thorn between him and the command car was tilled by an unseen plough. A 50mm cannon shell hit the ground and rose, spinning like a cricket ball but apparently more slowly, bounced again and buried itself in the sand 800 yards to the left with a noise that reminded him of those jolly screaming fireworks of Bonfire Night before the war.

The Honey halted a little short of the armoured car and Geoff reported to the tall man who jumped down from its upper works. An equally tall figure beside him was introduced as the Battery Major, Major B. A. G. Jones. It is probable that Brigadier Waller was going to thank Geoff Armstrong and the HAC for coming at such an opportune moment. Certainly he must have felt a flood of relief at the sight of reinforcements – known to be hardened soldiers – at such a moment. Perhaps his words were slowed by the shock of Armstrong's appearance, for his face, flushed with sun and fever, was topped off by an Indian-style topee. An incongruous sight in the desert where men went bare-headed. A sight immortalized some days earlier by an army photographer when Geoff Armstrong had his brief encounter with the Auk. An idiosyncrasy known to his infantry as the distinguishing mark of their gunner.

But the exchange of words was brief, for at that moment, the command car was sliced by a 50mm shell as a tin of corned beef is sliced by a kukri. The carver ran lightly over the driver's legs and, without obvious hurt, they assumed an angle of detached surprise. To be close to such an impact is momentarily to lose the power of coherent thought. To recreate it after many years from the later memories of those who were there is impossible. But, Driver O'Connor's place in history must be recorded. *The Royal Artillery Commemoration Book* shows that he died the next day, 3 July, from these wounds, wounds which were received at the very turning point of the battle … at the moment when the line which had been broken in the Deir el Shein, had held at Pt 64 until both ammunition and armament were all but gone, now received invaluable reinforcement. With Geoff Armstrong's seven guns, Robcol was now stronger at 1630 Egyptian time than it had been an hour earlier. In Westminster, Churchill had not yet sat down.

Driver O'Connor's mortal wounds enable us to pin down this critical moment in the confused day's battle as about 1630 hours because it was recorded not only by Geoff Armstrong as he came up, but also by B. A. G. Jones and the Brigadier in their private diaries.

The HAC swung into action on Robcol's right (which would put them just north of the ridge in low ground). One has little doubt that their position was hull down to a ridge about 1,000 yards away and that in this chosen saucer of ground, they had little reason to worry about the battle which raged about them. Nor would they have much time for introspection as the records show that they 'fired 600 rounds before dusk'.

Two days later, I was privileged to take the surviving guns of 83rd/85th Battery – after repair by the artificers – to form a troop of 11th HAC and, sitting in a Surrey study many years later, I remembered the casual affectation of the voices which came over the air from their OP tanks – a casualness which was perhaps born of fear almost conquered and an affectation which enabled the enemy to pinpoint their identity however well they observed wireless discipline, which they seldom did.

I would give much to recapture the messages which passed through the ether that day. But alas, all one knows is that they fired 600 rounds. And yet, even that one fact makes the sinews tauten: 600 rounds from seven guns is nearly 90 rounds per gun. At 25lbs per round that means nearly one ton of metal manhandled across the desert by the two ammunition members on each gun and finally rammed by the No. 4 into the chamber of the gun.

One other fact we know about the acting commander of 11th HAC: we find him at one point on the left of Robcol, talking to

Bob Loder-Symonds, acting CO of the 1st RHA. What one would give to hear Loder-Symonds's description of this conversation, but this brilliant solder was later killed in Java. He only appears at one point in the accounts of Robcol's action, but his intervention is critical. Geoff Armstrong hears him 'persuade his armour to stand by refusing to withdraw his guns'.

Geoff Armstrong later wrote to Brigadier Waller:

> I am convinced that the stand Robcol made on Ruweisat Ridge coupled with the sturdy support of 1st RHA on the left literally saved Egypt ... I don't think the conduct of Bob Loder-Symonds has ever been sufficiently known or appreciated. I am the only living witness of what happened. On the day I arrived behind you with all that was left of the HAC, your column was getting badly punished ... and you could easily have been outflanked on your left and destroyed. 1st RHA was covering your left rear and as I arrived at Bob's RHQ he was on the blower to the few tanks in front of him who wanted to come back to rally.
>
> He told them in my presence that whatever happened his crowd would 'bloody well stick' and exhorted them to stay out front until dark. He shamed them into staying and I moved my guns up to your right rear under the ridge. It was the turning point.

The Brigadier writes: 'Loder-Symonds of 1st RHA came up and said that he had persuaded the 9th Lancers to move up closer on our left and the Honeys to stay on our right and asked us not to retire. I replied we had no intention of retiring.'

CHAPTER 10

Robcol and 2 July 1942

0400 hours. That the Brigade Major was 'called' at this ungodly hour, we know from his diary, previously quoted. What military activities were covered by the phrase 'continued to organize things' we do not know.

One can imagine the bustle in the little cluster of men and vehicles which took place between the entries. Vehicles revving up and pulling apart from the protective closeness of night to the protective distance of day. Perhaps sticking in loose sand or in some lightly scratched slit-trench and being dug out, amid much swearing – straining and spinning as it touched the sand-mat and finally gripped. 'For Chrissake, keep her going and don't stop till you're on that hard rock.' The feel of the spade hilt in one's hand reminded one of the need to take a short constitutional – only to have to return for some out-of-date copy of *Union Jack*. Bedding must be rolled up and camouflage nets shaken out. With four hours to spend before the move, every vehicle will have its 'brew-up' and perhaps its 'burgoo', though the next day B. A. G. Jones will record 'no breakfast, but I got a shave'.

Over in 11th Field, RSM Nobby Clark would have been one of the early risers and one can see him still strolling around the RHQ area, poking at sleeping signallers with his silver-mounted stick. Today, his splendid moustache deserved an extra twirl for today his beloved Royal Eleventh Field Regiment will make history. But, he does not yet know it. In fact, he knows, like all of us, very little. Walk over and wake Captain Tomson, the Adjutant, or perhaps 'Pip' Mott, the Signals Officer. Any signal come in by night?

Young Katti, the Intelligence Officer, may have slept a little longer. At any rate, the first entry in the regimental war diary (which he is unlikely to have filled in until later) is 0600 hours. All we learn from it, which we don't already know, is that the column now contained two troops of 113th Light Anti-Aircraft Battery in addition to 11th Field and C Company, 1st/4th Essex.

At 0700 hours, Brigadier Waller reported to General Ramsden. All we know of the orders he received is from a single entry in his diary: 'order to move out as a column, contact 1st South African Division and if possible, New Zealand Division.'

A glance at the map will show the width of front which the little force was asked to cover – something well over 10,000 yards with a total of 25 guns.

But it seems probable that we today are better informed on the where-abouts of the South Africans and the New Zealanders – and certainly the Germans – than General Ramsden when he launched this small force into the blue. Whatever his state of knowledge, it is clear that Ramsden pointed his puny arrow straight at the heart of the Afrika Korps.

What do we know of the advance that saved the Delta? The Brigadier recorded the first steps as: 'Moved off 08.30 along Ruweisat Ridge. About 10.00 hours, reached a point some 2,000 yards SW of Pt 64 (8827) – actual position about 880277' while B. A. G. Jones noted, 'We moved forward about 08.00 and went into action about 10.00.'

The 11th Field Regiment War Diary (WD 397/4) confirms, '10.00 hours – Robcol ordered to advance on bearing 260 degrees for 13 miles to contact enemy along Ruweisat Ridge. Enemy contacted SW of Pt 63 (885279). Regiment deployed' while the 83rd/85th Field Battery RA War Diary (WD 407/43) notes, '09.00 hours – column ordered to advance on bearing 260 degrees for 13 miles to make contact with the enemy reported in the area. 877282.'

Although our surveyors, and the maps they worked from, are not accurate to a few hundred yards in eastings and northings, and the maps do not agree on the height of key trig points to one or two metres, and although our watches are equally not synchronized to within one or two minutes (or even half an hour), the orders are clear.

If you had in front of you the 1:250,000 map Egypt and Cyrenaica – El Daba, from Pt 97 at the south-western end of the Gebel Bein Gebir, 260° and 13 miles brings you, as it will later bring Geoff Armstrong's 11th HAC, to Pt 64 (Pt 63 on some maps). Pt 64 dominates the depression of the Deir el Shein which the enemy took last night and the whole landscape between the ridge and Alamein. If General Ramsden's orders are carried out, a small plug will have been inserted into the break in the Alamein line.

How to describe this plug? I can only speak for the back – and that only as in a mirror darkly. Memory, after many years, throws up shadows of that which we would like to see more readily than that which we did see. In my case, the difference may not be acute since I was certainly in the rear. Having led the regiment for 1,500 miles, now as 'back-stop Charlie', the whipper-in, I was surrounded by 3-ton ammunition trucks, fitters and signal vehicles. Perhaps my low position in the column merited a few more minutes in bed. Who knows? Certainly, as we moved off, my own position was not a martial one.

In front of me stretched two lines of guns, almost certainly the four guns of D Troop in line abreast in front and the five guns which now made E Troop in similar line behind. On the flanks, the anti-tank 6-pounders which Tommy (the Adjutant) had picked up a few hours earlier and maybe the Bofors guns of the 113th Light Anti-Aircraft Battery. In front, at some distance, a line of armoured cars. Cars of particular design – Tatanagars, product of Indian workshops. On the right, hugging the ridge, 'Clem' Clements, in 'RD'. Next to him, Lawrence Boyd in 'RE'. Between the two, Major J. N. 'Duggie' Douglas in 'X' car. To the left of this column, Major John Ashton, between his two troop commanders in similar vehicles with B and A troops behind in similar desert formation.

Despite its unusual shape, the Tatanagar armoured car was loved by all who travelled in her – but her wireless set, the 101 set, was to radio telephony what the 2-pounder anti-tank gun was to ballistics. Useless!

The OP cars are in touch with each other some of the time, but – as the speed of the advance carries them out of sight of the guns – contact with the main column becomes first difficult, then impossible. Slight adjustments to the tuning knob become major sweeps as the signallers realize that contact has been lost. Picture yourself a signaller in the middle seat of one of these OPs – you tuned onto the 'net' of the GPO's truck before setting out. Wireless silence is ordered for the march. As 'RE' advances along the southern side of the ridge, all instincts tell you that the troop commander is about to call for fire from the guns some distance behind. This will be a test of all your years of training. For this moment, you suffered Friz Fowler's map-case around your ears, Pat Waterfield's sarcasm as he sent you 'down the line'.

Of course, Lawrence Boyd's not a regular like Friz or Pat – only a Calcutta jute-wallah – but he wasn't stuck for words when the line went 'dis' on that last exercise near Mosul. They tell me he has a liver like asbestos from all that trekking in small boats up the Hoogli river, drinking whisky in the midday sun. Besides there may not be much time for our own sakes – Lawrence looks happy enough sitting up there, but I'm a eunuch if there isn't a Mark III just over that blasted ridge. Just check Nobby's carrier-wave. Christ, it's gone! Not a bloody peep. What the hell do I do now – break silence and get shot by my own side or stay 'chup' and get shot by the Jerries?

In the seat, raised to the left of the driver's head, one can imagine Lawrence Boyd sunning himself. It was cold and damp as the column set off, but now the sun struck through to warm bones accustomed to the sun of India. Bones which on Lawrence's youthful frame stretch the skin, as if seeking the sun's warmth. Funny how damp and cold the desert can be – nice and warm now, but there is no prize for fidelity to anyone who loves 'till the sands of the desert grow cold'. Funny show altogether really – going shopping with a 25-pounder on tow when we passed through Cairo. Three days ago, four? Make something for my next letter-card anyway – shopping in Cairo with a 25-pounder. Didn't seem to reduce the prices.

Still, if I'd stayed in Cowley Camp in Cairo just because there wasn't a truck handy, I don't suppose we'd look forward to tonight's meal as we do. Always assuming we get a chance to brew-up tonight of course. That poor bloody RAF chap we passed on the way back from Mersa Matruh won't need any rations tonight. Pity we couldn't give him a decent burial. That's how we got lost and missed the column. Bloody lucky to find them again – somewhere near Daba, I imagine. About there that the Auk came steaming past. He seemed to know what's going on, anyway, grinning all over his face. Don't know what the Auk looked so chuffed about. Don't really know that I'm feeling so good about myself, come to that. It's a fine troop commander who loses three guns before we really get into action – and a first-class BSM. Still, I've got five guns behind me now.

Pretty tired some of the new boys looked – but good chaps. Wish I could remember their names and where they come from – Keelan, Wilkinson – can't remember the others. Think at least one was from 32nd Field. They should know the form anyway. Unless they've had it by now. Didn't even have a chance to check if they've got things like aiming posts and telescopic sights, let alone their names.

Steady, driver. Stop. Back her up to the ridge – Captain Clements seems excited about something. Christ, look at that!

Lawrence Boyd looked down into the Deir el Shein from a feature on the ridge which we can now identify as Middle Pt 63, about 2,600 yards short of Forward Pt 63. The saucer at the eastern end of the depression was a 'black mass of vehicles' crawling like maggots around an ageing piece of Stilton. 'RD' was already stationary and Clem had his glasses to his eyes, glasses which gave rectangular shape to the crawling maggots and showed their feelers to have the straight lines of gun barrels or the spiky protuberances of mounted machine guns. Lawrence was surprised to find that Clem had pulled up against a third armoured vehicle – smaller than the Tatanagar – a little beetle-shaped scout car. Lawrence never did find out quite what he was doing there, nor where he came from. Probably the advanced screen of the 22nd Armoured Brigade – though he could be one of the South African armoured cars from the brigade north of the ridge – but, in that case, Lawrence would certainly have expected him to speak with some slight accent. In any case, he seemed to have been there some time, even to know exactly where he was, and to speak with the slightly insufferable air of authority of those who know their 'knees are brown'.

'What on earth's all that?' asked Lawrence.

'That's the German army, my boy,' said the cavalryman.

But, the signaller's fears were well grounded. There, with the whole German army stretched out before their gaze, and before the critical stare of the unknown cavalryman, both troop commanders fumed at wireless sets which gave no response. As they watched, two maggots larger than the rest detached themselves from the crawling mass, followed by two more and then more … and their black shapes crawled towards the onlookers. By the time they realized that the 101 sets would get no answer, the advancing wave was getting close to the ridge and would have been identifiable with experience. There seemed little point in staying simply to enjoy the view, so the OP trucks pulled backwards down the ridge – leaving the little scout car to use his greater mobility when he thought fit.

A short distance under the ridge, Clem and Lawrence stopped by two Tatanagars of similar shape, but identified by the pennants on their wireless serials as 'X' car containing the battery commander of the '3s and 5s' – 'Duggie' Douglas – and the regimental commander's vehicle. Lawrence reported the approach of the tanks and their inability to do anything to stop them.

'Whose tanks are they?' asked Colonel Mac.

'Jerry presumably,' said both Clem and Lawrence together.

'Are you sure?' said the CO and, when neither could give complete assurance, 'Go back and find out.'

More experienced observers would have recognized the essential small points of difference between a German and a British tank, known where to look for the British roundel or German swastika, or simply have lied bravely. Clem and Lawrence were not yet up to any of these refinements of their craft, and one cannot just go up to an advancing tank and ask it to identify itself. So, the two troop commanders just 'hung around' (to use Lawrence's own words). However, they were not left long in indecision. By now, some of the tanks were advancing to the south of the ridge and when one of the leaders stopped and took a shot or two at the little cluster of vehicles, their unfriendly nature was assumed.

Somehow a message was got back to order the guns into action. As the OP wireless set still refused to work, one assumes that the order was passed through the CO's or battery commander's set. Fire was called down on to a map square to the south of Forward Pt 63, but as Lawrence 'hadn't a clue where the guns had got to' and as, to his eyes still unused to the desert, his only map was completely inadequate, it is unlikely that this fire caused much damage to the enemy at this stage. At least Lawrence was, many years later, modest enough to doubt this. Perhaps the CO's wireless, or Duggie's was functioning more efficiently and they were able to correct the fire. Certainly the RHQ had communication back to Robcol, who also received orders in their turn from some higher HQ, presumably 50th Division.

As B. A. G. Jones's diary records: 'About 10.00. There was a good deal of movement in front and we fired a lot. Rob Waller and I sat on top of our wheeled carrier well up behind the leading troop position.'

The Brigadier again: 'Our OPs on Pt 64 ridge looked down into the abandoned 18th Indian Infantry Brigade box. This they said was full of MT and some 25 pounders. Here we were ordered to stand fast and await orders. About 11.30 we beat off an attack by Boche infantry.'

While the 11th Field War Diary adds, '10.00 hours – Enemy contacted SW of Pt 63 (885279). Regiment deployed.' I believe this to be the map reference of the guns.

The 83rd/85th Battery War Diary:

> 11.30 hours (Ruweisat Ridge) Large enemy leaguer observed north of ridge. Battery ordered into immediate action in 882278 and effective fire was put down on enemy MT concentrations.
>
> 12.00 hours (Ruweisat Ridge) Enemy infantry put in an attack which was easily repulsed by D Troop, whilst E Troop engaged the withdrawing MT.
>
> Many casualties caused to enemy personnel and vehicles.

Obviously someone knew what was going on – or thought they did. Perhaps it was Clem, whose wireless set relented. I have every reason - as we shall soon see – to know that he re-established contact about this time. For a while, he probably observed alone – or with just Duggie to give him support. Lawrence, fuming as only a Calcutta jute–wallah can and waving the fingers of his hands outwards like fins in an action which is, even many years later, pure Lawrence – came back to the gun position and found the regiment in action some distance back on the southern slope of the ridge. Here he changed the offending wireless set and returned to the ridge where he 'engaged MT and other targets with some success'. Perhaps this was during the rather ineffectual 'infantry attack' about 1130 hours.

Shortly afterwards however, the tanks which had already been reported advancing to the south-west of the ridge must have threatened to outflank the gun position on that side. Lawrence continued that 'during the course of the morning, I was recalled and sent out south west of the gun position from where I engaged further targets. About midday, I returned to the ridge'.

If the situation appeared clear up front, at the back of the column it was unashamedly obscure. The one man in a field battery who should be able to fill in all the gaps in the above commentary is the Command Post Officer.

A Command Post Officer has his place in the line of march, a place which allows him to help in siting the two troops and within minutes, even seconds, to survey them in with increasing accuracy until they can fire together. He is the nerve centre of the battery's intelligence and the skilled surveyor who guides their indirect fire. In Flanders mud, he would expect to be a busy man. When the guns engage tanks over open sights, there is little he can do to help.

As Robcol advanced in extended order expecting to meet tanks any minute, this particular CPO, your author, was at the back of the column 'whipping in'. With vehicles which have just marched some 1,500 miles without full maintenance, this was a job that took time and patience. The guns were some way ahead, stretching down the crest leading from the Gebel Bein Gebir.

In an open space, a column of sand spurted upwards and fell slowly – the crash of sound which followed immediately was brusque and angry. The sound of a high-velocity tank gun was quite different to the 81mm mortars and field artillery one had heard in France. It was immediately followed by an air-burst and another crack. I should have been feeling superior. After all, this was the regular's baptism of fire. We, Terriers, were sent out to let them have the benefit of our experience of six weeks' fighting with the British Expeditionary Force in France. But this was quite different. No survey instruments to give me a sense of belonging. One was out of position in the established order of things – one does not belong. *Crack* again. I moved forward, behind the guns. Here at least one was no longer 'off-side', but the feeling of helplessness did not abate.

The guns, in positions where their trails dropped and over which I had no control, were already firing actively. I did not know at what. Presumably over open sights. As a more familiar rumble came back, to burst several hundred yards behind, I realized that this was no place to stand and stare. Dig! Dig furiously! But spades made little progress against the rock which I struck a few inches below this accursed ridge. Lie panting in the shallow scraping. Scrabble with bruised fingers and then feel shame at showing such naked fear.

Bombardier Young came up in 'Monkey 2' with a line – a line which would ultimately run past the guns to the OP and down which Lawrence would, for a few minutes of undisturbed communion, pass orders to the guns – before it was cut to ribbons in the next salvo from the Deir el Shein. Lucky Young with a job to do, a job which would keep him from the panic of the idle. His pale face and lank forelock showed a man engrossed in the job for which he had trained so long. Only this time, his mistakes would not be punished by the lash of Friz Fowler's map-case. Funny to think that, in a few months, Sergeant Young would be posted home and would call on one of my brothers. He said nice things of me, offered opinions which I treasured more for the circumstances in which they were formed; but, today, he could have little regard for the pale young subaltern from whose command post he ran his line. Worse was to come.

Clem's ranging over, he ordered, 'Battery, fire!' But the guns were not linked. The CPO had not done his job, not even thought of the survey for which the CPO existed. Blind panic seized me as D Troop fired. E Troop have no 'correction' enabling them to add their weight of shell. Somewhere in the gun position lurked the shadow of the second in command, Pat Waterfield, who had on an earlier occasion shown his scant regard for 'weekend soldiers'. From some blessed source came the answer. My command post assistant? Bombardier Young? As I write,

I can still feel the horror of the problem, but the solution was clearer now than then. The gunner's rule! E Troop was about 400 yards left of D Troop – the range was about 3,000 yards – E Troop right 8 degrees. They were a little behind D Troop so, E Troop – add 100. Easy! But 25 years cannot erase the feeling of inadequacy at the time.

If I had been a better CPO between 1000 and 1100 hours, 2 July 1942, I would now be able to describe the gun positions with more authority. The many scraps of evidence sometimes conflict. I have struck the balance of probabilities, strengthened by my own incomplete view, in putting forward this picture of a situation which I should have known for certainty if I had seen clearly then. *The Salonika History* states: '78th/84th Battery were on the left and 83rd/85th Battery on the right. RHQ was between the batteries and slightly to the rear. 265th Anti-Tank Battery had been put out as a screen forward and to the flanks with orders to fire from the portees.'

Lawrence Boyd added: 'Carriers of the 1st/4th Essex were about 500 yards in rear. In the 3's and 5's, D Troop were on the right, E Troop on the left.' The enemy, had advanced to the left and, at one time, threatened to outflank the regimental position. C Company, 1st/4th Essex and the 113th Light Anti-Aircraft Battery were in the area near the guns.

As the morning wore on the enemy continued probing the position, with occasional intermittent heavier shelling. B. A. G. Jones recalls, 'We had a few shells, but ate our lunch in peace,' while the Brigadier added, 'From 12.30 onwards there was a good deal of desultory fire on both sides and German MT showed to the North West.'

I suppose we too ate something, though the taste of the meal has not survived. I am surprised to find no account of heavy fighting in this period. My impression was of a struggle that went on all day, but such accounts as I have found do not support this. Perhaps, as the sun rose in the sky and started to fall again, we even slept a little.

At the two or three trucks which comprised Robcol HQ, there was at least one brief interlude. 'About 13.30 a Liaison Officer from 50th Division arrived and told us to move forward and take post SW of 1st South African Division. No withdrawal unless 1st South African Division moved.'

At this point, the Brigadier's writing gets a little scrappy, even irritable. He goes on: 'As this would have put us in the 18th Brigade box where the Boche were, got on the blower and asked that as the Boche were on the ground allocated, I proposed only to move from present place as and when I thought it advisable. As the Boche seemed strong in front of me, could I have latitude regarding standing fast on 1st South African Division south.'

The answer to both was yes. 'From about 12.00 hours, 22nd Armoured Brigade had begun to collect behind our left. They now (between 14.00 and 15.00 hours) moved forward so that their right was a few hundred yards behind our left, their line being refused.' The Brigadier reports dryly, 'Towards 15.00 shell-fire became pretty heavy and casualties began to rise.'

While the 11th Field War Diary records: '15.00 hours enemy tanks seen approaching from the west. 15.30 hours Battery positions attacked by the enemy. Engaged by own guns. Regiment under heavy shell-fire and MG fire throughout engagement.' And the 83rd/85th Battery War Diary shows, '15.00 hours (Ruweisat Ridge). Tanks seen approaching from west and identifed as hostile by OP's. They halted hull-down and D Troop was ordered to engage with HE cap on. Both troops under very heavy shell and MG fire throughout the engagement. Two of D Troop guns received direct hits and two enemy tanks were destroyed by the troop.' *The Salonika History* records that:

> he put in his tanks – these were reported by the OP's and engaged as they came over the ridge, the opening rounds being fired at 2,900 yards, over open sights. By this time, the positions were being subjected to a certain amount of shelling and this became heavier as the tanks closed. The tanks continued to work close to the gun line particularly on the right flank towards Ruweisat where the ground was higher. A few vehicles were soon hit and set on fire and casualties to personnel began to mount. As the accuracy of the tanks improved, some guns received direct hits.
>
> 265th Anti-Tank Battery was heavily punished. Several portees were quickly hit before the guns could open fire and casualties were heavy. D Troop on the right, which under Captain Clements had previously caused some severe casualties to the German infantry, now came under direct fire and two guns received direct hits. Captain Clements was badly wounded and casualties to personnel were severe. The guns meanwhile were taking toll of the enemy's tanks and several could be seen on fire.

It was a desparate situation. Colonel Mac told his men that the guns must fight it out where they stood, and so they did. Victory for them was to hold the ridge until nightfall. A document in the library of the Imperial War Museum describes the layout of the gun positions in words identical to those used in *The Salonika History*:

> At 11.30 hours fire was opened on the leaguer, by both D and E Troops. The immediate reaction to this was an infantry attack on the ridge in the OP area. D Troop engaged the infantry while E Troop continued firing on the vehicles. Several of these were on fire by now and there was considerable confusion. The infantry attack was soon stopped and the enemy broke and ran.
>
> A second infantry attack was staged, this being a more determined effort. Casualties were caused, but it was carried forward until it was 1,000 yards from the OP. The infantry then went to ground, engaging the OP with rifle and MG fire. Some remnants ran back. By this time the enemy MT had disappeared into the heat haze and out of range. No further targets were seen for some time.
>
> At 15.00 hours, D Troop OP reported tanks approaching and both D and E Troop OP's were closed down. Under considerable attention from the enemy, it was also seen that lorried infantry were following up the tanks.
>
> The tanks halted 3,000 yards from D Troop which was on the right flank. This was the only troop which could engage over open sights. 22 tanks were counted from this position. The range was too great for effective anti-tank fire, but despite this, the guns chose their targets carefully and laid accurately. Enemy fire on the position was increasing.
>
> At the same time, B Troop also engaged these tanks. Visibility was poor but the fire appeared to be effective as the frontal advance was stopped. A period of quiet ensued. During this period, B Troop was flanked by enemy tanks which brought down both direct and indirect fire on the position. An ammunition vehicle was set on fire. Under cover of the flanking fire other tanks had advanced to about 2,000 yards range and had taken up hull-down positions."[1]

The timing of this attempt to outflank Robcol on the left of B Troop under cover of a frontal attack on 83rd/85th Battery from the right front is, in all accounts, identifiable as around 5 o'clock. At this hour in London, Churchill was sitting down in the Palace of Westminster, his Vote of Censure won.

While B. A. G. Jones records, 'About 16.00 the attack on our position developed. The shelling got really hot and 11th Field had a good many casualties,' the Brigadier's notes show, 'A determined tank attack developed about 17.00 from the NW. It was accompanied by heavy and accurate shelling.'

Immediately before this entry for 1700 hours (and after one for 1500 hours) the Brigadier records the arrival of the first help for Robcol: 'A Honey Regiment moved across our front and took post under the Ruweisat Ridge to our right rear.' The identity of these 'Honeys' (M3 Stewart light tanks from the US) has been a little vague. They are clearly shown on the Brigadier's battle map at about 881279 and identified as coming from the 22nd Armoured Brigade – some 3,000 yards to our rear. When interviewed 25 years later, he called them 'The Bays' but the appendix on the 22nd Armoured Brigade shows that they were a mixture of brave survivors from many regiments. As we shall see, the 22nd Armoured Brigade did not endear themselves to the commander of Robcol that afternoon. However, this feeling is directed at the Grants behind our guns. The Brigadier will credit the Honeys as providing at least 'moral support'.

Lawrence Boyd describes the position:

> Clements and I were eventually fired at, at close range by the leading tanks and we prudently withdrew along the ridge and eventually arrived at the gun positions where the two troop commanders took over direct control of their guns.
>
> 83rd/85th Battery were in position with E Troop of the left and D Troop on the right. E Troop were in box formation with three guns forward and 2 back. About 200 yards separated the forward flank guns. The ground was hard and rocky and digging was impossible. I took over Right Section (3 guns) and (Lieutenant Bill 'Slim') Slight Left Section.

I quote verbatim from the various reports I have found because each observer saw different things and from a slightly different vantage point – but each one has a number of events in common e.g. The Adjutant's ammunition 3-tonner. These enable us to set the happenings in a logical sequence which was far from obvious at the time. Then, all was confusion and all interest centred on one's personal struggle.

Firstly, 'After a short interval we came under fire from tanks in a semi-hull down position at about 1,000 yards range. Our return fire seemed to have a deterrent effect but I do not remember inflicting any definite damage at this stage. It very shortly became necessary to limit the expenditure of ammunition but the enemy did not attempt to close. Captain Tomson, the Adjutant, then arrived with a 3-tonner of HE which was most welcome.'

And then, 'The next phase was an attempt by enemy tanks and lorried infantry to by-pass our left flank. The range shortened and we were offered better targets. The threat was met by Stewart tanks who came up behind and to our left. A tank versus tank battle developed in which we joined; we appeared to be in the middle of it and an uncomfortable half hour or so ensued. I remember at least 2 enemy tanks being disabled and considerable damage to the infantry. The enemy eventually withdrew but our ammunition was again very low.'

Most accounts are clear that, some time between 1630 and 1700 hours, death missed the commander of Robcol by inches. Who knows what the course of history would have been if the German gunner had squeezed his firing mechanism just a little stronger. The Brigadier was standing just beside his driver. His record says,

> 17.00 hours: About now a 50 mm entered the front of my carrier and carried away part of [the driver] O'Connor's calf. It also smashed the controls and I had to change to McCarthy's carrier. The Assistant Adjutant of 11th Field (I think) very gallantly brought up a truck to get me away. By then I was alone, sheltering behind the carrier which the chap who had hit it was trying to do the same again. There was also a good deal of MG fire and shelling. Unfortunately, he [the Assistant Adjutant] came so fast that he couldn't stop and ran slap in to the back of the carrier, putting his truck completely out of commission. I couldn't help saying: 'What on earth are you doing!' Poor lad, he was very crest-fallen.

While B. A. G. Jones writes, 'Our carrier was hit by an Anti-Tank shell [47 mm] which hit O'Connor in the legs badly and also severed the electrical connections and so was immovable. I got another vehicle for him but found that he had been towed out.' The story of the Assistant Adjutant is a good one and I would dearly love to meet young Katti again – bright, likeable young subaltern with the face of youth matured slightly by a well-shaped dark moustache – to find out what he remembers of this incident. I know that he was not far away.

It was about this time that I received the order to leave the comfort of a hole in the rocky sand because the guns were nearly out of ammunition. How I received the order I can no longer remember. Reason states that it came by line; emotion recalls the battle-bowlered face of Duggie. However it came, the order was unwelcome. Who would leave such a glorious, though shallow sand-hole to wander around an unknown, unfriendly desert to look for an echelon one suspects is not there. Somehow, I made my first positive contribution to 2 July.

From somewhere, Young appeared in the Monkey truck. Even the excuse to move to the rear to look for ammunition was without comfort for the crest behind our basin was clouded by bursting shells. Somewhere in this wilderness, I passed Robcol HQ and, if I did not ram the Brigadier's car, the memory of our mad scrambling ride precludes surprise at the Brigadier's story. Somewhere Young and I found the ammunition lines. Some driver answered our call. Shortly, we were driving back to the troop position with an ammunition 3-tonner following. A few yards short of the position, our cable-laying 15 cwt took a trench at speed. One wheel stuck fast and the memory of the next few minutes is one of my few certain recollections of that afternoon. I can clearly recall the effort with the sand-mat which failed to move the lorry.

I remember jumping on to the bulky ammunition lorry and, from the running-board, urging the driver towards the black blobs, towards the guns. I remember dropping off about 100 yards short of the position and making my way back on foot to the command post – uncertain whether I was a hero or a coward. Later I realized that I was both, and feel a little sad that neither of the semi-official accounts even mentions my small part, even though the Adjutant and the RSM are noted for bringing up ammunition at the time. Perhaps I missed a page in history by not making those last few yards to the hungry guns.

Before we follow the RSM over that frightening distance, let us go back for the last time to the scene around the Brigadier's stricken Tatanagar. Because this attack in which his armoured car was hit was so clearly the moment at which the Germans lost their last chance to win the battle. We have seen how little there was to spare until this moment. We sense the oratory of Churchill in London. We have seen the Honey's intervention only minutes before. The Essex are marching to join their committed C Company. The 11th RHA are marching to the sound of gunfire. Both will arrive, and record the fact, before the dust around the Brigadier's shattered Tatanagar has settled.

They arrived not a minute too soon. Throughout the afternoon, the two forward troops, D and E, had suffered heavy losses. Their trails had fallen where they happened to be when first contact was made. We have already seen them engaging tanks over open sights at 2,000–3,000 yards. This is the range at which a tank's medium machine gun will rake the ground in wicked fashion and a 25-pounder will only win when a direct hit is scored on some vital point. Neither the troops nor the guns had had time to choose their ground; and Geoff Armstrong of 11th HAC, arriving at the sound of gunfire, will be appalled that guns can be sited so unfavourably. But, we knew no better that day.

It is clear in any case that the bulk of the teatime attack fell on D Troop, the most exposed guns when action commenced.

The Imperial War Museum document states,

> The first major casualty in D Troop was No. 3 gun, which received a direct hit. Most of the detachment were badly wounded. Any slightly wounded were distributed amongst the other gun teams. Despite the efforts of the Adjutant and the Battery Captain[2] to bring up further supplies, ammunition began to run out. Casualties increased. These were evacuated by ammunition vehicles returning for further supplies or special vehicles sent up with that objective.[3]

D Troop's four guns were genuine representatives of 11th Field – men who had come with me from India. With No. 3 gun knocked out, three 25-pounders remained in D Troop.

> No. 1 gun then received 3 direct hits, four of the detachment dying from their wounds. At the same time, Captain Clements was wounded. Shortly after No. 1 gun was hit, the 2 remaining guns received hits.
>
> At 18.00 hours Brigadier Waller, Commanding Robcol, was compelled to order Lt Col McCarthy to withdraw B and D Troops a few hundred yards to the right rear. The casualties had been heavy. There was no move until these orders were received. The positions vacated had been maintained through the day. B and D Troops then withdrew, D Troop leaving behind one gun completely knocked out.[4]

A map reference 884282 yields a significant sidelight. In Brigadier Waller's diary – backing on to his description of the evening of 2 July – is a pink message form. It seems to have come by hand as it contains no transmission details. This fact is noted because 50th Division liaison officers are mentioned in several histories – one wonders if 50th Division had any wireless communication at all! The Brigadier noted, 'Received about 20.30 on 2nd July from 50th Division.' The message, which we also noted in an earlier chapter in the context of Ackcol, stated: 'Latest information enemy tanks concentrating 880280. Assist our armour by bringing all available fire to bear if not already doing so. Ackcol being ordered to close up to friends on your north.'

What a wealth of information these 32 words convey. 880280: the Brigadier has written against this, 'That is behind our right – luckily they weren't! The actual area of our battle with them was around Pt 63, about 874279.' The Brigadier's own map reference is slightly misleading, the enemy tanks came from 874279. Pt 63 is 87602794.

It is also possible that the Brigadier's understandably sharp reaction to this message is based upon a further slight miscalculation. His battle map shows 'Robcol: 2nd July: 10.00 – 21.20 hours' as extending up to easting line 8784, refused back down the ridge along northing 2795, but this is almost certainly the line of the furthest advance of our OP cars. The 83rd/85th Battery War Diary records that the battery went into action in 882278. This would put the enemy tanks on the north side of the ridge about 2,000 yards from our guns if the map reference is correct. Perhaps 50th Division's information was less inaccurate than the Brigadier has given them credit for.

A final alternative is that 50th Division were reporting our own tanks as enemy. In the description of the actual fighting at about teatime, a force of Honeys wandered across the battlefield. They were, in fact, the only British armour to which the less inarticulate members of Robcol will give any credit that day. The Brigadier's map, across squares 880278 and 880279, carries the words 'Honey Regiment: 22nd Armoured Brigade: p.m. 2nd July'. If the map is accurate, the 'enemy tanks' were our own Honeys, or the two forces were close enough to hurl insults across the ridge at each other.

In any case, it is fair to assume that 11th Field was bringing all available fire to bear on any enemy tanks in its vicinity at the time the message was received. The Brigadier's note reads, 'see back of page to note what was happening at 20.30 when this was received. I may be a little bitter.'

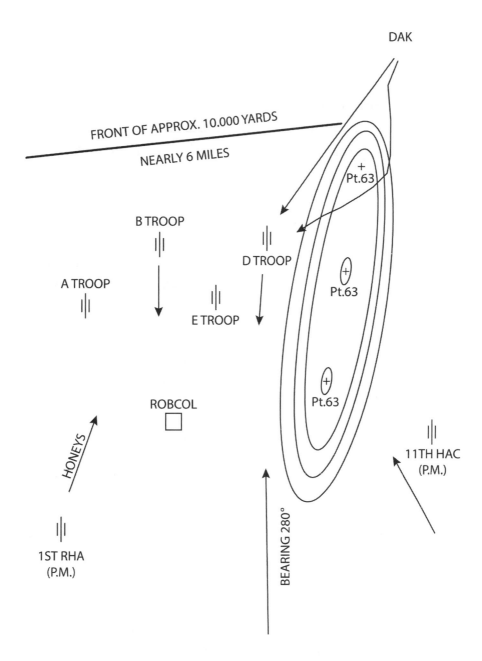

Gun Emplacements, Ruweisat Ridge, 2 July 1942. (Courtesy of Graphic Performance)

CHAPTER 11

A Visit to the Guns and Nightfall

When the 'flap' around the disabled command car had died down and Driver O'Connor had been evacuated to the care of 11th Field's medical officer, the Brigadier and B. A. G. Jones climbed onto the roof of one of the HQ 15 cwts. There they sat, kicking their heels against the canvas roof, staring through their binoculars towards the sun slowly sinking against the ridge. From their pose one would have imagined them at Epson or Ascot, cheering home the winner of the Royal Artillery Cup. But today's champagne was served in a 'piyala' – a battered enamel mug – and its sweetness came from the liberal lacing of sugar which the driver of their newfound home had added. Instead of chicken sandwiches, there was bully on hard tack.

It seemed a funny way to fight a war to men who, for years, had suffered the disciplines of peacetime exercises. Before 'the balloon went up' umpires and instructors in gunnery had instilled an instinctive reaction against showing even the smallest part of one's person in the wrong direction. Cigarette smoke could be seen for hundreds of yards, a lighted match for miles. Yet, here in the desert, the normal method of observation was to stand on top of a truck, puffing happily if one had 'the makings'. With no reference points to indicate the scale, with little cover for the attacker, and with heat haze to confound visual judgment, one could expose oneself freely to the enemy with little fear of accurate reprisal.

From the Brigadier's observation post, the ground sloped gently downwards to the crest of the ridge. In the distance, the stationary black specs of enemy vehicles indicated the limit of their advance against D Troop's first position. Once or twice, as the heat haze swirled, one imagined that one could see the black shape of No. 3 gun where it lay surrounded by its detachment. The other guns of D Troop were now out of sight, hidden safely in the depression to which they had been withdrawn.

E Troop guns were clearly visible, still answering to the OP's call for action. On the left, puffs of smoke told of A Troop also finding targets on which to range. B Troop, like D Troop, had now found lower ground. To the right rear, the six guns of the HAC had come up into a perfect position, 800 to 1,000 yards behind a crest over which the enemy would advance at his peril. Funny how in a desert which, at first sight, seems so featureless, little folds in the ground suddenly become apparent. And that is where experience tells. If only D Troop had found a position like that for the first action, they would never have suffered so badly. As the motto on the Brigadier's diary says, 'Learn from the mistakes of others, you haven't got time to make them all yourself.' In any case, Geoff Armstrong had got the HAC into good ground. They'll take some shifting from there.

To the left rear, the RHA are firing 'Gun fire'. From the whine of their shells, they are pasting the Deir el Shein. Hell of a cloud of dust over there – and that black smoke is encouraging. Looks as if they've 'brewed up' something all right. Only hope to God the prisoners from the 18th Indian Infantry Brigade have been got away.

Suddenly there's a little flurry of activity in E Troop. A 3-tonner races up to the position. Can 3-tonners race? Certainly the driver is not standing upon the order of his going! Puffs of smoke appear from a number of innocent-looking mounds on the ridge. The ground around E Troop spurts into the appearance of an irregular bed of flowers as the shells burst. Dust drifts over the position. The 3-tonner disappears from sight into an unsuspected gully. Only its squat roof shows – and smoke and dust drift over this sign of its presence. E Troop's guns bark and the ridge vanishes into a cloud of dust. Neither side shows sign of having suffered in this little scurry. Slowly the dust drops and the desert is strangely silent. Now and then the sound of metal boxes being thrown onto sandy rock indicates that E Troop's ammunition is being safely distributed.

'BAG, you are improperly dressed,' said the Brigadier jumping down from the 15 cwt's roof. He fumbled in the back of the truck and brought out his flat serge hat with the scarlet band of his rank. 'Brigade Majors RA on parade will wear a brassard on the left arm.'

Humouring the senior officer, Jones searched, grumbling, through his valise. Eventually the brassard was found, and he emerged 'properly dressed'.

'Right, now we look a bit more like soldiers, let's go and see how the chaps are getting on,' said the Brigadier. 'Follow me.' Setting off on foot towards the enemy, the two figures soon disappeared from view among the camel-thorn of the next barely discernible hollow in the sand.

'Hey, Chalky, come and take a dekko at this! An effing general!' called the lookout on E Troop, No. 3 gun from the layer's seat where he had been keeping an anxious eye towards the ridge.

'Eff me, so it effing well is. An effing general in the middle of an effing battlefield – doesn't he know that there's an effing war on?' grumbled Chalky, looking up from the blackened tin in which the water was just coming to the boil, ready for the precious tea leaves.

'Hey, sergeant, dekko jaldi!'

The sergeant switched from a horizontal to a vertical position in one natural movement, borne of long practice in the guardrooms of Indian summers. By now, he was getting used to such suprises – only a few hours before, he had saluted the Auk in the middle of no man's land. If this unknown brigadier chose to wander about in the middle of a ruddy battle, he knew what to do. The sergeant was a regular soldier. His reaction was instinctive.

'Detachments rear!' he barked, to the considerable surprise of the other two gun members, who, busy sorting ammunition behind the gun limber, had not yet noticed the approaching visitors. Despite their surprise, the gunners did not need a second order before giving instinctive obedience to the instinctively given command. There in the desert, with empty cartridge cases and ammunition boxes scattered around, they drew up in two ranks opposite the towing-eye of the gun. The char must wait upon this peculiar inspection.

'Detachment 'shun!' came the order and they stood to attention, suddenly acutely aware of missing sidearms and, in one or two cases, of missing shirts. In their nakedness, they suddenly felt conspicuous. How many German eyes were watching their unexpected gun drill? Wonder if the Boche can make out the Brigadier's red tabs and that flaming armband. When such a feeling comes upon you, only the habits of the parade ground will prevent you from putting a maidenly hand across the groin where instinct tells you that the impact must come. But standing to attention behind your gun, such human frailties may not be allowed to show.

Nor did they show on the faces of the Brigadier and the Brigade Major as they came on with measured pace across the sand. Erect they came, as on the parade ground at The Shop. Twenty-five years later, when B. A. G. Jones talked to me of the Brigadier's example, he eloquently described himself as following 'walking all pinch-bum' and, listening to his unusual adverb, I felt my knees close involuntarily and my stomach muscles tense.

'Stand easy, sergeant'', ordered the Brigadier. 'You're putting up a damn good show. Hold them here till nightfall and we've got them. The HAC's just gone into action behind you and there's a lot more coming up. What range are you firing at?'

"The major's been firing at MT at two to 3,000 yards, sir. But just now I'm laid on that black speck two degrees left of the tar barrel at 1,600 yards. I think it's a tank or a Boche OP and, when the bastard comes again, he's mine."

'Better get back to that brew-up before that happens, sergeant. Keep it up and good shooting,' and the Brigadier marched off in the direction of the next gun.

'Eff me!' said Chalky to himself as he threw the tea leaves into the boiling mess-can.

'Effing good show;' said the sergeant, watching the Brigadier's departing back. 'Hey, you two, get that flaming limber shipshape before the old boy comes back and gives you a rollicking.'

On No. 2 gun, the sergeant looked across at No. 3. 'Christ, the old man's gone doolalley,' he thought. 'Doing flaming gun drill in the middle of a flaming battle!' Then he caught sight of the red tabs and the red brassard.

'Get your bloody boots on,' he shouted at a gunner who was enjoying the luxury of sand trickling through his athlete's foot. 'Jeldi now, before the bloody Brigadier arrives.'

'Bloody what?' said the gunner.

'Bloody Brigadier, I said, jillo ... Detachments rear!' Only five men fell in behind No. 2 gun, and if an attack had come at that moment, they would have been passive spectators of the action, at least until the enemy got within rifle range. However, as the Brigadier repeated his words of encouragement, the artificer screwed back the cap on the recuperator system.

'I think she'll hold for a bit, sir,' he reported, 'but I'd like to strip her down properly before she's fired much more.'

The Brigadier pointed to the space between the gun shield and the sand: 'Several of D Troop's casualties have come from bullets and splinters flying under the protective shield. I know you can't get down far in this wretched rock, but if you can't dig in, then why don't you fill ammunition boxes with sand and build up. You'll be glad of the protection next time they come.' The sergeant cursed himself for not having got round to this earlier.

When the little procession got to the next guns, the detachments were smaller: four men on a gun, finally two men only in one detachment. Two men behind a gun with a shield riddled like a vegetable colander, but as the sergeant assured the Brigadier – the sights were still true and the firing mechanism undamaged.

The growing awareness of the gunners' sacrifice etched itself into the faces of the Brigadier and his Brigade Major as the macabre drill was repeated at each successive gun, relieved before they got back to the HQ 15 cwt only by a slight departure from the military manuals at the last gun they visited.

'Detachments rear!' came the cry, as before. Four men sprang to attention behind the gun as the two officers approached, but by now the Brigadier was anxious to get back to his signal truck and the communications of command. He strode past the four men without stopping for his usual encouraging word. Between them, the four men bore no shirt. Three wore steel helmets, but the sergeant was both shirtless and hatless. An enormous man with black hair all over his chest, a 'curry pot' bulged over short shorts such as South Africans wear, which ended high above hairy thighs stretching downwards into the black abyss of ammunition boots. Somehow in the action, half his face and his right chest had got covered with the black marks of exploding cordite. As the Brigadier and the Brigade Major marched by, ready to acknowledge the salute which had come from all other detachments, the sergeant called his men to attention. His right arm quivered towards a salute, a salute which no regular soldier would give with his head uncovered. Slowly his arm stiffened at the shoulder, but the gesture, once started, must be completed. A grin spread over his smoke-covered face, his arm abandoned its lateral movement and he presented a horny fist with thumb stuck up to the sky in a gesture which in any language means the same: '*Tik hai, sahib* … All's well, sir.'

'Take that man's name, major!' said the Brigadier with a fine show of military intolerance. The Brigade Major walked across to the parading subsection and spoke quietly to the No.1: 'Well done, sergeant, keep it up.' The two erect figures continued their promenade, back to the comfort of the solitary 15-cwt truck.

Into the evening

B. A. G. Jones records, 'The shellfire now forced us back about 1,000 yards – our withdrawal was covered by smoke from 3rd RHA.[1] We went into action again and stayed till dark.'

There is no further record of D Troop that day. I believe they stayed on the battlefield till dark, a little to the right rear of E Troop, tucked up against the ridge. If so they can have played only a small role in subsequent events. One gun, surrounded by slowly stiffening bodies, was left where Robcol first met the DAK. D Troop can have had little more to add to the fighting – particularly as Clem had, by now, been carried off bleeding profusely from the groin.

As the Brigadier wrote, 'About 18.00 hours I was compelled to shift the two forward troops a few hundred yards to the right rear.

Their casualties had been heavy and I wished to get them onto fresh ground and out of the line of the present shelling.' In conversation at Wyaston Leys, the Brigadier also mentioned a smokescreen from the RHA.

The Salonika History states, 'When one gun of D Troop had been completely knocked out and three temporarily disabled, this troop withdrew with their three useless guns to 400 yards behind E Troop. The fourth gun had to be left as it was immovable as well as irreparable.'

The 83rd/85th Field Battery's War Diary records, '18.30 D Troop withdrew owing to lack of ammunition and E Troop engaged tanks which advanced about 1,000 yards on D Troop's withdrawal.' This is confirmed in a letter I received in 1951 from Lawrence Boyd, 'In the late afternoon, D Troop withdrew, leaving us uncomfortably isolated. I had no orders and as we now had a reasonable supply of ammunition, I decided to stay.'

What a wealth of information this short paragraph reveals. E Troop is now isolated – and feels it. Lawrence has no orders – and even my respect for both Duggie, Mac and Brigadier Waller cannot hide the fact that in a better organized war he would have had some contact with authority. But to report this is to forget our primitive communications at that time. In London many years later, Lawrence described to me how he 'wrestled with the telephone'. It can only have been the line which Bombadier Young laid to the command position and to me.

Again, I am left wishing that I could have played a more heroic part in this story! In any case, it did not matter, for E Troop saw it out, but, before we attempt to describe their last defiance, we must take a final look at our near neighbours.

To our right, 11th HAC are in position just north of the ridge, firing strongly from safe ground. They have half-filled the gap left by the South African Brigade. To our rear, the RHA are marching steadily forward to plug the hole more securely. The Acting CO of 11th HAC has reported to Brigadier Waller.

Geoff Armstrong notes on Robcol: 'Meanwhile, Battery Commander liaises with 1st RHA on Robcol left and hears acting CO Bob

Loder-Symonds persuade his armour to stand by refusing to withdraw his guns' whether the tanks stayed or not. These are bitter words but it cannot be denied that, although we received some encouragement from the appearance and actions of the Honeys, the sight of a small force of Grants standing, apparently idle and unconcerned, to our left rear throughout the afternoon perplexed the men who served the guns. We did not know that at the time, they were the last real tanks in Egypt and that they were under orders not to engage.

As the Brigadier records it:

> Loder-Symonds of 1st RHA came up and said he had persuaded the 9th Lancers Grants to move up closer on our left and the Honeys to stay on our right and asked us not to retire. I replied we had no intention of retiring.
>
> About 19.00 or perhaps 19.30, there was a lull and I went across to see Carr of 22nd Armoured Brigade in a jeep. My main objective was to get him to stand by us and to find out whether he was staying on the ground after dark or withdrawing. He said his orders were to move back after dark.
>
> On returning about 20.30, I found that our forward troop (now E Troop) had again been attacked by tanks which got to within almost 300 yards and shot down most of the gunners before they were driven off. All this within a few hundred yards of the 9th Lancers Grants who made no move.

This is an ugly moment to report and I have no wish to cause pain to the many gallant cavalry officers who served under Brigadier Carr on better days. But my tribute to Brigadier Waller demands that he receive full credit for standing fast when others were less steadfast. His diary for 4 July returns to this incident: 'Bill Carr very apologetic about not supporting us more on 2nd. Blames (a) Royal Tank Regiment (RTR) chaps for not going up more freely (b) order not to get the Grants shot up.' The actual order from XXX Corps was, 'The armoured force will be in Army reserve and will not be committed to battle against enemy armour until a really favourable opportunity has been created for it by the action of the infantry divisions.'

We can see the effect this paragraph had on the armour at the height of the battle for Ruweisat. It was a specific order and the cavalry must be excused for reading it literally. Years later, Brigadier Waller would clash with a famous armoured commander in the gardens of Buckingham Palace about the meaning of 'really favourable opportunity' and sadly repeat the story to me at Wyastone Leys some months later.

The second reason is, however, valid enough, remembering the losses of the 22nd Armoured Brigade who had had a hell of a time. The diary of 4 July continues:

> General Lumsden on same theme – obviously expected me to be a bit 'old-fashioned' about it, and anxious to explain the limitations of armour. I said my experience with armoured troops was fairly considerable and I quite understood what they could and could not be expected to do. He added 'of course, too many guns have been lost.' Actually, although on the night of 2nd July I had told General Norrie – without naming the Regiment – about our forward troop, I had not, nor had I intended to say more to Lumsden about it.

Perhaps this is also one of the reasons why the story of Robcol has never been published. But, if you think Geoff Armstrong and Brigadier Waller insufficient evidence, let me add one more paragraph to this painful episode, from B. A. G. Jones's diary, 'All this happened just South East of Pt 64 of Ruweisat Ridge, where a thing happened typical of the action in later days. The leading troop of 11th Field was all but run over by Boche tanks. The 9th Lancers Grants were about 600 yards from them and did nothing to help.'

Returning now to E Troop, isolated, without orders but still firing dauntlessly, his diary continues,

> The enemy tanks, seeing D Troop withdrawing, advanced but they only advanced a short distance before they were stopped by fire from E Troop. At no time did the tanks manage to get nearer than 300 yards to the Troop position. No praise is too high for this Troop which was made up of elements from four different Regiments. The ammunition situation was desperate.
>
> About this time, the scene was enlivened by a D Troop ammunition lorry turning up somewhere near No. 2 gun (Sergeant, later BSM Wilkinson).

Lawrence Boyd's letter of 20 October 1951 added, 'This was an anxious period, relieved at last by the arrival of RSM Clark with another ammunition lorry. The RSM spent a considerable time on the gun position and took over as layer on one gun, leaving only, I think, when wounded. I remember his presence with gratitude. He cheered and encouraged us all.'

Jones again:

> Then in the late afternoon, the enemy fire was concentrated on E Troop commanded by Captain Boyd. This troop inflicted heavy casualties on the enemy but was badly mauled itself. Two guns were put out of action by direct hits. Ammunition was nearly exhausted but the Adjutant, Captain Tomson, brought up supplies to the troop position from 11th HAC under heavy fire. Heavy casualties to personnel were also incurred. Just before Captain Tomson arrived, Lieutenant Slight, who was already wounded, blew up one gun with himself in the layer's seat with the final two rounds in the position.'

This puts 'Slim' Slight's sacrifice as late afternoon as the 11th HAC arrived at about 1630–1700 hours.

The Salonika History states that

> Sergeant Keelan of this troop, who was one of those gathered in two nights before, was the only man on his gun who was not a casualty. He continued to fight his gun alone under intense fire and for his gallantry on this occasion received an immediate award of the DCM. It was Sergeant Keelan, too, who under intense machine gun fire, gave RSM Clark training on the new No. 29 [sighting] telescope.

I can see Nobby Clark now, twiddling his splendid cavalry moustache: 'Now, what's all this 'ere?' Despite his delight in all things hallowed by the gloss of time, despite his lack of the Certificate of Education which alone would have allowed him in time of peace to be the Colonel's No. 1 soldier, despite his belief that soldiering ended with the horse, Nobby had an acute mind and considerable dexterity. He 'proved such an apt pupil that he stepped into the layer's seat and scored three successive hits'.

Both these incidents are confirmed in the Imperial War Museum document:

> Sergeant Keelan, one of the NCO's gathered in two nights before, was the only man on his gun not a casualty. He fought his gun under intense fire and, for this, he was awarded an immediate Distinguished Conduct Medal. It was this NCO who, during the heat of the battle managed to instruct the RSM in the use of the No. 29 telescope, a new piece of equipment.[2]

Lawrence Boyd's letter continues,

> A further attack developed towards evening. We came under heavy fire, I think mainly observed fire from hull-down tanks. We concentrated our return fire

on a tank on the ridge which was obviously acting as OP. We hit it but it did not blow up. No. 1 gun (I cannot remember the No. 1's name but he was later a BSM in the Regiment [Keelan]) was hit and slightly damaged and 2 of the detachment were killed and one wounded. I spent most of the remainder of the action with this gun and remember doing some rather ineffectual laying. Both guns in Left Section were by now out of action. Lieutenant Slight and the Assistant Gun Position Officer (AGPO) had both been hit and the detachments had withdrawn. All Right Section guns were in action but ammunition again very low. Eventually as light began to fail, I checked ammunition and found there was no HE left and I thought we could reasonably go.

While the 83rd/85th's War diary adds, 'E Troop withdrew at dusk having expended all ammunition. They had obtained 3 direct hits on enemy tanks and two of E Troop's guns had been hit. Several vehicles of the battery were also destroyed in this action, the unit having borne the brunt of the attack for five and half hours.'

The Brigadier's diary:

> We got out the three workable guns, the fourth and fifth had had a direct hit. The casualties in this troop had been very heavy. It contained one gun from 515th Battery and the No.1, Sergeant Keelen was the only man left on it. He had kept his gun in action, loading and firing by himself. On the order to withdraw, although wounded, he limbered up and withdrew the gun safely.
>
> About 21.30 the armour had all moved off so we followed and leaguered at Pt 97.
>
> Casualties about 80 K/W/M including 5 Officers.

While B. A. G. Jones's diary shows, 'Well in our 2nd position we held their attack and eventually moved back to Pt 97 to leaguer. I slept like a log for the trip back was difficult and I was dead beat. The Brigadier was really magnificent in the battle and cool as the proverbial cucumber.'

The 83rd/85th Battery's War Diary records, '21.45 Robcol withdrew to Leaguer at Pt 96 (429890). Casualties – killed 5 BOR's, wounded Captain W. J. Clements, Lieutenant Boyd, Lieutenant W. E. Slight, Lieutenant E. P. L. Sturdee, Lieutenant A. M. McGregor, 2nd Lt P. Curry and 75 OR's.'

The Imperial War Museum document adds:

> When the light began to fail, enemy shelling also died down though the position was still under small arms fire. At 21.30 hours, Captain Boyd, as all HE had been

expended, ordered his troop to withdraw. This was accomplished with the aid of one tractor and the OP vehicle. One gun had to be left on the position as, in the time available, it was not possible to move it. The next day it was recovered by 2nd RHA and is now one of the centre pieces in the Army Hall of the Imperial War Museum.[3]

At Wyastone Leys, 25 years later, the Brigadier found the last sentence difficult to understand. He doubted that the E Troop gun was recovered by 2nd RHA as he had a clear memory of going back to the gun position with Geoff Armstrong of 11th HAC and finding our lost gun with the gunners bodies stretched around it. However, this riddle is resolved when one remembers that D Troop lost a gun, knocked out quite early in the day, and 'Slim' Slight had blown up one of E Troop's guns 'about tea-time'. Brigadier Waller and Geoff Armstrong will have seen one of these two total wrecks on 3 July. It is almost certain that 2nd RHA recovered Slim's gun. As D Troop were leading, it is unlikely that 2nd RHA will have got forward to their position. Our last hypothesis is that a third gun was left on the battlefield that day – the second gun of the Left Section of E Troop. This view is compatible with Lawrence's letter:

> For some reason unexplained, we could only find one tractor. I ordered No. 1 and No. 3 gun (Bombardier Lane) to withdraw with the tractor and my OP vehicle which was on the position, telling the tractor to return for the remaining gun. This was accomplished without further loss and I left the position in the tractor. We were fortunate that shelling ceased as darkness fell though I remember some small arms fire. I regret that the Left Section guns were left on the position, both out of action. I believe they were retrieved next day. We left the gun towed by my tractor with the Regimental Light Aid Detachment [who were also responsible for recovery of equipment].

Perhaps the confusion is caused by the fact that E Troop had five, not four, guns. The Imperial War Museum document states, 'Out of the nine guns with which 83rd/85th Battery started the day, 2 were complete wrecks, 6 were repairable, and one was serviceable. This gun joined 78th/84th Battery the next day.'

At this point, the narrative becomes personal once more. I cannot, with truth, identify the guns which we have tried above to define more exactly. I can however state with certainty that we left Ruweisat confident that we had removed all guns capable of firing. The above records show that, as darkness fell, gunfire ceased though there were occasional bursts of small-arms fire as stragglers left the battlefield to west and east.

So the memory of that nightfall on Ruweisat is burnt into my mind. At least I had found the strength to walk abroad. I patted the rounded nose of a Chevrolet 15 cwt, grey and sand-coloured. It was no longer frightening that a piece of hot metal struck it, slowly and without force enough to penetrate the thin metal. Duggie was there, wearing – I think – a battle-bowler (which we had not yet learned to discard). He was rabbit-faced, and brave, as ever. Was the 15 cwt towing a gun? I cannot swear to this but I believe this was how the third gun of E Troop left the battlefield when only two towers were available. The approaching night had banished fright and I made a business of being conscientious. Duggie was certain that everything which could move was on the move. We would be the last to go. We moved east to Pt 97 and the brief moment of clear memory was clouded by tiredness.

Later, B. A. G. Jones would describe the Brigadier's gallant salute to the men around the destroyed guns of both D and E troops as dusk fell on 4 July. Both the Brigadier and Geoff Armstrong, while paying their last respects to the dead, would ultimately be chased away by fire from a 50 mm gun.

Epilogue

The desert sun, blood red in the dust of battle, slowed down as it sank towards the western end of Ruweisat, touched the ridge and picked up speed in final eclipse. It was a sight which, from only slightly differing angles, the men of 11 Field would watch with awe for four months.

When, on 2 November 1942, Eighth Army finally advanced, we no longer had any doubt. Sundown on 2 July had witnessed the turning of the tide. But we did not know it at the time. We knew that we had stood firm and felt some pride. But, as the din of battle dropped to an unnatural quiet and both sides pulled back to attend to the chores of food and replenishment before total darkness made this difficult or impossible, our biggest feeling was one of relief.

Throughout the night, men lay where they had fallen.

In the Deir el Shein, the Germans, pulling their bright green and ochre desert shelters around them, fell into the postures of exhaustion in the false security of the shadows cast by their vehicles on the desert sand. Under this thin covering of sand, stubborn rock would resist the efforts of their evening trenching tools trying vainly to scratch some shelter from the bombers which they knew must come. Utterly exhausted, they cannot have scratched for long. Nor would their sleep be long disturbed even by the RAF; in their condition most would stir only lightly, dreaming, even at the whine of that which would bring lasting quietness.

In the British leaguer on Pt 97, similar patches of shadow held similar mounds of wool and canvas, hiding the same exhaustion.

On The Ridge lay the last gun of D Troop, a strangely asymmetrical shape, bearing little kinship to the smooth machinery on which we had trained for battle. Around it, in poses like those of the sleeping living, lay the bodies of No. 3 subsection. Ringing them at a discreet distance, German uniforms, stiffening in the night air, numbered the enemy who had shared their last journey. On The Ridge and in the hollows imperceptibly leading to the position, the black shadows of panzers, mark IIIs and IVs, with smoke still drifting from one or two charred hulls, stood tribute to their marksmanship.

Perhaps an occasional figure groaned, or let out a sharper cry. One imagines stretcher-bearers scavenging in mercy, just as one knows that in the sleeping leaguers, artificers are hard at work on guns and vehicles, batteries were charging, telephone cables being checked for the next day's battle. In the RHQ trucks, the Adjutant, Tommy Tomson, attempted to compile a casualty return: 'Provisionally, sir, I make it 12 killed and 62 wounded including seven officers in the 3s and 5s with 26 men still missing. They report their ration strength for tomorrow at 87. I haven't got the score yet from the 8s and 4s, though I don't think they've had quite such a rough time.'

Professional pride will have led him to seek an accuracy from which his humanity must have revolted.

The Salonika History records that, at one time during the fighting, the total strength of the regiment was down to 167. The '8s and 4s' did not escape all that lightly, though most of their casualties came the next day when according to the regimental war diary, they lost seven killed and 32 wounded.

On the desert tracks back to Burg el Arab and Amiriya, the last 3-tonners jolted over the uneven desert carrying the last of the wounded, grunting at their painful progress, back to the hospitals of the Delta. Some miles nearer The Ridge, the squat, armoured shape of 'RD' chugged along – painfully on its wounded wheels, stopping at too frequent intervals to cool its boiling engine. Daylight was well advanced before gunners Paul and Chambers eventually faced a tired ordnance officer in a workshop outside Alexandria and, by their show of belligerence, persuaded him that of all vehicles in the Eighth Army, 'RD''s repair merited highest priority.

Some time later that day, 3 July, Chambers, Paul and 'RD' reported back to the regiment fit and ready for action.

But, of all this activity in the darkness, there is little record and tiredness has erased all memories. We only know that as the sun rose on 3 July, both leaguers stirred more slowly than is prescribed by desert lore for those who wish to see their children's children.

In the Deir el Shein, the DAK counted their runners – 26 tanks left out of the 55 which had attacked the day before. Some may be back in running order within hours. One last, all-out effort for Alexandria. If only we can get back onto that accursed ridge before the Tommies wake from their slumber!

On Pt 97, the Brigadier and his Brigade Major have made a similar count. 11th Field is down to one battery – 78th/84th – though 83rd/85th are working desperately on their non-runners. Some of their six disabled guns may be back in action by nightfall. 11th HAC is in good heart. Geoff Armstrong looks a bit feverish (they think he wears that blasted topee to hide the colour of his face), but his guns are still in splendid shape.

'BAG, for God's sake, make sure we don't go short of ammunition today.'

The Essex now had three good companies to protect the guns. Those chaps who came up last night (3rd RHA, the nucleus of Ackcol) look a useful addition. Thank God they've got some 6-pounders with them. If only we can catch Jerry before he gets back on to The Ridge!

From Pt 97, the '3s and 5's watched Robcol move off as it had done only 24 hours earlier – only now it had gained a little in strength, while the DAK was a little weaker. The crisis was past, even though the patient was still in a critical condition.

It was still touch and go, none the less. The DAK in the Deir el Shein had a shorter distance to go. The '8s and 4s' met the DAK head on as the '3s and 5s' had done the day before. Once more the leading troop got 'bitten off' very near to the position where D Troop had 'caught it' the previous day. Once more the leading troop, after suffering heavy casualties, received orders to withdraw. But this time, with the experienced HAC anchored in hull-down positions in the shelter of the ridge, they withdrew to comparative safety.

3 July was the '8s and 4s'' day. For every act of gallantry and sacrifice of which you have read in the preceding pages, our sister battery produced its ample counterpart. The one sound gun of the '3s and 5s', that of Sergeant Wilkinson, accompanied the'8s and 4s'. Twice wounded early on 2 July, he and his detachment were immediate volunteers to fill the place of an '8s and 4s'' non-runner. On 3 July a near-miss blinded him with sand and he had to be evacuated.

Once more, the line held. The patient suffered no relapses. But, by now the attack was a little less strong and the patient a little less weak. On the right, Ackcol had plugged the gap left by the 1st South African Brigade's withdrawal the previous day. In the centre, the 1st Armoured Division was a little stronger and more aggressive than on 2 July. To the south, the New Zealanders had closed up from Alam Nayil and, making a magnificent sweep into the Deir el Mreir, wiped out the whole of the divisional artillery of the Italian Ariete, thus threatening the DAK's right flank. That night when the time came to leaguer, Geoff Armstrong said to the Brigadier, 'They want the best seats, we have them.' The column leaguered on the guns. That night only the German rendezvous lay away from the field of battle.

On Pt 97, the artificers tightened up the recuperator systems of the guns of 2 July – with satisfied grunts. The '3s and 5s' – if only on a small scale – were back in business once more. In the next days, the '3s and 5s' made up a troop in 11th HAC until enough guns were back in action to justify their separate existence once more. A Lieutenant F. R. Jephson was appointed D Troop commander.

At 2200 that night of 3 July, 1st Armoured Division passed a signal to Robcol.

Less than two hours later, Rommel decided to call it a day. The next day, the Afrika Korps made a last despairing gesture in the direction of Alexandria.

Rommel had not only been stopped but was now forced to take defensive measures to safeguard his own supply lines. For, like ourselves earlier, the enemy now found themselves at the end of a very long supply route, and although Alexandria might be only 60 miles from Alamein, their nearest port – Tobruk – was 350 miles behind them. By

The Auk's message of congratulations to Robcol, dated 3 July 1942. (Author's collection)[1]

4 July the enemy advances – at least temporarily – had definitely been halted. Now moreover, the 9th Australian Division had arrived fresh from Syria to reinforce the South Africans in the north. As there was not sufficient infantry to man the whole line in strength, the majority were concentrated in XXX Corps between the sea and Ruweisat Ridge, while the 7th Armoured Division occupied the gap between Ruweisat Ridge and Qattara Depression, leaving the 1st Armoured Division in reserve.

As recorded by Joan Bright:

> That day [3 July] had really marked the end of the danger period. The enemy forces, having failed, but only just, to bounce the Eighth Army out of its final stop line, after their tremendous advance, had now perforce to wait for reinforcements and supplies.
>
> If we were utterly exhausted, so were they, and already there were signs that, although on their side they had success and bright hopes, their morale had sunk lower by far than ours.
>
> Those days were probably the finest in all the history of the great Eighth Army. For weeks it had retreated, fighting by day and travelling by night, after one of the most vicious pitched battles in history. There was little equipment left and on

reaching the completely unprepared Alamein Line the survivors had had to turn and stand and fight while defences were dug, minefields laid and newly landed reinforcements brought in. They fought with the courage of desperation, beating off attack after attack and falling asleep over their weapons in between. In the terrible thirst and glare of the desert summer they had endured, giving no ground. The Afrika Korps had expended itself as a wave breaking upon solid rock.[2]

Some time on 4 July, in some hospital or casualty station, a Bombardier Johnson made his last great sacrifice.

5 July, no attack came.

On 2 July 1952, in a world almost at peace, *The Times* 'In Memoriam' column carried these words:

> RUWEISAT RIDGE – In memory of 104 casualties of 11th Field Regiment RA. 10 years ago today, when Rommel's tanks were stopped by 78th/84th and 83rd/85th Field Batteries RA, unsupported by other arms, at 1,500 yards range.

Whose act of commemoration this was, we do not know. It was not Brigadier Waller – though he remembered still. It was not the Brigade Major – now Brigadier B. A. G. Jones – though his memory was also fresh. It was not Colonel Mac. Nor was it Geoff Armstrong, for his memories are still of a day when the Honourable Artillery Company marched to the sound of our gunfire. 'Unsupported by other arms' – though true in the sense in which it was written – is ungracious to those other arms who shared our trial without the satisfaction of being able to give support; it can therefore not have come from anyone outside the regiment. 'At 1,500 yards range' suggests it was someone who was wounded before the tanks closed on E Troop. '104 casualties' shows someone who believed he spoke from detailed knowledge. Above all, though, the few lines of tribute show someone who remembered. Someone who remembered, and as I was to do years later, someone who wished to remind the unconscious world of Robcol's sacrifices and of Robcol's achievements.

In Wyastone Leys, Brigadier Waller stared across the beautiful valley of the Wye, a small paper cutting in his fingers. Seated at the desk at which I was later priviledged to make the first notes for this history, he carefully pasted the cutting into a yellowing, much-thumbed AB 119 – Army Signalling Scribbling Book (Instructional Purposes Only). The pages of the AB 119 left little space for the comment the Brigadier wished to make – needed to add. Only the back inside cover allowed space for that which he had to get down on paper. It carried for us all, the following lines to those who, as foreseen by his ancestor, 'uncommended died, in some desert where no men abide':

*'Lines written on 2nd July 1952 after reading an 'In Memoriam'
notice in* The Times *for that day:'*

The red sun sinks beyond the Deir el Shein,
Soft darkness covered you: the tumult died;
The soaring lights marked out your stubborn line,
Beneath the shadow of Ruweisat Ridge.

What was the worth of your stout hearts that day?
Who tells the sum of all your sacrifice?
But for your staunchness, who can say?
The autumn victories had never been?

Is that the answer to your sweat and pain?
Your requiem in the Desert's dusty breeze?
When the bells peal for Alamein,
Remember these.

In the text, I have been privileged to quote two poems from Brigadier Rob Waller. His words 'When the bells peal for Alamein, remember these' closes a story which can have no other ending.

Before the covers finally close on this book, I would like to offer you a second, final poem by B. A. G. Jones. It was written in the desert just after the events of this story and does not fit easily into the narrative, but it illustrates thoughts known to everyone who took part.

War in the Desert – Summer 1942

No high ideas are mine about
The rough and bloody work of war
I fight because I have to fight
On this or on some other shore.

But in this vast unending space
There are no animals to maim
No homes to break, no fields to burn
With hate and devastating flame.

No innocent and harmless lives
To wreck. We never see
Fleeing from all he loved and owned
The hopeless, broken refugee.

So while I have to take a share
In this or in another war
May all my battles then be fought
In some great desert evermore.

And more, I pray in times of peace
No monuments or graven stones
Will be erected here to mark
Our battlegrounds, our brother's bones.

These moving sands will couver o'er
Our dead. No trace there'll be
In future years of scars of war
In all this wide sterility.

This endless waste of sand and dust
Let us fight here if fight we must.

In Recognition

Seldom can the Military Cross, the Military Medal and the Distinguished Conduct Medal have been won by three men serving the same guns as these three did on Ruweisat Ridge on 2 July 1942. Fate brought them together in E Troop, 83rd/85th Battery, 11th Field Regiment RA for less than 48 hours before they were parted by the wounds that each of them suffered that day in Robcol's action on Ruweisat. They came from very different backgrounds.

Captain Lawrence Boyd, MC

The son of a clergyman, he was educated at Winchester. He served in the Calcutta Light Horse and was commissioned on 28 December 1940. He was posted to 11th Field Regiment RA in Meerut and went with them through Iraq and Iran. In June 1942, they were ordered at short notice to march the 1,500 miles to help replace gunner losses in the Cauldron of 5/6 June 1942. By then, he was troop commander of E Troop and having lost three of his guns in the night breakout from Mersa Matruh, arrived at El Alamein with only one of his own guns behind him.

As we have seen, four guns of E Troop were to come from other regiments. Two were led by Captain Eric Foster of 164th Field Regiment RA. This regiment only existed for a few days, from 17 June to its end at Gazala. It was formally disbanded on 1 August 1942. A further one gun came from 515th Battery under Sergeant Keelan and another under

Sergeant Wilkinson. Boyd had hardly had time to learn the names of his gun commanders before the column moved off along Ruweisat Ridge. After the war, he worked for British Steel, and then spent several happy years in retirement. He died 'while fishing in Scotland'.

> On 2nd July during the attack on his column near the Ruweisat Ridge, this officer showed most conspicuous courage and devotion to duty. He fought his Troop with success all day largely contributing to driving off an attack by infantry. When it was attacked by enemy MKIII and IV tanks and heavily machine-gunned and shelled he set a splendid example to all ranks by his complete disregard of danger. Although himself twice wounded he took command of a gun when the No. 1 was killed. He continued to fight his guns until two of them were put out of action and all his ammunition was expended.[1]

Sergeant George Wilkinson, MM

Born in a mining village in the north-east of England, it was the depression of the 1930s that led him to take the King's Shilling. He served with 13th Field Battery RA in Aldershot between 1933 and 1935, transferred to the expanding Anti-Aircraft branch and was posted to 8th Anti-Aircraft Battery in Peshawar, then on to Port Sudan, protecting British interests during Mussolini's invasion of Abyssinia. Peshawar again in September 1936, then Calcutta and towards the end of 1940 to Karachi to create a training depot for the Indian Army. One of two Urdu-speaking anti-aircraft specialists he was posted to a Punjabi regiment armed with 18-pounders! Back with 8th Anti-Aircraft Battery RA at Easter 1941, he then went to Basra in Iraq and then to 157th Field Regiment RA equipped with 25-pounders. Rejoining his old battery, now called the 164th Field Regiment RA, it was the breakout from Mersa Matruh that led him to join E Troop, 83rd/85th Battery on 1 July 1942.

> This NCO had set a very high example of courage and devotion to duty throughout the whole period of operations. On July 2nd South of Ruweisat Ridge when his Troop was attacked by tanks, BSM Wilkinson, then No. 1 of a gun, was twice wounded. In spite of this he continued to direct fire of his gun under heavy gun and machine gun fire until dark when he was ordered to withdraw. Although he had several opportunities of being evacuated with the other wounded, he was in action with his gun on the following day and continued to command his gun efficiently again under heavy shell fire.[2]

Sergeant John 'Jack' Keelan, DCM

Although his name was spelled correctly on his citation, he has often been refered to as Keenan. He was definitely a useful man to have at one's side in a scrap. Stockily built and speaking with an accent which suggested his physique owed something to a Durham coal mine. Like Sergeant Wilkinson, he came to E Troop 83rd/85th Battery from 164th Field Regiment RA. *The Royal Artillery Commemoration Book* also shows Jack Keelan as coming from 515th Battery, 165th Field Regiment RA. Other records show 515th Battery as forming part of 164th Field Regiment RA, which with 157th Field Regiment RA and 97th Field Regiment RA were the guns of 10th Indian Infantry Division.

Keelan had become separated from his unit, the 515th Battery in the retreat from Mersa Matruh. In my research, I found that Sergeant Keelan had died before I could properly trace him. I understood that after the war in the desert, he served with The Welsh Division in Western Europe, lost a leg in the crossing of the Rhine and had died in the early 1970s.

> During the action on Ruweisat Ridge on 2nd July this NCO behaved with great coolness and showed an excellent example to his detachment. His Troop was shelled severely for several hours and finally attacked by enemy tanks. He controlled his detachment and supervised the fire of his gun with great steadiness and determination and set a splendid example to all around. When a shell killed four of his detachment he continued to fire his gun alone until the last round was expended. Although wounded and still under heavy fire from tank cannon and machine guns, when the Troop was ordered to withdraw he brought his gun safely to the rear.[3]

Bombardier Johnson

Of all the devoted band of E Troop, none displayed more shining and indomitable courage than Bombardier Johnson. It is here that tired memory can play tricks, but it is at this moment that awareness of him springs to mind. I cannot now imagine, before the first day of action on Ruweisat was over, that Duggie and I talked of heroes. It was no moment for small talk but it is and always has been with this minute of 2 July 1942 that I connect Bombardier Johnson. I can record the fact, I cannot explain it.

In Lawrence Boyd's letter to Lieutenant Colonel Colville of 20 October 1951, he wrote:

I have not included in my account any mention of Bombardier Johnson who continued to act as No. 1 of his gun after his arm had been blown off. He died shortly afterwards and received no award. I was told of the incident afterwards and I hope you have been able to obtain a first-hand account. His magnificent conduct should never be forgotten in the regiment.

This was my text when I turned to Jim Manning and 'The Times Diary' in 1967. Bombardier Johnson had always been on my mind. Despite my research, I had been unable to find any address which would have allowed me to follow up.

As Duggie and I spoke of him – the mental picture is too sharp for doubt – his tortured body would have been approaching Alexandria on some clumsy 3-ton lorry. A few hours later we spoke of him more earnestly. Both Duggie and I were anxious that his sacrifice should be rewarded. But, we were 'new boys' in the desert. We did not know then that dead heroes qualify only for a Mention in Dispatches or a Victoria Cross. A Mention seemed pathetically inadequate. We could find no independent witness to justify a Victoria Cross. As Bombardier Johnson died on 4 July 1942, the Africa Star which many families cherish, carries no '8'.

The layer on Sergeant Franklin's gun, he almost certainly came with him from 32nd Field Regiment RA. Many years later as part of my research, John Mayes would write to me from Australia saying, 'I remember Bdr. Johnson's amazing performance. Apart from bravery and devotion, I have often recalled that as an example of the natural instinct of a well trained soldier.' The Imperial War Museum document and *The Salonika History* both record "Bombardier Johnson, another NCO in E Troop had his left arm shot off earlier in the day. He continued to lay and fire with his single arm, refusing all aid. This very gallant NCO died in hospital two days later.'

Bombardier Johnson's sacrifice was as deliberate as that of Titus Oates and by one of those coincidences with which life abounds, the BBC has just helped me recall Scott's words even as I worked on this draft,

a brave man and a gallant gentleman – it is splendid to pass however with five such companions as I have – for my own sake I do not regret this journey – had we lived, I should have had a tale to tell which would have stirred the heart of every Englishman.

The Men of Robcol

If this book has a hero, it is the '3s and 5s'. Not the military unit, but the men whose spirit made the numbers live on long after 11th Field Regiment RA and Robcol had fulfilled the function for which they were brought together. In another sense, Rob Waller is the hero and the guns themselves also fill an heroic role. But neither Rob Waller's unquenchable leadership nor the material magnetism of the guns would have sent ink to the pen which writes of the guns of Robcol if the men who served the guns had proven inadequate.

The 83rd/85th Field Battery War Diary

This gives us a good start. 1 July 1942, Officers of the Battery at the beginning of the month:

Battery Commander	Major J. M. Douglas
Battery Captain	Captain E. J. S. Foster (from 164th Field)
D Troop	Captain W. J. Clements
	Lt. E. P. L. Sturdee
	2nd Lt. R. Bentham
	2nd Lt. J. Mayes
E Troop	Captain L. L. Boyd
	Lt. W. E. Slight
	Lt. A. M. McGregor (from 32nd Field)
	2nd Lt. P. Curry (from 164th Field)
Battery HQ	Lt. F. R. Jephson

Of the Battery's officers, seven came from India with the Battery. The Battery Commander had joined a few weeks previously in Iraq, and Foster, MacGregor and Curry, with one Warrant Officer and 55 Other Ranks, had joined in the last few hours before the battle.

By nightfall on 2 July, seven of the eleven, Major J. M. Douglas, Captains Clements and Boyd, Lieutenants Slight, Sturdee, McGregor and Curry had been wounded though neither Douglas, Sturdee nor Curry were evacuated. 55 Other Ranks had been wounded with 12 killed and 26 reported missing. Of those missing that day, 19 managed to return to the Regiment by 5 July. All this, out of about 300 men engaged in the action.

265th Anti-Tank Battery

Under a short-lived organization introduced in May 1942, Field Regiments consisted of two Field Batteries and one Anti-Tank Battery. 11th Field Regiment therefore had a third Battery, 265th Anti-Tank Battery between 25th May and 14th July. This Battery came from and returned to 83rd Anti-Tank Regiment RA. The Battery War Diary shows 6 Officers and 96 Other Ranks. Five officers have been identified:

Battery Commander	Major P. R. Paul
	Lt. M. J. H. Morton
M Troop Commander	Lt. R. W. J. Hull (from 32nd Field)
N Troop Commander	2nd Lt. M. Budd
O Troop Commander	2nd Lt. R. A. Smith

Although accounts differ, each of the three Troop Commanders were wounded on 2 or 3 July.

Further notes on the men of Robcol

This is an inadequate headline to describe the men, yet space precludes including all the notes and interviews collected as part of the research. This section therefore summarizes some of the knowledge in either my own words or the words of others who were there. This is by no means a complete summary.

Lieutenant Colonel John Ashton: He was Commander of the 78th/84th Battery on 2 July 1942. On 3 July, his Troop 'did very well' – it was their day. After the war he became a Justice of the Peace (JP). He died aged 63.

Gunner Barker: He was a layer on No. 1 gun, D Troop. Clean shaven, about 21 years old. A very quiet, shy person, he was hit badly.

2nd Lieutenant R. Bentham: Bob was self-reliant. He was only recently down from university as a geologist. This had taken him for months on end to the frozen North. After the war, his travels would take him back again to these cold deserts. All my pictures of Bob centre on his pipe, an ordinary briar with no pretentions. He was a quiet, dependable man. Remembered on 2 July by 'Tug' Wilson as, 'smoking his pipe, strolling from gun to gun giving encourage-ment' while 'Chalky' Whyte called him 'the best man among us'. His obituary, carried in *The Times* during August 1968, was by Lord Shackleton, then Leader of the House of Lords.

Gunner J. Bethell: Delivered ammunition to E Troop. He responded to my article in *The Gunner* as a Chelsea Pensioner.

Captain Lawrence Boyd: Commander of E Troop. When Keelan's gun suffered a very near miss which killed the layer and two others, Boyd took over as layer until he was also hit. He was also later Mentioned in Dispatches. By the mid 1960s, he was a most respected sales executive with the British Steel Corporation in Yorkshire and looked younger and fitter than he did in 1942.

Signaller Chamberlain: Supporting D Troop communications.

Regimental Sergeant Major 'Nobby' Clark: Apart from the references to Nobby in the main text, Sergeant Wilkinson wrote, 'The RSM came onto the gun position carrying his swagger stick and walking about unconcerned with shells dropping around him as though he was inspecting the barracks, until he got into the No. 3 seat and had to be told how to use the sight.' He was later Mentioned in Dispatches. After the war he served in the War Department Police. He died in July 1992.

Captain Bill 'Paddy' 'Clem' Clements: Commander of D Troop. He was one of the first in 11th Field to see the enemy. He was acting as No. 1 on a gun when he was wounded. He was later Mentioned in Dispatches. 'Nobby' Clark said that he 'was front page news' in 1951–2 having disappeared from his regiment. He had a heart attack in 1967 and died in August 1982.

Sergeant George Coates: A respected NCO in the '3s & 5s'. He went 'into the bag' in Mersa Matruh with B Echelon. He was a pay clerk and OP Assistant. He had earlier joined the army, arriving in India in 1935. He died in March 1995.

Joe Corrie: In 155th Light Anti-Aircraft Battery, part of 4th Indian Division, he was also trying to find Jack Keelan.

2nd Lieutenant P. Curry: Only joined 11th Field from 164th Field a few hours before the battle. His story with the Regiment is short – I remember seeing it myself. On 5 July at Alam Baoshaza at 0530 hours he was reported missing when an ammunition lorry in which he was travelling was misdirected into an enemy occupied area! It was all I ever saw of him.

Artificer 'Tiffy' 'Taffy' Davies: See Lane below. He was maintaining the guns under fire. Working as part of the LAD team.

Gunner Dickson: A gunner in the '8s and 4s'.

Major J. M. Douglas: 'Duggie' was a brave man. I remember the spirit of one who drove himself to do things that he would not ask others to do for him. I knew him through four months of Alamein, through Mareth, Tunis, Italy and Greece where he left us to command 1st Field Regiment RA. My memory is of a man who looked frail, but a man on whom one could lean with confidence, a man of level temper and low voice, the Commander of the forward Battery on 2 July. Although wounded that day, he remained on the position. He was later Mentioned in Dispatches, twice.

Sergeant Egglestone: D Troop, No. 1 Gun. John Mayes, the D Troop leader, got out of Mersa Matruh with him. They shared Egglestone's Quad/Gun Tower in which to ride to the battle. The gun received a direct hit. Three of the gun team were evacuated, but Sergeant Egglestone died with his stomach torn open by a piece of shell casing.

John Mayes recollects that Egglestone was leading the Left Section guns, and 'I remember dragging Egglestone to a position in rear of the Command Post ... I have a clear recollection of him pleading with me to shoot him.'

Captain Foster: From 164th Field. He replaced Jimmy Breakell as Battery Captain.

Sergeant Artificer Charles Found: For his efforts in replenishing ammunition, repairing the guns under fire and evacuating the wounded, he was awarded the Military Medal.

Sergeant Franklin: From 32nd Field with his gun. A very direct person, yet taciturn and laconic, he was a very good soldier. He was keen to get back to his own regiment after the battle. His gun in E Troop was destroyed by Lieutenant Slight with the last two rounds, but before that, the gun had been hit, the layer, Bombardier Johnson and Gunner Parrott both seriously wounded. Sergeant Franklin later went to Italy and was wounded which necessitated having an arm amputated.

Gunner Harris: A gunner in the '8s and 4s'.

Gunner Hartland: A gunner in D Troop.

Gunner Tom Hignett: Joined 11th Field in Meerut in April 1941. After the war, he was commissioned and in 1990 was a captain. He died in 1991.

Sergeant Jeffs: One of D Troops guns was under his command. A photo taken on 4 July 1942 describes him better than my pen can hope to do. It shows too one of the most benign smiles I have ever known. He had sailed the South Pacific in a schooner with his father and brothers. A tough, experienced NCO, a slow-spoken, quietly spoken man, he was a first-rate soldier who got results but seldom raised his voice. The epitome of a Kiwi, he was a Fiji islander and my memory of him is welded with that of Queen Salote, Queen of Tonga, the Friendly Isles. 'Chalky' Whyte recollects 'the night of 2nd/3rd July was the only time I saw him knocked up'.

Sergeant 'Johnny' Johnson: No. 1 in D Troop, he came with us from Meerut. He was no longer young but he was a smart old soldier. His gun team was always well turned-out and efficient, as good as any others in this regular regiment. I can see his face, creased with the whiskers which good soldiers sometimes tolerated on active service and the whiskers are white. On 2 July, he commanded one of the guns in the forward section of the British Army.

Sergeant Jack Keelan: He was from Liverpool. Wilky comments: 'His gun [in E Troop] had a direct hit and his gun team were killed or wounded. He escaped because he was directing the fire of his gun from a standing position five yards or so to the right flank. Later I saw him trying to fire the gun alone. After collecting ammo, I joined him with some of the lads.' He was seen by 'Chalky' Whyte as 'ideal in action. Whyte and Keelan got Captain Boyd out when he was wounded.

Gunner Ron Kinsville: He was taken prisoner, wounded, in the breakout from Mersa Matruh but managed to get free a few days later. He was in B Echelon. He died in May 1995.

Sergeant 'Shady' Lane: No. 1 of a gun in D Troop. He was noted for his tattoos. The recoil mechanism on his gun was not functioning properly, so Lane and the Artificer 'Tiffy" Davies worked on it under machine-gun fire. John Mayes recalls this and says that 'Tiffy Taffy Davies stands out' because of this action. 'Tug' Wilson also joined his gun. Lane was able to get his gun out that night and was with the Battery on a gun the next day.

Sergeant Lang: No. 1 of a gun in E Troop. His gun was destroyed. Towards the end of the day, he came back with a towing vehicle and helped the wounded Lawrence Boyd get three Right Section guns out with only two towing vehicles. The Imperial War Museum identifies the 25-pounder on display as this gun.

2nd Lieutenant John S. Mayes: Seen as 'a frail man' he ended his career as Adjutant in Salonika. He was given compassionate leave to find his parents who had been interred by the Japanese. He joined Butterfield & Swire and spent many years travelling the Far East. Living in Australia, he provided many written and typed notes which contributed to this story. Unloading ammunition at the front with the 'camouflage net beside me dancing like a live thing with machine gun bullets'. This must have been one of the E Troop's Left Section guns.

It is likely to have been the gun that Lt. 'Slim' Slight later blew up. 'I remember that we were firing off stuff which we knew couldn't take the place of the armour piercing which was so scarce.' He was later Mentioned in Dispatches.

Lieutenant A. M. McGregor: Joined 11th Field only a few hours before the battle, coming from 32nd Field. I do not think that I ever saw him. Lawrence Boyd did see him a few days later at the Convalescent Depot in Nathanya, suffering from a wound which made it very difficult to sit down.

Lieutenant 'Pip' Mott: Was traced after the war with Colonel Mac's help to the War Office, then a major, still in Signals. Before the war, he had been in shipping in Calcutta, volunteered in Bangalore, joined the Regiment early in 1942 in Baggush before going back to India with the 4th Indian Division at the end of the war. Late on 2 July, communications had been destroyed between RHQ and E Troop and he was sent forward to find out what was happening. At that moment, John Mayes appeared in RD, an armoured OP carrier, so they went together. John had been sent back by Lawrence Boyd to get orders and to find tractors to move E Troop's last guns. Together, they brought at least one gun out. He was later Mentioned in Dispatches.

Gunner George Moody: One of the 83rd/85th gun teams.

Bombardier Obie O' Brien: Was a boy soldier, a Midlander who had joined up in 1935. A signaller, he was in the command post when an armour-piercing shell cut him in two. John Mayes described how 'all the command post people were in complete shock and amazement'.

Signaller O'Shaughnessy: He 'struck terror into any young Orderly Officer'! He was an Exchange Operator and signaller in the M1 Signals truck. Despite this, he brought up ammunition at least twice, once to D Troop and once to E Troop. He died in October 1977.

Gunner Parrott: Received a wound across the chest from a direct hit that came under the gun's shield. He died three days later in hospital.

Sergeant Major Pearce: Brought up ammunition and delivered it to the rear of the guns. Sergeant Turberfield and 'Tug' Wilson then manhandled it to the guns themselves.

Sergeant Rippingdale: One of the gun commanders in E Troop.

Gunner Roberts: A gunner in the '8s and 4s'.

Sergeant 'Sherry' Sheringham: No. 1 on No. 4 Gun. An Anglo-Indian, he had conjunctivitis in both eyes on 2 July. The crew included Bombardier Bowran (No. 3), Gunner Hartland (No. 4) and a Driver Dowthwaite. He was another who 'came good in battle'. After the war, he became a prison officer and shortly before he died, wrote to me full of pride about the Regiment and the battle on 2 July 1942.

Lieutenant E. P. L. Sturdee: 'Tug' Wilson describes the incident when Lt. Sturdee was wounded: 'Lt. Sturdee was standing behind my gun, when a splinter ripped across his chin. "Look at what I've got," he said!' He may have been wounded by the same shell that killed Obie O' Brien. After the war he went into local government. He died in 1981.

Bombardier Tate: One of the gunners, he was wounded and was carried to the Command Post.

George Titley: Of 31st Field. He also tried to contact Keelan only to find out that he had already died.

Sergeant Turberfield: During the tank attack, Turberfield was in the Command Post as GPOA with 'Tug' Wilson and said, 'We are not much use here.' They went from the Troop Command Post to the guns, joined Lane's gun and also brought in ammunition. 'Chalky' Whyte referred to him as 'the perfect NCO'. He was later Mentioned in Dispatches. After the war, he was commissioned and became a captain and an instructor. Signaller O'Saughnessy said of him: 'He gave us confidence, he was everywhere.'

Sergeant David Tydeman: He was sent back by Colonel Mac to 1st Army HQ where he found Brigadier Friz Fowler who organized Indian Field Ambulances, about 12 vehicles, to help with evacuating the wounded. 11th Field's Medical Officer was having difficulties coping with the volume of wounded while the Regimental Aid Post was in the open and under fire. He was later Mentioned in Dispatches. After the war, he was commissioned.

Gunner Johnny Walker: Was in B Echelon and E Troop.

Gunner Walters: A driver in B Echelon.

'Badgie' Watkinson: A shell landed between his legs and he died on his way to hospital.

Gunner Watts: A gunner in the '8s and 4s'.

Gunner David 'Chalky' Whyte: Started in Anti-Tank and wanted to go to Hong Kong but instead went to 11th Field RHQ and later to 83rd/85th Battery. Considered himself a 'cautious anarchist'. He was with me from Mareth to Enfidaville in North Africa. Later he was sent to the UK to train and pass on his experience. He was demobbed in January 1946. He was recommended for a Military Medal, but it did not come through. He became GPOA in D Troop and later No. 1 on the No. 4 gun. He suffered eight splinter wounds and was taken to 9th Hospital in Alexandria. He died in September 1988.

Signaller Fred Wilkins: A signaller in the '8s & 4s'. He knew Sergeant Artificer Charles Found.

Sergeant George 'Wilky' Wilkinson: His 'Ammo Book' of jottings was one of the most poignant contributions I have been privileged to read in all the years I have been trying to find out the truth about 2 July 1942. His endurance kept the last gun firing as dusk fell on Ruweisat. It was the only serviceable gun of the '3s and 5s' on 3 July and both he and his gun joined the '8s and 4s'. This despite the fact that he had been wounded twice on 2 July. He was then wounded a third time on 3 July and had to be evacuated. Among many other things that he wrote, he talked about 'the silence when darkness came …the awful feeling of tiredness I experienced when it [the day] was over' and 'What a bloody rotten business is war. It makes us into murderers and frightened, cringeing cowards – we're fighting for freedom, but I'll never be free again – I'll be a prisoner to my thoughts for the rest of my life.' 'Wilky' died 7 November 1985.

Bombardier Harry 'Tug' Wilson: Red tape prevented his gaining a commission as the war ended before it came through. He was for a period my OP Assistant. He was in the Command Post as GPOA with Sergeant Turberfield and left with him to join Sergeant Lane's gun. He later went back to the gun position to bury some of the dead. After the war, he owned a draper's shop.

83rd/85th Field Battery Gun Summary

Summarizing the guns and their commanders was a complex task as the more information that was collected, the more varied the recollections of those who were there. First let us look at why on one page, one can read of nine guns, on another of another of 17 guns, and on yet another 25 guns.

83rd/85th Battery consisted of nine 25-pounder guns, D Troop having four and E Troop five guns. When the DAK came around and over the western end of Ruweisat Ridge on 2 July, D Troop in particular were in their direct line of advance. On 2 July they therefore took the brunt of the action and the casualties, and were the key to stopping Rommel. This book's main concern therefore has been to understand and explain these events. The four guns in D Troop were original in that they largely came from India with the Troop. The five guns in E Troop consisted of one original, one from 32nd Field, one from 121st Field and two from 157th Field.

Who else was on the battlefield?

78th/84th Battery: Consisting of eight 25-pounder guns, four each in A and B Troops. Their day was 3 July, when supplemented by the one operational gun from 83rd/85th Battery, they continued the good work started the day before. This story must however be told in another book. These two Batteries comprise the 17 guns.

265th Anti-Tank Battery: As we have seen, in addition to the guns above, there were six 6-pounder anti-tank guns dispersed in front.

113th Light Anti-Aircraft Regiment also provided two Bofors anti-aircraft guns. This comprises the 25 guns.

1st/4th Essex: Originally only C Company of this Regiment was spread out around the guns to provide protection for the gunners from enemy infantry attacks.

11th HAC: During the afternoon, Geoff Armstrong and his Troop of seven remaining 25-pounders arrived and took up a strong position to the right of the ridge.

1st RHA were behind Robcol's HQ and to the left, but quite some distance from the action.

22nd Armoured Division: During the afternoon, the Honeys and the last available Grants (at the time) appeared behind 1st RHA. The Honeys then drove across the gun line in support of the guns.

What do we know of the disposition of the individual guns?

Some notes on the individuals listed can be found in Addendum 1. The bulk of the early attacks fell on D Troop, the most exposed guns.

D Troop: There is broad agreement on the gun dispositions. The Troop was under Captain Paddy Clements who was wounded during the day.

No. 1 Gun: Commander, Sergeant Jeffs. After No. 3 Gun, this gun received three direct hits, four of the detachment dying from their wounds.

No. 2 Gun: Commander, Sergeant Lane. Shortly after No. 1 Gun was hit, this gun was also hit.

No. 3 Gun: Commander, Sergeant Egglestone. This gun was the first casualty, receiving a direct hit. Most of the detachment were killed or badly wounded, including Sergeant Egglestone. Slightly wounded men were distributed amongst the other gun teams.

No. 4 Gun: Commander, Sergeant Sheringham. Shortly after No. 1 Gun was hit, this gun was also hit.

Casualties were severe. When ordered to do so by Brigadier Waller, they withdrew with three useless guns to about 400 yards behind E Troop, leaving the fourth total write-off in situ.

E Troop was under command of Captain Lawrence Boyd. Both he and Lieutenant Slight were among the wounded. There are different recollections of the gun dispositions between Boyd and Sergeant Wilkinson. This outline follows Lawrence Boyd's memory, but as the Troop only came together during the night of 1/2 July, no one's recollections can be definitive. Sergeant Wilkinson has No. 1 Gun, Lang; No. 2 Gun, Keelan; No. 3 Gun, Wilkinson while No. 4 and No. 5 Guns are as below.

No. 1 Gun: Commander, Sergeant Keelan, from 164th Field Regiment. This gun was well forward (some 150 yards) and was the only gun still firing at dusk. The gun received a very near miss which killed the layer and two others. Keelan then continued firing the gun alone.

No. 2 Gun: Commander, Sergeant Wilkinson, from 164th Field Regiment. The gun was to the rear of No. 1 Gun. This gun was hit, two of the detachment killed and one wounded. This was the Battery's only serviceable gun on 3 July.

No. 3 Gun: Commander, Sergeant Lang, came from 121st Field Regiment. The Imperial War Museum identifies the 25-pounder on display as this gun.

No. 4 Gun: Commander, Sergeant Franklin, came from 32nd Field Regiment. Bombardier Johnson was the layer on this gun. This was the gun blown up later that day by Lt. Slight.

No. 5 Gun: Commander, Sergeant Rippingdale. The original 11th Field gun.

No. 1 Gun was some 200 yards to the left of D Troop. When D Troop withdrew behind E Troop, Captain Boyd took over the Right Section (Guns 1–3) and Lt. Slight took over the Left Section (Guns 4–5).

By 1900 E Troop had only two guns still firing. An hour later, only one gun was still firing, No. 1 Gun of Sergeant Keelan.

By 2030, the tanks were within 300 yards of E Troop but darkness brought a halt to the fighting. E Troop had taken the brunt of the attacks for five and half hours.

Out of the nine guns with which 83rd/85th Battery started the day, two were complete wrecks, six were ultimately repairable, and only one was serviceable. This gun joined 78th/84th Battery the next day.

2 July 1942 as a Turning Point in the War

In Chapter 1 only a limited number of authorities were quoted in support of the claim that 2 July 1942 was 'the day we stopped losing the war'. Here is a further selection:

The Chief of the Imperial General Staff (CIGS), Field Marshal Alan Brooke, 1st Viscount Alanbrooke, KG, GCB, OM, GCVO, DSO & Bar

Sir Arthur Bryant in *The Turn of the Tide* quotes from his diary of 28 June 1942: 'The Middle East situation is about as unhealthy as it can be, and I do not very well see how it can end.' In *The Montgomery Legend*, page 35, R. W. Thompson makes it very clear that 'The CIGS knew that a false move by Auchinleck could lose Egypt in five minutes'.

Major General Sir John Kennedy, CGMG, KCVO, KBE, CB, MC

Director of Military Operations at the War Office from 9 October 1940 and worked closely with Alan Brooke, giving a clear picture of impending doom and of its likely consequences. In *The Business of War*, page 209, he quotes General Sir John Dill, CIGS between May 1940 and December 1941, as saying at this time: 'Unless the Middle East is reinforced strongly and fast, we shall be defeated there, and our combined efforts will not enable us to win the war for years.' He appeared to be against any plan to hold Tobruk and quotes on page 219, a note he dictated in April: 'From the purely military point of view, the retention of Iraq and Persia is perhaps more important to us than the retention of Egypt itself ...' He identified the critical hours – though, on page 249, he can give no details of what had taken place in them: 'By 1st July, Rommel was only 60 miles from Alexandria. We hoped that, greatly extended though he was, he might be checked at Alamein, but, after so many disappointments, we could not be very confident ... However, by 3rd July, it looked as if Auchinleck would be able to hold Rommel, and even deliver a counter-stroke.'

Sir David Hunt, KCMG, CMG, MC, OBE

Montgomery's Director of Military Intelligence, he served Auchinleck, Montgomery and later Alexander. In his book *A Don at War* he says: 'The 2nd July 1942 is the day which to my mind has always been the decisive day of the first battle of Alamein. There has been some argument and discussion about this in the various historical works which have dealt with the battle, but certainly the impression left on most people actually on the spot was that the 2nd marked the climax. Up to then we were on the defensive and desperately so, from then on our thoughts and actions turned decisively to the counter-offensive.'

Marshal of the Royal Air Force, Arthur, Lord Tedder, CGB

Tedder's HQ at this time, was some distance from Eighth Army HQ. But, in his book *With Prejudice*, page 309, he clearly identified the critical date and, at the same time, showed that its importance was not immediately understood: 'Though we did not then know it, Rommel's push had met its real breaking point on 2nd July.'

Field Marshal, Harold Alexander, 1st Earl Alexander of Tunis, KG, GCB, OM, GCMG, CSI, DSO, MC, CD, PC, PC (Canada) and Field Marshal Sir Claude Auchinleck GCB, GCIE, CSI, DSO, OBE

The opinion of both these men can be dealt with by extracts from Brigadier Waller's diary. This diary, written at the time, is the final proof of what happened as seen by the man in direct command of the troops in contact with the enemy. However, the contemporary record is enlivened by later comment, often in red ink and not always complimentary to the British higher command. Two of these later interjections occur on the pages recording events on 2/3 July:

Extract from Alexander's Despatch period August 1942–May 1943, page 839. 'The enemy had … defeated the Eighth Army and … driven it back to El Alamein. There it stood and on the critical day of 2nd July, defeated the enemy's most desperate attempts to break through. By this stand (the survivors of the old Desert Army) gained the vital time … for the arrival of the fresh divisions and improved tanks which were to turn the scale of battle!' The words in brackets are omitted at this point in the diary but this extract obviously made a deep impression on the Brigadier as he repeats it in full elsewhere in the diary. At the same point, Brigadier Waller quotes Alexander, page 841, 'Ruweisat Ridge … It was here that the decisive battle of 2nd July had been fought.'

The Brigadier then goes on to say, 'Auchinleck's Despatch does not even mention the fighting on 2nd July!! See my diary – this day truly was decisive and so the Court of Enquiry, under the presidency of Jumbo Wilson, which sat to enquire into the Campaign, recognized.' (18th February 1948 Brigadier Rob Waller).

Auchinleck may be forgiven. He had sent the congratulatory message refered to earlier, and that day he was not only Commander of the Eighth Army, but also Commander-in-Chief of the Middle East. His Boswell, Connell, was too busy defending his subject from foul calumny to spare a thought for Robcol, but he had no doubt about the date. In *Auchinleck*, page 628, Connell records how, just before the battle, the Auk signalled Smuts: 'On the eve of what may prove to be the turning point of our campaign of the western desert …' Smuts replied in a cable dated 3 July. By the time that Smuts sent his reply to Auchinleck's message, the first decisive phase of the first battle of El Alamein had been fought and won (page 627): 'With all their faults, Auchinleck and Eighth Army had, by that Thursday evening, held Egypt and held the Middle East.' That Thursday was Thursday 2 July, the day after 'Ash Wednesday'. Connell also records that the day before, Auchinleck had decided: 'These damn British have been taught for too long to be good losers. I've never been a good loser, I am going to win.'

He also, on page 654, says, describing the comic episode of Aziz Ali al-Misri, the pro-German Chief of Staff of the Egyptian Premier, who escaped from Cairo in an Egyptian Air Force plane with two other officers: 'They presented themselves on July 3rd at Rommel's headquarters and were received as "leaders of the Egyptian Liberation Movement". They were a little on the late side. It no longer lay in Rommel's power either to help them or to make use of them.'

Lieutenant General Sir Brian Horrocks, KCB, KBE, DSO, MC

Let us now see how one of Montgomery's Corps Commanders generously looks at the same hours: Horrocks, *A Full Life*, speaking of the Auk: 'Few generals have ever had such a load to bear. At this time, the situation in the Western Desert looked disastrous. Our troops and the German Afrika Korps were both moving eastward at full speed, sometimes in parallel columns. A defensive position had been prepared at Alamein, but as only the 2nd South African Division and an Indian Brigade were available to man it, this was by no means impregnable. It wasn't even certain we should get there first with the remainder of the Eighth Army. Let alone be able to retrieve from the existing chaos sufficient battle-worthy formations to hold this position. I have always felt that the decision to stand and fight on the Alamein position was a bold one as it involved bringing the only available reserve, the 9th Australian Division, forward from Alexandria with the risk that it might also become involved in the rout.'

'The decisive nature of the initial struggle which now took place at Alamein has never been appreciated by the general public, though

General Alexander made the situation plain in his dispatch of 5th February 1948, in which he wrote, "By this stand the survivors of the old Desert Army gained the vital time necessary for the arrival of the fresh divisions and improved tanks which were to turn the scale of battle." Had the battle-worn, exhausted and bewildered Eighth Army not succeeded in halting Rommel's drive, we should most certainly have lost the Delta and Egypt, and the Mediterranean would then have become an Axis Centre. It can be agreed with justification that this heroic stand was the turning point of the war.' The potential disaster is then described as earlier in this text. 'It was the desperate fighting in the first fortnight of July when the Eighth Army rescued Egypt, which paved the way for our subsequent victories.'

Marshall, Roosevelt and Churchill

In *The War and Colonel Warden* (Colonel Warden was Churchill's war-time codename) Gerald Pawle describes Churchill at the White House on 21 or 22 June, page 174: 'Hardly had they reached the White House before the grave news arrived. Tobruk had fallen; 25,000 Allied troops had been taken prisoner; and Admiral Harwood warned that in view of the growing enemy air threat to Alexandria he was sending the Mediterranean fleet to greater safety south of the Suez Canal. Reports from American observers suggested that Rommel would be in Cairo within a week.'

From *The Montgomery Legend*, page 48: 'On June 30th President Roosevelt asked Marshall for an evaluation of the situation in the Middle East ... Marshall replied that he thought that the British would withdraw to the Upper Nile; that the Eighth Army would be destroyed, that Rommel would occupy Cyprus and Syria, and eventually seize the Mosul and Basra area, and much else besides ...'

American Intelligence (Army G-2) thought that Rommel might reach Cairo in one week. Army Operations gave him two weeks. In the upshot, Marshall and his experts thought that the next 48 hours would provide decisive answers, and they were right. It is significant, therefore, that on 2 July they did not feel inclined to change their opinions. It may have been difficult as early as 2 July to assess at long range Auchinleck's victory at Alamein, but two days later, the Americans were becoming aware that their worst fears would not be realized.

On 2 July, Roosevelt signalled Churchill 'Good for you', but he was referring to the political victory not the victory in the desert. Churchill, too, was still in ignorance. In fact, according to *Auchinleck*, page 651, on 3 July, he signalled to Harry Hopkins, 'I hope one day I shall have something more solid to report.' Better news must have reached him some time that night for on 4 July he signalled the Auk: 'I cannot help liking very much the way things seem to be going.' Does Churchill's phrasing in Volume 4, page 385 suggest that he was having some difficulty accepting the victory of the man he had already half-decided to replace? Such a feeling would be as typical of the great man as his later praise of Auchinleck's decisiveness 'once in direct command' and his own acknowledgment. 'As early as July 2nd he made the first of a series of counter-attacks which continued until the middle of the month.' Even in his sad dismissal notice of 8 August he recognized: 'You stemmed the adverse tide.'

The Eighth Army was well served by its war correspondents, and by the BBC. Three of the best known have written books in which they clearly appreciated the climax which came at the beginning of July. Unfortunately, none of them appears to have been in the desert on 2 July, although each gives evidence of an intimate knowledge of events a few hours earlier (probably 30 June) and a few hours later (probably 4 July). They were of course, largely dependent on their Conducting Officers for the opportunity to view events spread out over a wide area. They also had a duty to get their news back to their papers. On 30 June communications in the desert were very sketchy. 1 July became known as 'Ash Wednesday' when, in Cairo, GHQ officials were burning confidential documents. The Flap was itself news. And at least one of them had a wife and baby son to worry about in Cairo. He succeeded in getting them on a train to Palestine and gives a vivid description of Cairo at that time. Whatever the reason, none of them was on Ruweisat Ridge during the critical hours. They appreciated what had happened, but could not describe how.

Fred Majdalany: The Battle of El Alamein

Page 18: 'By July 1st, Rommel had been effectively stopped by a hurriedly occupied and incomplete defensive system that takes its name from the adjacent railway halt of El Alamein sixty miles from Alexandria ... it was a considerable victory, though at the time it seemed more like an extremely narrow escape.' He is 24 hours out in his view. On 1 July the Alamein line was broken. It was not re-established till nightfall on 2 July.

Alexander Clifford: Three Against Rommel

'Desperately now Auchinleck needed time, time to unload the eighteen ships that were already sailing up the Red Sea with reinforcements, time to bring the fresh Australian and New Zealand Divisions down from Palestine, time to evolve a deeper defence plan in case the desert could not be held. Desperately he needed time, but he could not afford to pay for it.'

Churchill's Volume IV, page 386, illustrates the anxiety which he felt about the fate of these reinforcements. On 4 July, writing to General Smuts, he speaks 'of 8th Armoured Division with 150 tanks, landing now; the 44th British Infantry Division should land July 23rd and the 51st a month later. Whether these Forces will be able to play their part depends on the battle now raging'.

As Clifford reports, pages 283/284, 'So Auchinleck kept his army and stole some of the time he so urgently needed. But, things were very, very desperate during those last days of June. As matters stood, the chances were that Britain would lose Egypt ... The crisis came at the very beginning of July ... The line was weak, but it was elastic, and it was tethered at both ends by the two fixed boxes. It gave, but it did not break.' And on page 286, '... four times this happened, on the first four mornings of July ... and on the fifth morning there came no thrust at all ... there was the turning of the tide. In those four mornings the crisis had come and gone.'

This book was published in 1943 and was written very close to the events as they happened. It is interesting, in view of *The Montgomery Legend*, to note that Clifford sensed the immediate effect on morale of this victory of the Auk's. From pages 293–300: 'Behind the crust of the Alamein line there was, in those chocking days of July, a feeling of freshness and renewal and rebirth. It was very perceptibly the end of one period and the beginning of another … After the first week in July, Auchinleck had begun to take the initiative in the desert … So through July we watched the Alamein front become established and strong.'

Of the Auk, he says, '… he had, I think, saved Egypt.'

Alan Moorehead: The Desert War

From Cairo, Alan Moorehead's view, though slightly inaccurate as to relative tank strength, is equally clear that Cairo was saved during the first four days of July. Page 165: 'Rommel's forces were roughly equal to ours when he began the campaign. Now with the fall of Tobruk he was twice as strong … As far as one could judge … we had about four divisions (Indian, British, South Africans and composite forces). Rommel still had over a hundred tanks and he was adding to them from captures and his own workshops at the rate of at least a dozen a day. We had practically no tanks at all.'

From pages 166–170: 'Only one barrier lay between them and the Delta – the Alamein Line, 150 miles from Cairo, 60 miles from Alexandria. The vanguard of the enemy arrived on the Line on the last day of June. Only now was the full extent of the danger realised. Churchill was in Washington when Tobruk fell, conferring with Roosevelt, and together they heard the shocking news that the whole British position in the Middle East was in danger of immediate collapse. It promised to be the greatest disaster since the fall of France. The loss of Egypt would precipitate a claim of misfortunes almost too disastrous to contemplate. It would force England back to the dark days of the Battle of Britain.

'With Egypt, would fall Malta and all British control of the Mediterranean. The Suez Canal would be lost and with it the stores and equipment worth 50 Tobruks. Suez, Port Said, Alexandria, Beirut and Syrian Tripoli might go. Palestine and Syria could not then hope to stand and once in Jerusalem and Damascus, the Germans would be in sight of the oil wells and Turkey all but surrounded. The Red Sea would become an Axis lake and once in the Indian Ocean, the Italian fleet could prey upon all the routes to Africa, India and Australia. India would be approached from both sides by the enemy. Finally, Russia's flank would be hopelessly exposed.

'All this was possible as the Germans came up to the Alamein Line on July 1st. And on that day, and the day following and the day after that, the Alamein Line was in no condition to resist any sort of really determined attack whatever. It was ready to crumble. Such troops as we had would fight – yes. But if the Germans came on the way they did at Tobruk there was no question but that the Line would break. Behind Alamein the road lay fair and straight into Alexandria, a two-hour drive. There was nothing much to stop the enemy on that road. In the desert itself, beyond Alamein there was nothing much to stop their cutting the Cairo road and driving straight to Cairo.

'During this anxious first week of July … (I believe that this was probably 1st July at or near the Auk's HQ) … One war correspondent reported that a small group of German tanks had broken through in the south and was headed straight from the Alexandria–Cairo road. A second said that firing had begun on the line and that in the opinion of one of the senior generals there it could be held only another twelve hours. A third said that two Axis thrusts were being made – one in the centre of the line, another in the north. The enemy tanks were coming round the south to isolate all the troops in the line itself.

'It seemed clear to me now that the battle had touched its crisis. Once the line went, Alexandria could not be held. Clearly … the next few hours were going to decide the matter one way or the other.'

And from pages 172–173, on the Alexandria–Cairo road: 'Even in the remote villages, the people guessed that something dramatic was happening in the war. For one thing, the Germans had been broadcasting in Arabic that they would be in Alexandria the following day. They even had the poor taste to suggest that "the ladies of Alexandria should get out their pretty dresses".

'Back in Cairo, we realised that already the crisis was passing. Like most great dramatic moments of the war, it was not seen for what it was at the time and all the finesse, the luck and dangers of this gamble were only realised when the game was done. Alexandria, perhaps the whole of the Nile Delta, had lain in Rommel's hand for a moment. He stood on the threshold of the greatest victory of the year.

'An Indian position was overrun in the centre, but the Indians counter-attacked ... On July 4th, the British position was intact. On the 5th
it was still intact and getting a little stronger. At the end of the week the
situation was definitely better ... By the opening of the second week in
July, the British were set to give battle on the line.'

An Italian officer's view

In his book *Alamein 1933–1962 – An Italian Story*, Paolo Caccia-
Dominioni, Count of Sillavengo, gives an extremely interesting account
of the desert from the point of view of an officer in the 31st Combat
Sappers. This unit served in the Folgore Division, which was easily the
best Italian fighting unit in the desert. As one who has always been
proud of 'having his knees brown', one reads with awe this book of a
man who knew the desert from 1933 to 1962. In 1933, he did a trip to
the Siwa Oasis with a number of friends, including one Peniakov (Lt.
Colonel Vladimir Peniakov), later better known as Popski, commander
of Popski's Private Army. On this journey, he passed near Alamein and
met an Arab who was prepared to make a two-day trek in the hope
of finding one abandoned petrol tin which was reported to be lying in
the desert. After the war, Sillavengo spent several years at Tell el Eisa in
charge of the Italian War Graves Commission.

In a diary entry for August 1942 (which since it comes between 12
and 14 August was probably written on the 13th), he writes on page
108: 'If it had not been for Auchinleck, the British would probably have
lost Egypt and Nubia by this time and been entrenched in Palestine
and the Sudan. But in a few hours, between dawn and dusk on July
1st, Auchinleck managed with shrewd disposition of fresh infantry and
artillery, to revitalise the army. He had stopped Rommel. He had broken
up subsequent enemy attacks, however shrewdly conceived.'

Although Robcol did not stop Rommel until 2 July, he is quite right
in attributing Auchinleck's <u>dispositions</u> to 'between dawn and dusk on
July 1st'. Brigadier Waller's diary for 1 July states, 'Early this morning got
orders to RV at Imayid station at 07.00, there to meet General Nichols. On
arrival, heard that I was to organise two columns from remains of 1st/4th
Essex, 2nd/11th Sikhs and 11th Field RA and any other guns I could get.'

Sillavengo's admission is the more poignant because on page 39, he also describes how near Fuka about 30 June, a Corporal Terravazzi, of the 37th Heavy Transport Group, drove on with great devotion to duty, even though wounded in the buttock, with two tons of black shoe-polish for the expected ceremonial entry into Alexandria!

The following diary entries were made a little closer to the actual fighting, page 48: 'July 1st 1942. A couple of days previously, even the day before, it might have been possible to press on towards Alexandria, by-passing El Alamein and leaving it to fall of its own accord at a later date. Perhaps by this time, we had missed the boat.'

Page 57: 'Hill 33. El Alamein, July 4th 1942. There was no doubt about it; we were at a standstill … a very grave view had been taken of the situation at Armoured HQ the previous evening; not only would it be necessary to give up the advance, it was debatable whether we should be able to hold on to the ground already won. Then the 21st Panzer was forced to retreat …'

Page 58: 'On July 2nd the confusion was general, circling to and fro about the perimeter of El Alamein – chaos unprecedented, as if the previous winter's events in the Marmarica were being compressed into an area one fiftieth the size … Two evenings before [he writes on 4 July] on the Ruweisat Ridge (visible from the observation post), the 21st Panzer had moved to the east to attack the British 1st Armoured Division and had itself been simultaneously assailed by Scottish troops [sic] from the north east [sic] and South Africans from the west.'

Majdalany quotes from Rommel's view

The Rommel Papers, page 13: The German High Command … did not realise that with relatively small means, they could have won victories in the Near East which, in their strategic and economic value, would have far surpassed the conquest of the Don bend [in Southern Russia].'

General Friedrich von Mellenthin on Rommel in *Panzer Battles 1939–1945*

He describes how, on or about 21 June, Kesselring flew to Adrica to urge Rommel to stick to the original plan of taking Malta before

Egypt: 'Rommel … admitted that the Panzerarmee had suffered heavily in the Gazala battles, but maintained that the Eighth Army was in a far worse plight and we now had a unique opportunity for a thrust to the Suez Canal. A delay of even a few weeks would give the enemy time to move up new forces …'

Kesselring flew back to Italy and, after frantic lobbying, Rommel's view prevailed, despite opposition from the Italian General Staff, German Naval Staff, Field Marshal Kesselring and General von Rintelen. The decision was taken to postpone the attack on Malta to September 'and throw everything behind Rommel's invasion of Egypt'. It is clear that this had been in his mind at least since Black Saturday, 13 June when, in his eyes, 'The 1st British Armoured Division was no longer in a fit state for action and left the battlefield during the night.'

On 15 June Rommel wrote to his wife, 'Dearest Lu, how much I think of you … perhaps we will now see each other in July after all,' and on the 27 June, 'P.S. Italy in July might still be possible. Get passports.'

On 29 June (while I was lost in the desert south east of Matruh on my 24th birthday) he was still thinking of an early end to the campaign: 'Now the battle of Mersa Matruh has also been won and our leading units are only 125 miles from Alexandria.' On the night of 29/30 June he himself was only 'about six miles west of El Daba'. And on 30 June to Lu, 'less than 100 miles to Alexandria'.

On pages 240–241 he is quoted categorically: 'We planned to get through to the Alamein line and overrun it while it was still incomplete and before the retreating remnants of the Eighth Army had had time to organise its defence. This line was the last bastion on which the British could oppose our advance. Once through it, our road was clear.'

In retrospect, he realized (page 260) that 'there had only been a few days during which we could have hoped to conquer Alamein and take the Suez Canal area'. These days were the first days of July.

The Rommel Papers, Chapter XI, page 243 is headed 'The Initiative Passes – Check at Alamein'. While pages 245–249 note that early on the 1 July: 'At about 0900 hours, the 21st Panzer Division ran up against the strong-point Deir el Shein, which was stubbornly defended by the 8th Indian Division, fresh from Iraq.' This was the 18th Indian Infantry

Brigade, not the complete Division. The same day: 'At 16.00 hours a report came in from Nehring [tank commander of the Afrika Korps] saying that the Afrika Korps had stormed the greater part of the Indian strong-point Deir el Shein. In the evening that battle at this point was over. Two thousand Indians had been taken prisoner and 30 British guns destroyed or captured.'

Still on 1 July: 'At 2130 hours that evening, I ordered the 90th Light Division to continue its attack through to the coast by moonlight. I wanted to open the road to Alexandria at this point as quickly as possible. The British defence in the threatened sector was strengthening hour by hour. During the night, the Luftwaffe commander reported to me that the British fleet had left Alexandria. This determined me to go all out for a decision in the next few days ... I was convinced that a break-through over a wide front by my forces would result in a complete panic.'

In fact, on 3 July 1942, when he wrote to Dearest Lu, although he acknowledged that 'the struggle for the last position before Alexandria is hard', he added. 'However I hope to manage it.' But this last ray of optimism was not to last. Von Mellenthin, his Chief of Staff wrote on 3 July: 'Some ground was gained on Ruweisat Ridge, but with only twenty-six tanks it was impossible to break through. When darkness fell, Rommel ordered the Panzer Divisions to dig in where they stood; everyone realised that the offensive which opened on May 26th, and which achieved such spectacular victories, had at last come to an end.' According to Corelli Barnett, the order to dig in was given at 2256 hours. At the same time, the Auk was sending an encouraging message to his men: 'From C in C to all ranks, Eighth Army. Well done everybody. A very good day. Stick to it.'

It had taken 24 hours to trickle through into the mind of the German commander, but the vital damage had been wrought on 2 July. Even now, there would be one last effort on 4 July. But that day, 3 July, he wrote to Dearest Lu: 'Unfortunately, things are not going as well as I should like them. Resistance is too great and our strength exhausted.'

Panzer Battles page 128 states that the same night, von Mellenthin confessed, 'We had just failed.'

On 4 July, 21st Panzer were taken out of the line to rest. Next day, as recorded elsewhere, there was no German attack. According to Connell in *Auchinleck*, page 654, von Mellenthin was, by the morning of 4 July, describing the position as 'perilous'.

On 3 July, Rommel wrote: 'After three days vainly assaulting the Alamein line I decided that I would call the offensive off for the moment after the next day's attack ... Reasons for my decision were the steadily mounting strength of the enemy; the low fighting strength of my own divisions, which amounted by that time to no more than 1,200 to 1,500 men, and above all the terribly strained supply situation ... We intended to return to the attack as soon as possible.'

Two months later he made a reconnaissance in force round the southern end of the Alamein positions, but the key position on the Ruweisat Ridge was never again in real danger.

'The line which was not a line' had been held.

The Order of Battle: A Research Summary

Orders of Battle, Second World War 1939–1945 (Volumes 1 & 2)

Prepared by Lt. Colonel H. F. Joslen (HMSO)

In this book, I have described the loneliness of Ruweisat Ridge on 2 July 1942. But, even though we know how small the force was which stopped Rommel that day, it must be acknowledged that so many years later, it was difficult to prove. To do so required going through every unit in the desert and showing that they were not there. In doing so, one hoped to find, by elimination, those who were there.

With few official sources to help in such a task, it seemed impossible. It might have remained impossible if I had not been lucky enough to visit the Royal Artillery Library at Woolwich. A short description of what was being attempted produced a confident answer and, when on arrival, feeling like an elderly cadet officer who was not quite certain of his gun drill, there was a row of books on the library table open at passages of interest to the search. One of them was the official *Orders of Battle*, which would either prove or disprove the case.

Although I first learned of this mine of information at Woolwich, these notes were compiled from a copy of the book borrowed from the Metropolitan Borough of Wandsworth, via the St Bride's Library.

The book lists every division and brigade in the British Army between 1939 and 1945. Starting with the establishments (on varying dates) of the armoured divisions, it lists in turn the eleven armoured divisions of the wartime army. Six of these in June/July 1942 were in the UK: the Guards Armoured Division, 6th Armoured, 9th Armoured, 11th Armoured and 42nd Armoured (formed in November 1941 from my old Territorial division, 42nd Infantry Division) and finally, 79th Armoured Division which was not in fact formed until August 1942.

Of the remaining five armoured divisions, one, 2nd Armoured Division, lost its Divisional Commander Major General M. D. Gambier Parry as a prisoner of war on 8 April 1941. It was disbanded in Egypt a year before this story starts, 10 May 1941.

A further division, 8th Armoured Division was 'at sea' on 2 July. In truth, they very nearly got into these pages. They arrived in Egypt after a two-month voyage on 5 July, as we have noted earlier.

We cannot leave 8th Armoured Division without some thought for their fate. Their brigades were numbered 23 and 24. Before the end of July, we were to watch, in horror, as 150 brand-new Valentine tanks of 23rd Armoured Brigade under someone else's command immolated themselves on a Ruweisat minefield and the 88s of the DAK. They never had a chance to accustom themselves to the deceptive light of the desert. So many of our hopes had rested on them.

To quote Lt. Colonel Joslen: 'In the six months the Division was in Egypt, it never operated as a complete formation.' The 8th Armoured Division was disbanded in Egypt 1 January 1943.

However, in August/September 1942, their artillery support – 5th, 11th, 104th RHA, 146th Field, 73rd Anti-Tank and 56th LAA contained at least some of the guns of Robcol. 73rd Anti-Tank was in the original 8th Support Group between 8 November 1940 and 12 July 1942.

We are therefore left with three armoured divisions which were in the Middle East in June/July 1942. They are: 1st Armoured Division, 7th Armoured Division and 10th Armoured Division.

10th Armoured Division were formed in Palestine by re-organization of 1st Cavalry Division on 1 August 1941 and existed until 15 June 1944 when they were 'disbanded in Egypt'. In September 1942, they were served by such distinguished Ruweisat veterans as 1st and 104th RHA and The Royals but no artillery is listed before September.

Orders of Battle makes it clear that 10th Armoured Division was not in action in July. The first battle in their list of credits is Alam Halfa, 30 August to 9 September. They formed part of the last defences of the Delta, and, they were in a considerable state of flux.

'In March 1942 owing to the paucity of equipment and scarcity of British formations in the Middle East, the Division was not up to establishment ... HQ Divisional RA formed on 7th May 1942 became part of Rees Force for the defence of Cairo bridgehead from 17th June 1942 to 20th August 1942; during this time 50th Division RA was attached to the Division as supporting artillery.' We have seen earlier that (a) HQ RA 50th Division was a contributor to the formation of Robcol on 30 June, 1 July and 2 July, (b) 50th Division artillery had been virtually wiped out.

'From 1st July 1942 to 17th July 1942 Divisional HQ formed HQ Gateforce. The Divisional Commander also commanded 1st Armoured Division from 19th July 1942 to 22nd July 1942.' The Divisional Commander from 26 June to 18 December 1942 was

Major General A. H. Gatehouse, yet another commander whose appointment dates from these critical days.

The facts in *Orders of Battle* are clear. The only unit from 10th Armoured Division which could possibly have intervened on Ruweisat was the 8th Armoured Brigade who left the division on 30 June 1942. They provided 3rd RHA for Ackcol.

Did they add other units to our battle? Yes, one small but very gallant unit from this brigade reached Ruweisat. Units under the command of Brigadier E. C. N. Custance in June/July are given as Nottinghamshire Yeomanry, Staffordshire Yeomanry, Grays (to 30 June 1942), 3rd Royal Tanks (from 12 July) and 1st Buffs (The Royal East Kent Regiment).

The *Historical Records of the Buffs* by Colonel C. R. B. Knight, OBE, enabled me to delineate 8th Armoured Brigade's part in this battle with some accuracy. The gallant stand of The Buffs anti-tank gunners on 1 July has been recorded at greater length in the section on the Deir el Shein. They were 8th Armoured Brigade's only human contribution.

We are left, as every desert soldier would expect, with 1st Armoured Division and 7th Armoured Division. Both were regular divisions, known as mobile divisions.

7th Armoured Division was in Egypt at the beginning of the war and served in North Africa from 3 September 1939 to 12 September 1942. Both 1st and 7th Armoured went from Africa to Italy. Yet another formation to change commander at this time as Major General J. W. M. Renton took over from Major General F. W. Messervy on 19 June 1942 and commanded the division for three months.

Looking more closely at the armoured losses in June we can see how severely the armoured brigades suffered and how four brigades exchanged their last fit tanks and amalgamated until they were little more than a single regimental group. Nonetheless, it came as something of a shock to find no troops listed under General Renton's command during 1st Ruweisat: 4th Armoured Brigade, from 4 January 1942 to 25 June 1942, 7th Motor Brigade from 9 February 1942 to 26 June 1942 and 5 July 1942 to 11 September 1942, 22nd Armoured Brigade from 26 July 1942 to 31 August 1945.

True, 11th Hussars are shown as under command from 10 April 1940 to 31 November 1943, but they were in Persia during the first days of July. At first sight, the division seems to have had no artillery until August 1942 but then one remembers that such units would be found in the divisional support groups. Before making this further search, let us note that 7th Armoured was under XXX Corps from 23 April to 20 June and under XIII Corps from 20 June until 26 November 1942. They are credited with attendance at Gazala (26 May to 21 June) and Defence of the Alamein Line (1 July to 27 July) but not at Mersa Matruh (26 June to 30 June).

1st Armoured Division arrived in Egypt on 13 November 1941 and left North Africa on 27 May 1944. They carry all three honours and were fortunate in that they were commanded throughout the first period by Major General H. Lumsden until he was wounded on 19 July. Major General A. H. Gatehouse, from 10th Armoured Division, then took over for three days until he too was wounded on 22 July. Brigadier A. E. Fisher was then Acting Commander until General Lumsden returned on 15 August.

Although our battle maps show 22nd Armoured Brigade and 4th Armoured Brigade under 1st Armoured Division on 2 July, the official list is quite clear. 2nd Armoured Brigade is the only brigade listed under 1st Armoured Division during first Ruweisat, though 201st Guards Brigade Group were in the division from 21 May 1942 to 14 June 1942.

Under divisional troops we find The Royals from 12 May to 13 September 1942. Again, no artillery until August/September and we must look again to the Support Groups after making one final note. 1st Armoured Division in less than one month came under:

XXX Corps from 24 April to 12 June,
XIII Corps from 12 June to 15 June,
XXX Corps from 15 June to 24 June,
Eighth Army from 24 June to 25 June,
XIII Corps from 25 June to 1 July,
XXX Corps from 1 July to 2 July,
XIII Corps on 2 July,
XXX Corps from 3 July to 10 July and
XIII Corps from 10 July to 26 July.

The support groups

A study of the Support Groups does not at first lead us to the units for which we are searching.

8th Support Group was at sea between 8 May and 18 July and was disbanded in the Middle East on 23 July.

2nd Support Group with, amongst others, the Northumberland Yeomanry, 2nd RHA and 104th RHA supported 2nd Armoured Division from February 1940 to April 1941 but was disbanded in May 1941.

1st Support Group played a similar role, sometimes with identical make-up, in support of 1st Armoured Division until it was disbanded in February 1942 – when it became 7th Motor Brigade Group, whom we have just seen were indeed under 7th Armoured Division in June/July 1942. At the same time, we learn why General Renton had no troops under his command during First Ruweisat. 7th Motor Brigade Group were under 7th Armoured Division from 9 February to 26 June, 1st Armoured Division from 26 June to 30 June, XIII Corps from 1 July to 5 July and returned to their home command, 7th Armoured Division from 5 July to 11 September.

They were thus present at Gazala, Mersa Matruh and the Defence of Alamein. During this time, they served under:

Brigadier J. M. L. Renton (promoted to command 7th Armoured Division from 19 June),

Brigadier, The Viscount Garmoyle who died of wounds on 3 July,
Brigadier T. Vaughan-Hughes for the one day of 3 July and
Brigadier T. J .B. Bosville from 4 July.

In June and July, their units were 2nd King's Royal Rifle Corps, 2nd Rifle Brigade and 9th King's Royal Rifle Corps and possibly 4th RHA. Extracts from the *History of the Rifle Brigade* enable us to chart their contribution to First Ruweisat with some accuracy, particularly as Lord Garmoyle's death is a sad reference point which is fixed in many histories. As in all accounts of this period, even this tragic loss is sometimes recorded 24 hours out – on 4 July – but there is plenty of evidence to fix it as 3 July.

The armoured brigades

The many changes in establishment, nomenclature, command and commanders we have met force us to continue our search by looking at the *Orders of Battle* for the armoured brigades, themselves called light, heavy, brigade groups etc.

Immediately we seem to have found a further reinforcement – 1st Armoured Brigade. However, it soon became clear that this unit 'was employed for the remainder of 1941 in equipping and training RHA units for operations in the Western Desert'. On 6 June 1942, the 1st Armoured Brigade was 'reorganised and designated 1st Armoured Brigade (Tank Delivery Troop)' and 'units of the Brigade Group are posted to other formations and the Brigade ceased to be operational'.

And now we come to a real identification. It is one which fits the battle maps and what we know to be true, but it is at variance with the divisional orders of battle which put 2nd Armoured Brigade under 1st Armoured Division and left us wondering about 4th Armoured Brigade and 22nd Armoured. The brigade order of battle shows clearly that:

2nd Armoured Brigade were Eighth Army troops from 23 June to 5 July, and that,
4th Armoured Brigade was under 1st Armoured Division from 25 June to 7 July with,
22nd Armoured Brigade under 1st Armoured Division from 7 June to 22 July.
The explanation is not hard to find. We have seen elsewhere that after the calamities of 5/6 June and 12/13 June, all four armoured brigades in the Middle East plus their tank reinforcements from 8th Armoured Brigade, were effectively reduced to one armoured regimental group.

These three brigade groups which interest us at the beginning of July, oscillated between 1st and 7th Armoured and Eighth Army in June/July. In the first 4 days of July:

2nd Armoured Brigade was nominally under Eighth Army from 23 June to 5 July,
4th Armoured Brigade was under 1st Armoured Division from 25 June to 7 July, and,
22nd Armoured Brigade was under 1st Armoured Division from 7 June to 26 July.

Since we must identify the remnants of these three brigades with particular care, the details of their make-up during First Ruweisat are tabulated below.

Brigade	2nd Armoured Brigade Group (Eighth Army)	4th Armoured Brigade Group (1st Armoured Division)	22nd Armoured Brigade Group (1st Armoured Division)
Commander	Brigadier R. Briggs. Succeeded by Lt. Colonel J. R. Macdonnell on 5 August. During August, 2nd Armoured Brigade had 4 commanders	Brigadier A. F. Fisher, who took over from Brigadier A. H. Gatehouse on 26 June and was succeeded by Brigadier W. G. Carr on 7 July	Brigadier W. G. Carr who switched commands with Brigadier A. F. Fisher on 7 July
Units	Bays (to 26 June) 10th Hussars (to 4 July) 9th Lancers (to 30 June) 1st Rifle Brigade (to 19 June)	1st Royal Tanks (3 June to 7 July) 6th Royal Tanks (7 June to 7 July) 8th Royal Tanks (7 June to 7 July) 1st King's Royal Rifle Corps (1 February to 7 July)	2nd RGH (to 16 September) 3rd City of London Yeomanry (to 16 September) 4th City of London Yeomanry 1st Rifle Brigade (from 19 June)
From 7 July	3rd/5th Royal Tanks 3rd Sharp-shooters 6th Royal Tanks 1st King's Royal Rifle Corps	1st Royal Horse Artillery (9 February to 7 July) Tp. 171st Light Anti-Aircraft Battery (21 May to 7 July)	2nd Royal Horse Artillery (25 June to 2 August) (successors of 107th Royal Horse Artillery – wiped out 6 June)
Between March & July 1942	11th Royal Horse Artillery 88th Light Anti-Aircraft Battery 4th Light Anti-Aircraft Battery		

Notes:

2nd Armoured Brigade: By 7 July 'the units in the Brigade had suffered heavy casualties and the Brigade was reconstituted'.

4th Armoured Brigade: In July 1942 (presumably after 7 July) 'the Brigade was reconstituted as a Light Armoured Brigade Group with two Armoured Car Regiments (11th Hussars and 12th Lancers) and one Regiment of Stuart tanks plus supporting units'.

22nd Armoured Brigade: acting as an armoured brigade group between March and September 1942.

Before making a final recapitulation, we must just briefly check the remaining armoured brigades. We have already mentioned:

8th Armoured Brigade's contribution of the Buffs anti-tank gunners. The remainder were under GHQ MEF from 30 June to 17 July.

9th Armoured Brigade were under HQ BTE from 10 May to 25 August. They were commanded by that brave soldier Brigadier J. C. Currie and were not in action until Montgomery's Alamein.

23rd Armoured Brigade's arrival on Ruweisat we have already mentioned. Between 8 May and 5 July, they were 'at sea'. Their sister Brigade, **24th Armoured Brigade**, took three days longer over the voyage.

74th Armoured Brigade was formed in the Middle East on 5 July 1942 as a <u>dummy</u> tank Brigade (from 39th and 101st Royal Tanks). A similar fate befell 24th Armoured Brigade in 1943.

This entry in the *Orders of Battle* is a frightening one. If Ruweisat had fallen on 2 and 3 July, their dummy tanks would have represented Cairo's last line of defence! In case you draw false comfort from the flag of 8th Division stuck in the map of Syria, let me assure you that this formation, formed on 2 June 1942 from the 5th Cavalry Brigade, had no troops under command except for 'Administrative units with RAC units attached from 9th Army'.

Another army tank brigade still claims our attention if our survey of the armour is to be complete.

1st Army Tank Brigade: had been in the desert for just over a year and, at the beginning of June was made up of:

8th Royal Tanks (to 3 June and from 10 July to 30 September),
44th Royal Tanks (to 3 June and from 26 June to 1943),
42nd Royal Tanks (to 8 June and from 27 June to 1944).

It is clear from the dates that a major tragedy occurred to this brigade early in the Gazala fighting. Its commander, Brigadier W. O. L. O'Carroll was taken prisoner of war on 1 June and his successor, Brigadier W. G. Richards, not appointed until 1 July. This is confirmed by the footnote. 'In June 1942 in Libya, the Brigade suffered heavy casualties and losses in tanks. The Brigade withdrew to the Delta to refit, while serviceable tanks with their crews were placed under command 32nd Army Tank Brigade for operations in the Tobruk area.'

These tanks did little good to 32nd Army Tank Brigade which was captured with 2nd South African Infantry Division in Tobruk and was never reformed.

This is perhaps a convenient moment at which to 'write off' another veteran desert formation. Formed in Egypt in February 1941, with the title 22nd Infantry Brigade, and known successively as 22nd Guards Brigade (March 1941), 200th Guards Brigade (January 1942), 200th Guards Motor Brigade Group (April 1942) and 201st Guards

Motor Brigade Group (May 1942) and served by many of the formations which made 1942 famous, the brigade was captured in Tobruk on 20 June 1942. It was reformed with the title 201st Guards Motor Brigade in August 1942.

Recapitulation – Armour, 2 July 1942

Eighth Army	2nd Armoured Brigade Group = 10th Hussars (with remnants of Bays, 9th Lancers, 1st Rifle Brigade). 11th RHA to join Robcol.
XXX Corps	None. Though 1st Armoured Division was under command 1 July & 3 July.
XIII Corps	1st Armoured Division = The Royals. 4th Armoured Brigade Group = 1st, 6th & 8th Royal Tanks plus 1st King's Royal Rifle Corps and 1st Royal Horse Artillery. 22nd Armoured Brigade Group = 3rd & 4th Coly, 2nd RGH, 1st Rifle Brigade plus 2nd Royal Horse Artillery. 7th Motor Brigade (from 7th Armoured) = 2nd King's Royal Rifle Corps, 2nd Rifle Brigade and 9th Kings Royal Rifle Corps plus 4th Royal Horse Artillery
General Headquarters, Middle East Forces	8th Armoured Brigade (from 10th Armoured Division), Buffs Anti-Tank & 3rd Royal Horse Artillery to join Robcol
Headquarters British Troops in Egypt	9th Armoured Brigade

We are still left with quite an imposing list but, after examining each unit in turn, we find only a handful of tanks and but few more guns.

22nd Armoured Brigade

22nd Armoured Brigade of 1st Armoured Division is already identified in many of the earlier pages. It is clear that by 2 July, Eighth Army's armour was tired, depleted and in unutterable confusion. This makes it difficult and sad for a gunner's description. How can one identify units which no longer have identity? How can one report facts which might, to those who were not there, suggest cowardice in men who fought Tigers with popguns? But I cannot tell the story of 2 July without accepting that – at the time – the infantry and the guns expected more from our armour than they were able to give. What do we know of the dispositions of our armour on 2 July?

Summary of extract from HQ 1st Armoured Division War Diary for July 1942 (WD 188/1)

2 July. 1200 hours. 4th and 22nd Armoured Brigades had formed up during the morning in the area 425889 on the Ruweisat Ridge ready to attack westwards. This

puts the two armoured brigades just north of Alam Baoshaza, i.e. just forward of Pt 96/Pt 97 with 9th Rifle Brigade well forward – probably in contact with 1st South African Division north of backward Pt 63.

1430 hours. 1st Armoured Division moved to 425889 (to area where 4th and 22nd armoured brigades were).

At about 1000 hours, Robcol was spread out, according to the evidence of the regimental and battery war diaries and the Brigadier's personal diary, in an area to the southwest of backward Pt 63 with forward elements at 880277 (OP's on the ridge looking into the Deir el Shein) and 83rd/85th Battery in action at 882278. That is, they were 15,000 yards west of the two armoured brigades forming up area. However, the Brigadier's diary shows that they moved forward to join the battle: 'From about 12.00 hours, 22nd Armoured Brigade had begun to collect behind our left. They now moved forward so that their right was a few hundred yards behind our left.'

An armoured division HQ, two armoured brigades – suddenly the desert seems over-populated. With Rommel down that night to 26 tanks, can one, even now, be overrating the contribution of Robcol? When one goes more deeply into the facts one can see how misleading the symbols on a map can be when the units are constantly changing from one formation to another as a result of disaster following disaster.

We can get a picture of 22nd Armoured Brigade by following the fortunes of 4th City of London Yeomanry, who served in this brigade from 1939–44. Their fortunes were recorded by the Earl of Onslow in his book *Men and Sand* from which I borrow freely in this attempt to dispel the fog of armoured war.

Mobilized in September 1939 with their first-line regiment, 3rd City of London Yeomanry and 2nd Royal Gloucester Hussars in 22nd Armoured Division, they arrived in the Middle East on 6 October 1941. By the 3 November 1941, they were down to 18 tanks from an establishment of 150.

It is important to record the bravery of their CO, Lt. Colonel W. G. Carr here. He had commanded them from the summer of 1939 and was wounded at Bel Hamed. In early 1942, he was promoted to brigade commander and General Staff Officer (GS01) of 1st Armoured Division. Frank Arkwright took over 4th City of London Yeomanry. We have seen that both Brigadier Waller and B. A. G. Jones were very critical of Carr's attitude on 2 July 1942.

Early in 1942 they received their first General Stewart (Honey) tanks and on 19 April they left once more by rail for the Western Desert. In the meantime, their A Squadron have been equipped with their first Grants.

The Grants went into action at Gazala and on 27 May, in the space of a few minutes, they lost six of their fourteen new Grants and fifteen of their old Crusaders. On 5 June, at Bir Aslagh they lost more than half of their existing tank strength in a couple of hours. On 6 June, they were overrun yet again. On 12 June, Onslow reported: 'Our total strength was only some 40 tanks under Colonel Arkwright, consisting of elements from nearly every armoured Regiment in the desert.' By nightfall, he put their tank strength at 'about ten'.

By 22 June, Tobruk had fallen. A Squadron picked up some more Grants from 8th Armoured Brigade near Fuka airfield. On 24 or 25 June, Onslow's C Squadron was combined with the remains of A Squadron. Honeys were taken over from 8th Armoured Brigade and acted as rear-guard as the Eighth Army fell back to Mersa Matruh. In the breakout from Mersa Matruh, 11 Italian tanks attacked and were all destroyed.

In the meantime, B Echelon had been surrounded and also destroyed and the survivors of the 4th City of London Yeomanry were now indistinguishable from the remnants of 4th Armoured Brigade.

This exhausted flotsam eventually passed through the minefields south of El Alamein and leaguered for the night of 30 June near the railway. It is not surprising that they were relieved at their orders to go into army reserve. 'But at dawn the next morning, this order was cancelled and the regiment was ordered to move south at once onto the Ruweisat Ridge, and north again at midday to support the 1st South African Division who were being attacked by enemy tanks. We had not been there long when we were ordered to move south again and then 6 miles west, this time to support the Indian Brigade.'

22nd Armoured Brigade have been criticized for their failure to give effective support to 18th Indian Infantry Brigade in the Deir el Shein. *Crisis in the Desert* page 298 elaborates, 'At that time, however, 4th Armoured Brigade was still unable to extricate its vehicles from the sand in which they were fast bedded, and about 13.20, when XXX Corps ordered the Division to go to the assistance of 18th Indian Infantry Brigade, the only tanks available were the 18 runners of 22nd Armoured Brigade. The armoured cars of the The Royals, confused perhaps by the sandstorm, reported that all was quiet at Deir el Shein, and 22nd Armoured Brigade took no action. It was not until the order was urgently repeated at 16.30 that the 4th City of London Yeomanry advanced and engaged the German tanks close to the wire of the box.'

As far as the survivors of 4th City of London Yeomanry were concerned, it was obvious that they had already passed the limits of human endurance. One final bitter pill remained to be swallowed. At dark, the order came from the CO to retire. They rallied on the tank flying his well-known double blue pennants. In the dark, they followed this tank for some 15 miles and halted for the night. Their beloved colonel, Frank Arkwright, was dead – killed somewhere near the Deir el Shein. Their last orders came from Harry Scott, the second in command, imitating the CO's voice. In the moonlight, the CO's body was lowered into the desert sand near Gebel Bein Gebir. The desert moon burned the scene into the minds of those who watched as the CO's batman played 'Gone Away' on a hunting horn. 22nd Armoured Brigade do figure on the maps of 2 July, but the strength of 4th City of London Yeomanry, as an example, was for a few hours spent.

A History of the Queen's Bays (the 2nd Dragoon Guards), 1929–1945

by Major General W. R. Beddington, CBE

The Queen's Bays (2nd Dragoon Guards) were not as such on Ruweisat as a unit on 2 July 1942. On pages 85–87, their regimental HQ is clearly identified as having moved back to Khatatba on 30 June. They deserved their rest – after serving in France in May 1940 and in the Middle East since November 1941 they had had to abandon plans for a rest at Sidi Bishr when orders to join 1st Armoured Division reached them at Amiriya on 24 June.

The Bays took over Honeys at Fuka. C Squadron received Grants. 'At twenty past four on the morning of 27th June, Regimental headquarters and 'C' Squadron moved twelve miles up the road [from Fuka] … Under command were also 9 Crusaders under Major Meyrick of the 9th Lancers.'

This is probably why the Brigadier's account talks of The Bays while B. A. G. Jones thinks the armour at Ruweisat was 9th Lancers.

'At eleven o'clock Weld and Knebworth re-joined with their composite squadrons of Honeys. At half-past twelve, the Regiment moved south-west to try and join the 1st Armoured Division.' They met and engaged an enemy column, lost two tanks, and leaguered for the night about 30 miles south of Mersa Matruh at just about the time that 11th Field were about to break out.

Page 84: 'Before the action, seven of the nine of 9th Lancers' Crusaders had dropped out with mechanical trouble. The Honeys were in very poor condition; many of the wireless sets were not working, and there had been no time to test the guns on any of the tanks.'

It would be surprising if this scratch force had been able to play a decisive role on 2 July, even if they had not had further battles to fight before they reached Ruweisat. On 28 June, they met up with Divisional HQ at 0830 and came under command of 22nd Armoured Brigade. C Squadron with their Grants joined 3rd City of London Yeomanry and the two Honey squadrons went to help 12th Lancers. Next day, 29 June, and the following night of 29/30 June, part of the regiment had further adventures with 2nd RHA and A Company, 1st Rifle Brigade, fighting as Draffcol, 'a long way west of the main forces and behind the enemy's forward troops'.

At breakfast time on 30 June, after breaking through enemy leaguers, they were back a few miles west of El Alamein. Draffcol was disbanded. Regimental HQ moved back to Khatatba, but the two Honey squadrons of The Bays and a squadron of the 4th Hussars were now amalgamated under Major, the Viscount Knebworth, to remain forward in the battle area. C Squadron's Grants remained with the 3rd City of London Yeomanry and moved behind El Alamein on the night of 30 June/1 July.

That day, they were sent forward, 'first onto the Ruweisat Ridge and then to the Miteirya Ridge to prevent an enemy break-through'. They were thus moving in concert with 4th City of London Yeomanry. Page 86: 'However, they were not in action until the afternoon, when they were sent to help the 18th Indian Infantry Brigade, hard pressed in the Deir el Shein. As they came into action they came under shell fire from the Germans attacking the "box"; they then engaged a column of enemy tanks and guns coming from the south, knocking out two of the enemy tanks without loss to themselves.'

At the end of the action in which 4th City of London Yeomanry suffered so grievously, they withdrew (page 87) 'four miles east to leaguer'.

'The next morning, 2 July, the enemy appeared to be massing for another attack on the positions around El Alamein ... the 22nd Armoured Brigade formed up south west of the Ruweisat Ridge soon after midday to attack west and then north with the twelve remaining Grants – six Bays and six Yeomanry. They met advancing tanks and were in action for the rest of the day. The enemy was stopped and lost several tanks.'

The flags on Robcol's front now take on a clearer perspective.

1st Armoured Division consisted of 4th Armoured Brigade and 22nd Armoured Brigade. The Grants which stationed themselves to the left rear of our guns, totalled 12 – six of them represented A Squadron, 4th City of London Yeomanry, though they were made up of elements from 'nearly every armoured Regiment in the desert', the other six were a composite unit formed of C Squadron, The Bays and 3rd City of London Yeomanry. The Honeys which came across our front at teatime, were a mixture of the remaining squadrons of these three regiments, possibly with oddments of 9th Lancers, 12th Lancers and 4th Hussars.

Crisis in the Desert page 294, shows that 'the DAK approaching the Alamein line on the evening of 30th June had 55 tanks, but on the morning of 2nd July could muster only 37 runners' while pages 309–310 state that by the evening of 2 July, '21st Panzer Division has 20, 15th Panzer only 6 serviceable tanks'.

The Grants, which we blamed for ignoring our battle, had orders not to get committed. From their War Diary, 1st Armoured Division had at 1415 hours, been placed under XIII Corps. This was because General Auchinleck had, according to Beddington, page 87, decided 'to regain the initiative by attacking with the XIII Corps (New Zealand Division and what remained of the 5th Indian Division), who were to wheel north around Bab el Qattara and, supported by strong air forces, take the enemy opposite El Alamein in the flank'.

Neither the Kiwis nor the Indians could be brought up from the south in time. It would therefore have been quite wrong for the armour to have got itself too deeply involved in our battle.

The arrival of the Honeys when things looked very black must therefore be recorded with gratitude. They could not take up a leading role, but by their very presence they gave fresh heart to tired gunners.

A History of the The Queen's Bays records the death of Major, The Viscount Knebworth, MBE and Corporal A. W. Sutton on Ruweisat Ridge. Their names are recorded with Robcol.

The Royal Artillery, Ubique Quo Fas et Gloria Ducunt

Wherever the fighting troops of the British Army go, they are accompanied by The Royal Artillery. The battle fell directly on 11th Field, and those who fought with them, because they were directly in the line of the Panzer advance along Ruweisat Ridge. But it must not be thought that they were the only gunners firing on the ridge that day. 11th HAC has already earned a separate mention, but other gunners played what part they could – their first duty being to give direct support to their own columns. The 25-pounders' range of over 13,000 yards allowed them to 'interfere' in other people's battles.

It was difficult to sort out the armoured regiments, but to identify the gunners accurately was ten times more difficult. Like the armour and the infantry, a regimental number often cloaked survivors from numerous decimated units. Furthermore, the establishment of gunner regiments changed. Normally a regiment consisted of 24 guns in three eight-gun batteries, but some regiments took on (or shed) a battery of anti-tank guns during this period. Furthermore, a three-battery regiment normally supported a brigade of three battalions (or armoured regiments) and both batteries and troops switched from supporting one unit to another at frequent intervals.

Let us see what we know:

1st Royal Horse Artillery (1st RHA)

Were to the left rear of Robcol on 2 July. They were commanded, temporarily, by Bob Loder-Symonds, whose meeting with Geoff Armstrong and whose intervention with the armour have already been recorded. When I went back for ammunition, I remember seeing them firing on our front. Maybe they fired the smoke screen when D Troop pulled back.

3rd Royal Horse Artillery (3rd RHA)

Geoff Armstrong says that on arrival, they reported to him and went north of the position, but that this was two or three days later. From *Crisis in the Desert*, page 306, it is clear that the South African authors believe that 1st South African Brigade was still in its position north of the ridge known as the HotBox at nightfall on 2 July. They state: 'the sweep which Rommel envisaged for the afternoon of the 2nd would bring his armour directly over the South Africans and the preliminary bombardment to clear the advance of 21st Panzer fell heavily on 1st Brigade. On the afternoon of the 2nd no movement within or out of the perimeter was possible until after dark.'

It appears that the misunderstanding between General Pienaar and General Norrie, as a result of which 1st South African Brigade moved back to 2nd South African Brigade Group at Alam Onsol, took place that night. This is confirmed by General Norrie's account on page 308, 'I did decide late at night … That it would be easier to put another unit there and to do it before dawn.

'XXX Corps then sent Ackcol, a 50th Division column with 3rd RHA as its artillery force, to take over the abandoned position.'

'When that force arrived just after dawn on 3rd July, it found a party of [German)] 90th Light in occupation of the "Hotbox" and drove them out, taking some 20 prisoners. Half an hour later, however, the shell-fire falling on the position became intense, and Ackcol fell back to a spot just south of the 2nd South African Brigade, losing some prisoners in the process.'

It is thus clear that 3rd RHA just missed Robcol's battle on 2 July but since they were undoubtedly one of the units rushing towards the threatened ridge during those critical hours, and since they stayed within sight of Pt 63 through the succeeding days when Robcol grew into Wall Motor Group, they deserve a place in this record.

Nostalgia gripped me again. This patch of sand was, so many years ago, my home for four months. A small blue square, map reference 88142818 marked a desert well, a *bir*. Alongside it was a small hillock of sand. A short distance west, on the other side of the track running off to Alamein station, was the OP tower from which I watched the barrage of 23 October 1942.

But second Alamein was only made possible by First Alamein and on 3 July, all could still have been lost. On that morning of 3 July, Colonel Akroyd-Hunt, looking up at the German tanks and OPs above them on the ridge, could little have thought that this stretch of sand had already seen the turning point of the war. Though they did not arrive on the battlefield until the day after that which is the subject of this book, they have their place in it because their story proves one of the facts which it is difficult to believe years later. Just as Robcol were the only troops on the main feature of the ridge during the critical hours, so Ackcol were the only troops on the northern flank of the ridge for several thousand yards after the 1st South African Brigade had pulled back to Alam Onsol.

The Guns of the Indian Divisions

At the time, it seemed perfectly natural that the CRA of 10th Indian Division and his Brigade Major, should assemble 'every available gun and all formations sufficiently cohesive to fight' as it is described in *The Tiger Kills*, page 146. Also that the resulting force, Robcol, should consist of 11th Field Regiment RA, so recently in 8th Indian Infantry Division and 1st/4th Essex, from 5th Indian Infantry Brigade normally part of 4th Indian Infantry Division, plus a handful of supporting troops from a variety of other arms. Years later, one asks oneself why HQ RA 10th Indian Infantry Division did not fight on Ruweisat with their own guns.

The reason is clear to see, but not easy to describe. To quote once more from *The Tiger Kills*, page 117, 'From this point onwards no record will be given of the multiplicity of formations in which the Indian and British units of the Indian Divisions found themselves. The 5th Indian Division for instance never functioned as a whole. Sometimes it had two brigades, sometimes one, on occasions none at all. Brigades of the 4th and 10th Indian Divisions also came under command, only to disappear again, while the gunners were for ever changing.'

From a number of sources, I have tried to 'unscramble' the sequence of events which led to Robcol. It is unlikely that my record is complete and for the omissions, I beg your indulgence. Even though incomplete, I believe it is at least accurate as far as it goes since I have carefully checked my sources. It is a jigsaw of four Indian divisions and an Indian Motor Brigade.

3rd Indian Motor Brigade: Their story is brief as they do not seem to have contributed to Robcol, unless it be through some straggler or survivor who 'crashed' our battle. The story of their defence of Pt 171, near Bir Hacheim on 27 May, is extensively covered in *The Tiger Kills*.

'The three Indian Cavalry Regiments had ceased to exist. Every anti-tank gun had been knocked out.' This was 30 2-pounders against 200 tanks. In those three hours of fierce combat the 3rd Indian Motor Brigade had been destroyed. The enemy however, had paid a price. Fifty-two enemy tanks were strewn over the brigade's battle position. This toll was exacted by 2nd Field Regiment, Indian Artillery, in their first action.

To understand the guns of Robcol, one must follow the fortunes of each of the four Indian divisions in the Middle East at the time. 5th Indian Division and 10th Indian Division both feature on the maps of June 1942, but you will look in vain for 4th Indian Division and 8th Indian Division. Nonetheless, both these divisions supplied units which played important roles. Let us start with the senior division.

4th Indian Division: Officially, they were resting in Cyprus. Here was 7th Indian Brigade, who appear on Ruweisat later when the line at Alamein is established and when 4th Indian Division take over from 5th Indian Division. But the Red Eagles (the insignia of the 4th Indian Division) 11th Indian Brigade got no further back than the Canal area in March 1942. They vanish from the map about 22 June, fighting gallantly on in Tobruk, 36 hours after the South African capitulation.

5th Indian Brigade spent their rest in Palestine and here were joined by Colonel Noble's 1st/4th Essex. On 6 June their rest was abruptly ended by a call to the Desert and by 14 June, after a 1,000-mile trek, they were under command of 5th Indian Division. By 18 June, they were with 10th Indian Division. By 25 June, they are in Mersa Matruh from which they broke out on the night of 28/29 June. Their story is heroic and they arrive, according to *The Tiger Kills*, page 143, 'almost intact, although much battered' at El Alamein. But, except for 1st/4th Essex, they disappear from this narrative at the Alamein control point where they are sent back to the Delta for a hasty refit. They will return to Ruweisat and join Robcol in a bare seven days, but 1st/4th Essex will be their sole representative in the early days.

What of the guns of this division? Their order of battle lists the following:

1st Field Regiment, RA served with them throughout the war, but at this period it seems to have been under 5th Indian Division. If they were still in action on 2 July, it must have been with 5th Indian Division in the south.

4th Field Regiment RA were between August 1939 and August 1940 with 4th Indian Division, but in the summer of 1942 were with 5th Indian Division.

25th Field Regiment RA were with 11th Indian Infantry Brigade in Tobruk. Wiped out, after a very gallant defence, 20 June.

31st Field Regiment RA were probably in Cyprus.

32nd Field Regiment RA are shown in the order of battle of 4th Indian Division as under them from June to October 1942, but in fact they did not join them until 4th Indian Division took up position on Ruweisat in August.

Four other gunner units also must be mentioned.

3rd RHA (Anti-Tank) will join Squeakcol on 3 July as field gunners.

65th Anti-Tank Regiment RA: September 1941 to April 1942, presumably supplied batteries for the field regiments under the organization of June/July 1942.

149th Anti-Tank Regiment RA: July 1942 to January 1946, the anti-tank regiment of 4th Indian Division, but, during the critical days, equipped with field guns in the Delta.

And finally:

57th Light Anti-Aircraft Regiment RA: September 1941 to August 1945 – and are discussed later on.

The second Indian division which cast a 'proxy vote' on Ruweisat was:

8th Indian Division: Under Major General C. O. Harvey, consisting of 17th, 18th and 19th Indian infantry brigades. This division was in Iraq and 17th and 19th Indian infantry brigades did not get into our battle, but 18th Indian Infantry Brigades march to destruction in the Deir el Shein on 1 July has already featured in these pages and was the indispensable prelude to 2 July.

It was, however, the guns of this division which provided the tools for the CRA of 10th Indian Division's intentions.

8th Indian Division's gunners were 121st Field Regiment RA (18th Brigade), 32nd Field Regiment RA (17th Brigade) and 11th Field Regiment RA (19th Brigade).

121st Field Brigade RA were, like their infantry 18th Indian Infantry Brigade, first across and, after action around Matruh where they arrived on 24 June according to B. A. G. Jones's diary, they died with their infantry in the Deir el Shein.

32nd Field Regiment RA arrived in the desert without their infantry and, after many tribulations, certainly provided two of Robcol's guns. They are covered in more detail later.

The 5th Indian Division: Major General H. R. Briggs's 5th Indian Division was flung piecemeal into battle at the end of May, bore the brunt of the fighting and by 2 July had ceased to exist – except as a number of columns in the south. The division was never permitted to operate as a division. In fact, at one stage, Divisional HQ with no troops to command, according to *The Tiger Kills*, page 117, 'withdrew to a quiet spot to the east of Tobruk ... to be out of the way'.

Divisional HQ was in any case overrun on 5 June. On the same day, its **9th Indian Infantry Brigade** and **10th Indian Infantry Brigade** were virtually wiped out in the Cauldron and were withdrawn on 10 June, although 9th Brigade recovered sufficiently to take some part in the action at Sidi Hamza on 25/26 June.

With these two brigades are lost the two field regiments of the division, **4th Field Regiment RA** and **28th Field Regiment RA**, both 'cut to pieces' in the Cauldron on 5 June.

The **3rd Brigade** of 5th Indian Division lasted longer and fared better, but the *jawans* of **29th Indian Infantry Brigade** finally were overwhelmed at Fuka on 28 June.

To quote *The Tiger Kills* once more, pages 117 and 145, 'Brigadier Reid could now muster only six companies of infantry. Twenty-three field guns remained out of three Field Regiments together with a few anti-tank and anti-aircraft guns. This small force represented all of the 5th Indian Division which remained in action. Yet, even this handful had to be divided into three battle groups [Scotcol, Gleecol and Reserveforce] in order to cover the utmost front.'

Reserveforce was overrun and destroyed on 28 June. The remains of Scotcol and Gleecol – two guns that came to 11th Field are '5th Indian Division' on the maps of 1 and 2 July!

The Tenth Indian Division brings us finally to Brigadier Waller's own division. 10th Indian Division consisted of 20th, 21st and 25th Indian brigades, supported by 97th, 157th and 164th field regiments. Like so many of the 'stars' in this drama, it had arrived from Iraq along the Nairn trail in May 1942. Odd notes in B. A. G. Jones's diary enable us to follow it into the June battle:

> 2nd June: Gambut. 157th on into battle. 21st Brigade still with us.
>
> 6th June: He visited 20th Brigade at Bel Hamet and heard that 157th Field and 1st Anti-tank Battery had been overrun. HQ RA moved back to Gambut.
>
> 7th June: He heard that John Marshall and four other friends had been killed. 157th and 1st Anti-tank Battery were for the present, non-existent. 4th and 25th Field Regiments were also overrun. 157th Field was his special concern "I could get no news whatsoever of 64th Battery ... 421st had at the end only one gun left in action and it without ammunition.

The diary shows clearly that, in the conditions under which Gazala was fought, HQ RA, 10th Indian Division were not in any position to control – nor even maintain good communications with the three regiments of their command and that the Brigadier's first divisional artillery disappeared outside his direct control. Since their loss led him to us, we may reasonably spend some time with these three regiments.

157th Field Regiment RA consisted of 64th and 421st field batteries to which 1st Anti-Tank Battery seems to have been added. 157th Field Regiment moved from India to Iraq, then Persia and back to Iraq again by August 1941. It was one of the earliest units to take the Nairn trail and arrived in Egypt with 10th Indian Division on 30 May 1942. On 21 June 1942, as Tobruk fell, the regiment was, according to the official order of battle, under command GHQ, MEF, and was disbanded in the Middle East on 11 August 1942.

Before it disappeared, it wrote a page of history in the Cauldron. The incident, which saw the end of 4th, 28th and 157th field regiments plus 107th South Notts Hussars in which my brother served, has been vividly described in other histories.

97th Field Regiment RA: The Kent Yeomanry was composed of 385th, 386th and 470th batteries. When the field regiments were re-organized on 25 April 1942, they lost 470th Battery which left to form part of X Field Regiment. On 31 May 1942, the two remaining batteries arrived in Egypt with the division. On 5 July 1942, they came under command BTE and ceased to be under the command of Indian formations.

The first reference to 97th Field in *The Tiger Kills* is at Sidi Rezegh on 16 June. When the garrison at Sidi Rezegh was ordered back to the frontier that night, only 12 of their 16 guns escaped with their infantry, the Rajputana Rifles.

As there is no further reference to this regiment in the Indian history, it seems likely that they withdrew with the three Indian brigades of 10th Indian Division. After a night breakout from Mersa Matruh, 60 per cent of the personnel of these brigades reached Alamein safely on 29/30 June and were sent back to refit. We know they were in Mersa Matruh from Brigadier Waller's diary.

However, with the critical shortage of guns, 97th Field were not sent back to the Delta with the infantry. 18th Indian Infantry Brigade were digging furiously in the Deir el Shein and, from *The Tiger Kills*, page 146, '… the remainder of the 97th and 121st Field Regiments, which had fought all the way back from Tobruk, arrived to give gun support'. Here it is likely that the guns went under.

164th Field Regiment RA: Of all the regiments in the desert in June, 164th Field Regiment has, in my searches at least, left the least trace. Initially it was known as X Field Regiment and, under that name it came to 25th Indian Infantry Brigade of 10th Indian Division.

It arrived in Egypt with 25th Indian Infantry Brigade on 4 June and on 17 June was redesignated 164th Field. On 1 August, it was disbanded in the Middle East. It is difficult to write of them with authority as RA records at Footscray failed, in this instance, to turn up any war diary. Probably, in such a short life, none was written. However, according to the 83rd/85th War Diary, among the reinforcements which reached 11th Field in their leaguer north of the main road at Alamein at about 1100 hours on 1 July was at least one gun from this regiment and Captain E. J. S. Foster, 2nd Lt. P. Curry, one warrant officer and 38 BORs.

CRA 10th Indian Division, Brigadier Waller, was therefore left on 1 July with only a small force – 17 guns and one company of infantry, but they came from the ends of the earth:

> 1st/4th Essex from 5th Brigade, 4th Indian Division by way of 5th Indian Division
> 11th Field with its original 13 guns from 19th Brigade, 8th Indian Division
> Joined by two guns of 32nd Field from 17th Brigade, 8th Indian Division, via 5th Indian Division
> One gun from 164th Field of 25th Brigade, 10th Indian Division, and
> One other gun from 121st Field (8th Indian Division) or 97th Field (10th Indian Division).

This force received its first orders from 50th Division and fought its main battles under 1st Armoured Division. Small wonder that this history has taken so many years to write!

83rd Anti-Tank Regiment RA: No mention of 83rd Anti-Tank Regiment RA will be found in any records of 2 July 1942, as on that date this regiment did not exist. None the less a number of those who were present that day owe their primary allegiance to this unit.

Formed at East Grinstead on 23 September 1941, initially its batteries were numbered 68th, 222nd, 262nd and 265th (from 67th Anti-Tank Regiment RA). But within a few days, 222nd Battery had been replaced by 224th.

In May, 224th Anti-Tank Battery with RHQ and 486th Battery of 121st Field Regiment moved to Persia. Here, on 25 May, RHQ formed Y Field Regiment RA which became known as 165th Field Regiment RA and may be assumed to have consisted, under the establishment which came into vogue at that time, of three field batteries and one anti-tank battery. This organization lasted from 25 May to 14 July when 83rd Anti-Tank Regiment RA were reformed in the Middle East in the anti-tank role for which they were originally formed.

On 2 July, the records therefore show 224th Battery regimented in Y Field (165th Field Regiment RA) and 68th Battery regimented in 121st Field Regiment RA. This regiment had in the last 24 hours supported 18th Indian Infantry Brigade in the Deir el Shein and had virtually ceased to exist.

262nd Battery were regimented in 32nd Field Regiment RA whose tribulations we shall follow separately to the point where they provide valuable reinforcements to 11th Field Regiment RA and 265th Battery with 11th Field. Their contribution to the battle of Ruweisat was therefore made anonymously – but it was a considerable one.

32nd Field Regiment RA: Lawrence Boyd's E Troop on 2 July was made up of five guns and he had not had time to strike up more than a nodding acquaintance with four of them. Two came from 32nd Field Regiment RA and we must ask ourselves what we know of them.

In some senses, a great deal, because 32nd Field was close to 11th Field for months, even years. In another sense, very little, for war brings great confusion and time does not help one to remember clearly.

Orders of Battle shows that 32nd Field Regiment consisted of 107th and 115th field batteries in Iraq and that these were joined by 262nd Anti-Tank Battery on 25 May 1942. 32nd Field was a sister regiment of 11th Field in C. O. Harvey's 8th Indian Division.

Its three batteries took the Nairn trail across the Syrian Desert shortly before 11th Field. At the end of May, 32nd Field was in a camp at Habbabiya under command of Lt. Colonel Tyndale Biscoe. From here they were about to make their first contribution to the battle of Ruweisat by posting Captain J. M. Douglas on 2 June 1942 to take over command of 83rd/85th Field Battery in 11th Field.

After four rather nondescript days at Sidi Hamza en route from Iraq, 32nd Field arrived at the airfield of Fuka on 27 June. It had already been evacuated and, after leaguering on the empty sand, they prepared to defend Fuka on the 28th. That afternoon about 1600 hours, the airfield was shelled. At 0800 hours 29 June, the hour at which 11th Field 'leaguered at El Daba aerodrome and awaited orders', the 32nd Field War Diary reads: '15.00 hours – orders received from control point Deir el Qattara to proceed to 91 sub area. 18.00 hours – arrived 91 sub area and camped for night.'

Here on 30 June and 1 July, this stranded RHQ collected in dribs and drabs and was ordered to hand them over to 11th Field. As these reinforcements are my main concern, I shall return to these orders but, before I do so, let us follow 32nd Field out of sight of Alamein.

They will return to share many trials with us in 5th Indian Division between the 3 September 1942 and 7 September 1942, and 4th Indian Division between the 8 September 1942 and until the end of the war.

On 1 July, after providing new strength to our E Troop, the war diary states that the 'remainder proceeded to Aminya and camped by 1st Reinforcement Camp RA'.

3 July 1000 hours, 'The BRA visited 1st Reinforcement Camp.' The decision is shortly taken that RHQ and a second battery will be reformed, because that day, while the BRA was visiting the remains of RHQ, 'Captain J. G. Corke RA arrived to say that nine guns were operating under command of Major H. W. Tilman, MC, RA in neighbourhood of Naqb Abu Dweiss.'

Tilman, 'Tilly', a name to conjure with if you belonged to my generation and loved high places. A great mountaineer, whose experiences on Everest in the years of peace, proved to be valuable stepping-off points for Brigadier John Hunt. Later, in the inscrutable ways of the British Army, Colonel Sir John and later Lord Hunt, conqueror of Everest and the man who took me up the hills of Benevento in 1943 together with many others from 4th Indian Division. The 1957 Blue List showed Tilman, H. W., MC, Lt. (Hon. M.) resigned 16 May 1949. Certainly in July 1942, he was no longer young and the war diary shows that this grizzled mountaineer – then Major H. W. Tilman, MC, RA – was in command of 107th/121st Battery of 32nd Field Regiment RA. Divorced from his HQ, his experience was undoubtedly one of the reasons that nine guns of 32nd Field were still operational.

If we return now to the Regimental War Diary, we read: 'Amiriya, July 1st, 0800: Lt. A. J. McGregor RA took 2 guns and 1 x 3 ton truck of ammunition to El Alamein to join 11th Field regiment RA.' Three hours later the war diary records: 'Alamein, 1st July (in leaguer north of the main road): 11.00 2 officers, 1 WO and 38 BORs of 164th Field Regiment and 1 officer and 17 BORs of 32nd Field Regiment posted. 5 guns received. E Troop reformed with these guns and personnel.' I believe that the five means four new guns to add to the one survivor of E Troop.

The battery did not even have time to record Lt. McGregor's initials correctly. The battery strength at the beginning of the month shows Lt. A. M. McGregor and the next day (with these initials) he is among the six officers listed as wounded.

57th Light Anti-Aircraft Regiment RA & 113th Light Anti-Aircraft Battery RA

To write of 11th Field without some thought for 57th Light Anti-Aircraft Regiment and 149th Anti-Tank Regiment would be unthinkable. The 4th Indian Division order of battle lists 57th LAA from September 1941 to August 1945 and 149th Anti-Tank from July 1942 to January 1946. If you have followed the dates in this story carefully, you will recognize a minor inaccuracy in this statement, but who cares. 57th LAA was the Bofors regiment of 4th Indian Division, and 149th, the number of our anti-tank regiment.

Trying to work out the moves of 57th LAA during the battle of Ruweisat, is a path which led me back over 25 years. On that morning in 1967 when I startled the attendant in the Imperial War Museum by my shock on identifying Bombadier Lang's gun, a little farther on from E Troop's 25-pounder stood a Bofors gun. Its caption reads:

> This particular Bofors gun served with the 57th Light Anti-Aircraft Regiment, Royal Artillery, during the Second World War. It saw action during the Battle of Britain, the fighting in the Western Desert and during the Italian campaign. At Casino, on 18th March 1944, this weapon shot down its 100th enemy aircraft.

Before the Rotunda was burned down, just over a year later, it had yielded a slim volume, *Short History of the 57th Light Anti-Aircraft Regiment, Royal Artillery*. It is difficult to imagine the history of this regiment in a few shallow pages when my draft on one day's fighting already approaches 100,000 words. Even my pride in 11th Field cannot limit my esteem for 57th LAA. Its three batteries, 169th, 170th and 171st LAA are credited with 103 enemy aircraft destroyed, 68 of them in the Western Desert.

It was no surprise to find evidence of their presence on 2 July. It would have been more of a shock to find them somewhere else. The little book, after describing earlier adventures, relates how they lost much equipment around Tobruk. But the *Short History* records, page 59, that 'by the 1st July the Regiment was manning its full establishment of guns again':

> The fighting around Mersa Matruh lasted until the 28th June, and by the 1st July, the Regiment had arrived at the Alamein line and any questions of further withdrawals were finished. For three days the fighting was intense and the enemy air-force was much in evidence.

Despite their exposed position, the record shows no fatal casualties between 26 June and 8 July. In fact, from 1 to 3 July, they appear to have sustained no casualties at all. But the difficulties of the conscientious historian are shown by the following passage which, from its position in the text, appears to be before 8 July:

> In one heavy Stuka raid on the Chestnut Troop, RHA who were being defended by B Troop, 171st Battery, Sergeant Guest's gun was straddled by a number of bombs. His tractor

was set on fire and the Bren gunner killed. The gun detachment were blown from the gun and most of them were injured. However, they regained their positions, including Gunner P. Jepson, the loader, who had been blown from the platform and had been seriously wounded in the neck and head. Nevertheless, he was one of the first to be in position again, where he remained servicing his gun till the raid was over when he collapsed unconscious over the breech.

For this action, Gunner Jepson was awarded the Military Medal.

The account of Robcol in the RA *Commemoration Book* identifies one troop, 155th LAA Battery RA, with Robcol. The four Bofors of 155th LAA Battery are also mentioned as being with the regiment until about 15 July in *The Salonika History*. However, the war diary of 11th Field is quite specific that on 2 July at 0600 hours Robcol consisted of 11th Field, 1st/4th Essex and two troops 113th LAA Battery and the presence of these two troops is mentioned again in the same source on 7 July.

It was therefore a thrill when I came upon the war diary of 113th LAA Battery of 27th LAA Regiment RA in the RA records at Footscray. Yes, they were indeed around 22nd Armoured Brigade HQ. They must have been spread out over quite an area of desert! On 30 June they seem, after marching 61 miles in an easterly direction the previous day, to have arrived somewhere near Alamein – though the indications are far from precise.

The battery commander, Major G. L. Moss, does not rank with Pepys and Evelyn as a diarist! Impatiently turning the pages to the hours which most interested me, I read, in toto: 'July 1st: 0600 Moved off approximately 12 miles east. 1200 Stopped and camped. July 2nd: 0600 Moved off on east course. 0900 Stopped and camped.' Has he grown so accustomed to recording progress only in an easterly direction that his pen can no longer form an initial 'W'? Did he indeed join Robcol from the west, rising like a Phoenix from the Deir el Shein? Or was this diary, like so many others, filled in from a memory too tired to find the detail of so many weary hours a matter of importance?

Certainly 113th LAA Battery was on Ruweisat. The 11th Field War Diary is confirmed by the entries for the succeeding days:

> July 3rd: 1630 Moved 2 miles north and 6 miles west. 1 Stuka destroyed and possibly one ME 109. North of C track by 1 AD HQ 1830 hours camped.
>
> July 4th: 1900 A and C Troops relieved and moved off to locate 50th Infantry Division also BHQ.
>
> July 5th: 0800 Came under command of 1st Armoured Division, attached to 57th LAA Regiment RA. A and C Troops joined Ackcol. B Troop remaining with 22nd Armoured Brigade.
>
> July 6th: 1800 … to pick up one gun from B Troop and proceed to Robcol. B and D Troops attached 22nd Armoured Brigade.

It is abundantly clear that 113th LAA Battery belongs to the story of 2 July, but – for lack of clearer identification – I have attached them, as they attached themselves, to 57th Light Anti-Aircraft Regiment RA.

76th Anti-Tank Regiment RA (237th, 239th & C Batteries, Anti-Tank)

Do not look on the maps of 2 July for the 76th Anti-Tank Regiment RA. They were not there. But, few people can have played such an important role unseen … and unacknowledged. First Alamein is littered with the bodies of this regiment but, after studying the battle for several years, I would not even have guessed at the unit's existence if Mrs McCarthy, when I visited Colonel McCarthy looking for signs of our old regiment in a Godalming attic, had not come across the nominal rolls of 76th Anti-Tank. A penny clicked, and half of Robcol was identified.

Their place here is assured by the fact that the three batteries of 76th Anti-Tank were split up and served in 11th RHA, 3rd RHA and 104th RHA. As each of these units served in Robcol, 76th Anti-Tank had perhaps more representatives on Ruweisat than 11th Field! Let us attempt to raise one corner of the veil on their anonymity.

239th Battery (11th RHA): Seven officers and 121 other ranks were in this battery as they landed in the Middle East on 29 November 1941. Most joined 11th HAC and in the battle of Gazala four out of seven officers are listed as casualties.

The date 29 May is familiar. It is the third day of 'Knightsbridge', and according to *Regimental Fire* pages 70–71, was the day Geoff Armstrong of 11th HAC won his MC. The name Fishburn in the list of wounded is equally familiar – we later played hockey together and two of our sons were together at university.

Of the 121 other ranks, the nominal role reveals more than half were casualties. But the survivors, although nameless, do belong to our story for they served the guns of Robcol. They also illustrate one reason why reconstruction of First Ruweisat has been difficult – a battery which fights a major battle after losing more than half its strength in officers and men does not spend much time on its war diary.

The second in command was given as Major R. F. Wright. As a temporary Lieutenant colonel, we shall find him commanding 149th Anti-Tank on Ruweisat. The colonel of 76th Anti-Tank is the man whose wife gave me an interesting nominal roll – Lt. Colonel A. O. McCarthy, MC, who took over 11th Field early in June. He too was wounded on 19 July 1942 but his wounds took him to 15th General Hospital. 76th Anti-Tank Regiment RA does not figure on the maps of Ruweisat, but the faded nominal roll shows how great was their contribution to Robcol.

Infantry Divisions

There was only one infantry division from the UK in the Middle East on 2 July 1942 although as we have noted earlier, there were also deception units with titles such as 7th Division, 12th Division and 8th Division in existence at about this time.

It may come as a surprise to some readers, though not to those who are versed in desert lore, that the number this division bore was 50 and their sign an interlaced pattern of two capital Ts – 50th (Northumbrian) Infantry Division, the Tyne Tees Territorial

Division. Recognized by New Zealanders, Indian and 'Desert Rats' as the workhorse of the British Army, their footprints have been blurred by better advertised formations.

A careful study of the order of battle reveals no division to dispute 50th Division's position as the sole British (UK) Infantry Division represented at First Ruweisat. They had little enough left to contribute – at least in the early days. Their offering made up in quality what it lacked in quantity, their Divisional Commander, Major General W. H. C. Ramsden (GOC 50th Division from 13 December 1940 to 7 July 1942), their CRA, Brigadier Claude Eastman and perhaps one gun and some Northumberland Hussars. General Ramsden was succeeded as GOC on 7 July by Major General J. S. Nichols who commanded 151st Brigade from 5 January to 21 June. From 21 June to 7 July, he commanded 10th Indian Infantry Division and his CRA, Brigadier R. P. Waller commanded Robcol.

The division is credited with Gazala, Mersa Matruh and the Defence of Alamein. Few credits are more richly deserved, though – as the battle advanced – their contribution dwindled to token strength.

First of the three brigades to vanish from the battle maps was **150th Infantry Brigade** consisting of the 4th East Yorks., 4th Green Howards and 50th Green Howards. On 1 June 1942, their commander Brigadier C. W. Hayden was killed and, to quote *Orders of Battle*, the brigade was 'captured by the Germans in Libya. The Brigade was never reformed'.

Second to go was **151st Infantry Brigade** consisting of 6th, 8th and 9th Durham Light Infantry. *Orders of Battle* gives no account of their passing but their honours finish at Mersa Matruh. They were not present at the Defence of Alamein.

The third Brigade, **69th Infantry Brigade** with the 5th East Yorks., 6th Green Howards and 7th Green Howards also lost its commander on 26 June when Brigadier L. L. Hassall was succeeded by Brigadier E.C. Cooke-Ellis. They are credited with attendance at Gazala, Mersa Matruh and the Defence of Alamein but personal knowledge strongly indicates that this last honour is due to their return to battle after First Ruweisat. On 2 July, I am quite certain they were reforming after their heavy losses at Gazala and Mersa Matruh.

As their CRA was a 'sponsor' of Robcol, their Divisional Artillery merits our attention:

72nd Field Regiment RA (to 1 June 1942). The date tells its own story: 72nd Field was wiped out with 150th Infantry Brigade.

74th Field Regiment RA and **124th Field Regiment RA** served with the division for longer – until the end of 1944, but Geoff Armstrong is our witness that they were not able to contribute guns to Claude Eastman's force on 1 July 1942.

The Northumberland Hussars Yeomanry (including 274th LAA Battery, 287th, 288th and 289th Anti-Tank Batteries and later 99th and 107th Anti-Tank Batteries RA)

There can have been few gunner units which suffered so many casualties in the war and yet Joan Bright's *History of the Northumberland Hussars Yeomanry* records 214 KIA, 423 wounded, 517 PoW.

They were commanded until spring 1940 by Lt. Colonel 'Dick' Straker. But, to the guns of Robcol his successor's name is of more interest. He was Lt. Colonel, later Brigadier 'Rob' P. Waller, MC. Colonel Waller came from G Battery (Mercer's Troop) RHA and had arrived in Egypt with them from India. He stayed with the NHY until Christmas 1941 when he became CRA 10th Indian Division. It was with them that he earned his DSO.

The history of the NHY is fully documented and beautifully described by Joan Bright who also had enjoyed the confidence of the Brigadier's diaries long before my own eyes were allowed to share his secret thoughts. Real yeomanry, Northumberland farmers, more at home with horses than with military diaries. However, it seems clear that when the NHY lost their horses and became mechanized, the unit chose to become anti-tank artillery.

274th (NH) LAA Battery: To quote a New Zealand colonel, page 69: 'You can say what you like about the Guards or anyone else. I saw a Regiment coming off a boat in Greece – you've probably never heard of them – they were called the Northumberland Hussars; everyone coming off those ships was dirty, unshaved and unwashed, but that Regiment came off clean – every man washed and shaved, every man tidy and respectable; it did me good to see them and I shall never forget it!'

Joan Bright writes, page 181, 'Rob [Waller] had fostered their traditions and built up a strong "NH feeling" in the Regiment – they were "not merely Yeomanry and county", they were "feudal".'

On 26 June 1942, they arrived in Mersa Matruh with 12 guns and during the night of 26/27 June, their D Troop was overrun with the 9th Durham Light Infantry Group and 293rd Field Battery RA. On the night of 28/29 June, the rest of the battery was in the second breakout from Mersa Matruh with 50th Division, BHQ and A Troop.

It is clear that most of the battery, that is to say BHQ and A Troop, were complete while B Troop and C Troop had one gun out of three each. They arrived on 28 June at Fuka to find it in enemy hands. They passed through the Alamein 'line' on the morning of 30 June on the way to El Hammam, with seven out of 12 guns, as the first enemy shells were fired into the Alamein defences.

Turning to the three anti-tank batteries, we find them in March 1942 split up and posted to Field and RHA regiments as were so many other anti-tank gunners in the re-organization of the time.

B Battery was wiped out with 107th RHA on 5/6 June 1942. At Almaza shortly afterwards, the remains of B Battery and 107th RHA were formed into a composite battery, 107th South Nottinghamshire Hussars Battery of 7th Medium Regiment. But this was after our story.

D Battery was already a composite battery. They were sent to join 4th RHA (7th Motor Brigade, 7th Armoured Division) and, if they feature again in this story, they will be found under 4th RHA (in the Ruweisat area).

C Battery went to 2nd RHA (21st Guards Brigade, 1st Armoured Division). On to Ruweisat with 2nd RHA, their route took them from 'Knightsbridge' (a defensive box at the Cauldron) and Halfaya to Mersa Matruh. Near Halfaya they met Brigadier Rob Waller and the 10th Indian Division, and eventually arrived at the Alamein Line. The quotations below are from Joan Bright and, as the next sentences are of particular interest, I have taken the liberty of quoting her at length.

> They had expected a formidable obstacle and were soon disillusioned by the few rather obvious pill-boxes dotted about, the shallow minefield and strand of barbed wire. After that to the south, there was nothing but sand and more sand … it was here that we were ordered to take up a position just to the south of Ruweisat Ridge … There was a serious shortage of troops and the defence of the vital Ruweisat Ridge, which was the key to the whole position, had to be left to the weakened battle groups …

They, like Robcol, were advancing against the enemy troops which had seized the Deir el Shein and the western end of the Ruweisat Ridge. They appear, however, to be following a line parallel to Robcol, a short distance to the south of Robcol's route, but 24 hours later than 11th Field. Bright's informant, Major R. I. G. Taylor, an experienced desert soldier, and a very brave man, in his own words shows that they were able to make little impression on the battle.

> A few miles without meeting opposition and we ran into enemy tanks. The terrain being devoid of any scrub or feature of any sort in this part of the desert, it was unwise to say the least of it, to approach the German Mark IIIs and IVs opposing us, and who appeared to have an ample supply of ammunition. I counted myself lucky when an enemy shell hit my truck first bounce, and failed to explode! Most of 'C' Battery's guns fired at least 80 rounds per gun, but I fear without much effect, as the range was about two thousand yards.

They do not appear to have suffered any casualties on 2 July. However, they were more heavily engaged in the remaining days of Ruweisat. 2nd RHA stayed on the Ridge or near it for another fortnight. When they returned to Almaza early in August, it would be C Battery's first taste of civilization for 15 months.

104th RHA Essex Yeomanry Regiment (339th and 414th Battery RHA, also 237th Anti-Tank Battery and later 463rd Battery and 519th Battery)

The RA *Commemoration Book*, 'On the morning of July 2nd Robcol was joined by a battery of 104th RHA (Essex Yeomanry) … within a day or two the force was much larger, including … the balance of 104th RHA.'

Both 339th and 237th batteries are identified in the Brigadier's diary as belonging to Squeakcol, part of Wall Motor Group into which Robcol grew, on 12 July 1942.

My knowledge of this unit is limited to an anonymous *History of the Essex Yeomanry 1919–1949* and to the fact that 104th RHA provided the colonel who took over command of 11th Field when Colonel Mac was wounded on 19 July 1942. Arthur Howell then commanded us for more than a year.

If 11th Field was sired by Friz Fowler, Arthur Howell was the father of the regiment. When thoughts run on to the great part played by Tom Page who commanded in the last two years of the war, it is obvious that they formed something of an Unholy Trinity. Each in his way earned deep respect. It was however quite a shock when starting this quest, to find Arthur Howell a wealthy London stockbroker and father of the Member of Parliament for my constituency! It was less hard, when I sat opposite him shortly afterwards at the memorial service to 'Gertie' Tuker, to imagine him as he was when he came to us on Ruweisat from 104th RHA.

This unit was besieged in Tobruk. At the beginning of June 1942, they were at El Adem with 1st Armoured Brigade, 1st Armoured Division. They were near Rigel Ridge supporting 9th Rifle Brigade with whom we later find them on Ruweisat. In the retreat, they were for most of the time under command of 7th Armoured Division, which had been allotted the task of protecting the left flank of the army without getting decisively involved. Their adventures make exciting reading. We must, however, just note one paragraph of the book, from page 61: 'Major Howell was captured by the Germans in the middle of the retreat, but was rescued by a gallant cavalry charge in armoured cars by Prince Albert Victor's Own (PAVO) Cavalry, an Indian Cavalry Regiment.'

Before they reached the Alamein Line at the beginning of July, 104th RHA had had heavy casualties in men and guns – they were exhausted and had reformed their remaining six guns into one troop. At the end of July, Arthur Howell left 104th RHA to take over 11th Field.

149th Anti-Tank Regiment, RA (432nd, 433rd, 299th and 513rd Anti-Tank Batteries RA)

149th are shown in the order of battle of 4th Indian Division from July 1942 to January 1946. Even without those dates, I looked for 149's number on the roll of 2 July because when you have shared many battles with a small group of men, you expect to find them at your side at all times.

In truth, they came to my aid even as I was searching. London is a lonely place when one has spent more than 20 years abroad. Alamein Night, on the 25th anniversary of Montgomery's battle, was even lonelier when one is attending for the first time in 21 years and see no face one knows. Groups of 1st Armoured greeted each other, the "Desert Rats" recognized each other with Cavalry accents. The 'Highway Decorators' made their usual clan-sounds, the nickname of the 51st Highland Division whose 'HD' insignia adorned road signs along their line of advance.

A group from 50th Division reminded me of my own Geordie miner-signaller, Bomdardier Sellars, whose shovel technique took me down five feet at Wadi Akarit on a forward slope registered by German 88s. But the Festival Hall offered no sign of friendship – I did not even recognize the man who carried the proud Red Eagle of the Panch Ab down towards Montgomery.

My footsteps were already acknowledging the nearness of Waterloo when Scouse voices caught my ear, grouped together around a regimental sign which carried familiar symbols. The Regimental Association of 149th Anti-Tank, the Cheshire RHA, was obviously still flourishing. Contact with people with a common background strengthened my purpose to write this story and, within a few days, showed me part of the way. 149th Anti-Tank Regiment RA had a history which was already on record – *Shabash 149* by E. W. Capleton with a foreword, page xi, by Lt. General Sir Francis Tuker, KCIE, CB, DSO, OBE: 'If one had to select the Regiment's finest hour it would be in July on the Ruweisat Ridge when, helped by four 6-pounders of the Kings Royal Rifle Corps, it taught the German Panzers a lesson that they never forgot and it showed the Eighth Army for the first time that our new 6-pounder, when skilfully employed, was the master of any German tank, rousing the Army's spirits from doggedness to elation.'

He was referring to the 149th's splendid action, with 5th Indian Division, on the Ridge on 16 July, but it was of course not quite the first time that skilfully employed 6-pounders had proved the master of the Panzers.

Shabash 149 is up to 48 hours out in its description of the vital hours: 'On the night of July 3rd, his armour rolled through the line. They overran 18th Indian Infantry Brigade ... took Deir el Shein and penetrated some 20 miles along the Ruweisat Ridge, to within forty miles of Alexandria.'

The 149th could not bear witness to 2 July for they were not there, but they were not far away. In fact, they were achieving their own minor miracle to come to our assistance. This yeomanry regiment, with Selwyn Lloyd as one of its first officers, trained to fire 25-pounders, had, on arrival in the Middle East in June 1941, been turned into an anti-tank regiment. By 2 June, they had lost all trace both of their RHA childhood and their anti-tank adolescence: they were simply 149th Field Regiment RA. Mid-June saw them at Khatatba, re-learning 25-pounder gun drill. At Khatatba, page 154 notes that they heard of the fall of Tobruk and the retreat to Alamein: 'As the Regiment pulled out of Khatatba and headed south towards Cairo with their 25-pounders, traffic jams formed with elements of the 9th Australian Division moving north to meet the enemy.'

This 'advance backwards' before the eyes of the articulate Australians obviously hit deep into the soul of the author of *Shabash*. When one has been besieged in Tobruk with Aussies, one does not like to hear Australian voices talking of 'Pommy bastards' going the wrong way, particularly when one is moving into the unknown with 25-pounders which the regiment has not fired since leaving England.

Shabash bore witness that, as Eighth Army arrived at Alamein, 149th Anti-Tank was deployed near Mena on the banks of the Sweet Water Canal with an OP on the Great Pyramid.

As Rommel closed on Cairo, 149th Anti-Tank prepared to receive him – but Lt. Colonel R. F. Wright's orders left his regiment somewhat short of Ruweisat Ridge. As they were denied the honour of 2 July, let us follow them in their own words on to Ruweisat: 'By July 3rd, some struggling Staff Officer intent on getting support up to the thin red line at El Alamein, suddenly remembered that he had a first-class anti-tank Regiment stuck in the cotton-fields near Giza.'

149th moved to Base Depot, Almaza, handed in the 25-pounders, picked up anti-tank guns. They were 6-pounders, which they had never seen before. 'At 22.00 hours July 7th, the Regiment was placed under four hours' notice to move ... At 16.00 hours on the 8th the last of the guns arrived. By 17.00 hours, we were off!'

149th Anti-Tank and 11th Field shared many adventures from this point on. It was sad to realize that – on 2 July – they just missed becoming part of Robcol.

2nd New Zealand Division

The Kiwis' long association with 4th Indian Division was to become one of the happiest memories of the war. It endured the rigours of peace and, even later, when the 4th Indian Division held reunions, there was always at least one Kiwi among the guests of honour. Even Montgomery, despite his lukewarm attitude to Indian regiments, picked a Kiwi and a Gurkha from 4th Indian Division among his three representatives from Alamein, in his 'First Fifteen Fighting Men' for the *Sunday Times* of 22 September 1968.

There is no one with whom 11th Field would sooner share the honours of 2 July than a Kiwi. At about the end of the first week in July, 2nd New Zealand Division were just south of forward Pt 63 and thus due west of us. The southern approaches to the Ridge were screened by them on the left of Robcol which, by now, faced north-west. They did not reach this position however, until after 2 July. On that date, elements of the division were able to fire on the Ridge, and indeed have been blamed by some for the 'overs' which made life uncomfortable for the southernmost South African brigade in the 'Hotbox'. But, they did not establish themselves in position to make any decisive contribution to the battle until 3 or 4 July.

Let us trace a few of the steps which led them, like us, to the magnetic attraction of Forward Pt 63 at this time. Major General Sir Howard Kippenberger KBE, CB, DSO and Bar, ED and author of *Infantry Brigadier* will serve as our representative of that splendid division – but he would be the first to point to the men who followed his lead.

September 1939 – Southern Battalion formed (the 20th New Zealanders). 5 January 1940 they embarked on *Dunera*, the 'first transport to leave New Zealand'. 12 February 1940, anchored in Suez Roads. March 1941, to Greece. April 1941, less 85 casualties (including three officers killed) to Crete. May 1941, return to North Africa. Twelve officers went back into a mess which 40 had left. Of 851 who went to Greece, two months before, only 300 came back.

After training at Baggush, Tobruk in November 1941, Sidi Regezh, Belhamed on 25 November and Kippenberger wounded and captured. He eventually reported to Freyberg at Baggush, to hear 'Colonel Kippenberger, you're a Brigadier'.

'The casualties of the Twentieth in this campaign were 24 officers and 537 Other Ranks, of whom 10 officers and 361 Other Ranks were prisoners, about 100 of those taken prisoner were wounded.'

It is about here that I must go across to Lt. Colonel Scoullar's book *Battle for Egypt, The Official History of New Zealand in the Second World War* to fill in the story. He began at Bagush (normally with two gs, but it is the same place) and had interesting comments on morale. On the third page of his book, we find: 'Letters to New Zealand from Bagush were generous in praise of British troops, especially of the tank units and the Royal Air Force.'

I dwell on this praise from those whose opinion matters to me, because as we have seen there was not much to praise in the external appearance of our armour on 2 July. As Scoullar shows in *Battle for Egypt*, Appendix II, page 386, in his description of the division in captivity: 'After the initial surprise, followed by humiliation and in some cases self-consciousness at finding themselves standing with hands up, disarmed, and no longer members of a disciplined, trained and ordered group, the majority of the men developed an anger which they directed vaguely at their officers, at the Army generally, and then more particularly at the British armour for its failure to provide the promised support.' It was not their fault, but this opinion cannot be ignored.

This was a period when the Desert battle extended over hundreds of miles. Scoullar writes of the capture of Bardia in January 1942 which released 800 New Zealand prisoners, including Kippenberger. On 14 January, however, the Axis forces advanced to El Agheila – a journey which ended only on 2 July.

It is obvious from the documentation that the order which started my journey from Ruwandiz was from the same source as that which reached Kippenberger on an exercise in the Syrian Desert on 13 June. By 14 June, he arrived at Baalbeck to find Divisional HQ already on the move. General Freyberg had already gone onto Cairo by air. 4th Brigade moved on 16 June, 5th Brigade on 18 June. The Brigadier and his unit commanders left for Cairo independently early on 17 June.

The South African Division

It is a matter of pride to South Africans that the first three German attempts to pierce the thin line at Alamein were made and repulsed on the South African sector despite the 1st South African Brigade being later withdrawn. For our story, their withdrawal exposed Robcol's right flank for vital hours until 11th HAC followed some hours later by Ackcol and 3rd RHA came to plug the gap.

Since this is the story of the Ridge, it is right to record that in the first two days of July, 1st South African Brigade Group – two batteries of artillery and a battalion strong, lost six killed, 27 wounded and four missing. Nineteen of these casualties came from 7th South African Field Regiment and, though we do not know their names, their passing must surely qualify this regiment for a place in this story.

These losses were suffered in a place which will always be known to South Africans as the 'Hotbox', and, since it is so important to this story, I have been at some pains to locate it accurately. The excellent cartographer of *Crisis in the Desert* clearly places it in a little kidney-shaped re-entrant just north of Ruweisat Ridge and just to the east of the eastern prong of the bifurcated barrel track which ran down from Alamein station. Brigadier Waller's battle map places them, 'approximately' at 884284, but shows no re-entrant. The 1:250,000 map El Daba allows us to bring them 2,000 yards to the south – the re-entrant shows clearly at about 884282.

The message from 50th Division indicating that Ackcol had been ordered to close up to our 'friends in the north' shows clearly the vital part played by 50th Division in organising resistance and the important role played by Ackcol (3rd RHA) in plugging the hole caused by the withdrawal of 1st South African Brigade.

In the north, 1st South African Division consisted of 3rd South African Brigade, 1st South African Field Regiment (1st and 3rd South African field batteries) and 7th Medium Regiment RA. They were just strong enough to man the western and south-western faces of the perimeter, leaving the eastern half of the box undefended. To cover the ten-mile gap between the wire and 18th Indian Infantry Brigade in the Deir el Shein, they organized, at the Auk's insistence during his visit on 29 June, two mobile columns each based on two batteries of artillery and one battalion of infantry. All other troops were sent back to Alexandria.

Below the box in the Deir el Shein, over some 30 miles of front, the New Zealand Division and 9th Indian Brigade of 5th Indian Division – joined next day, 1 July, by 7th Motor Brigade of 7th Armoured Division. This thin khaki line militarily had little significance at this stage.

Closing on the Alamein box at noon on 30 June was the German 90th Light Division and the Italian XXI Corps. In the centre, the DAK with 21st and 15th Panzer Divisions. During the first three days of July, Rommel's main attacks were carried out in the north by 90th Light Division against the actual Alamein box and in the centre by the two panzer divisions in a two-pronged attack through the Deir el Shein and along the Ruweisat Ridge. Despite the comparative weakness of 3rd South African Brigade, they were in prepared positions and, apart from occupying the sandy mid-riff left by the thinly padded positions, 90th Light made little headway.

On 1 July, Rommel records: 'Late in the afternoon I decided to put everything I could into supporting the southern flank of 90th Light Division's break-through attempt.'

This is the day which the South African historians describe as 'the crucial day in the whole desert campaign', but, as Rommel's attack in the centre was, at first, successful, I may be forgiven for christening 2 July not 1 July, as 'the day we stopped losing the war'.

90th Light tried in vain to get to the sea between 2nd South African Brigade Group at Alam el Onsol and the more or less fortified box occupied by 3rd South African Brigade around El Alamein station. They seem to have chased the 40-odd tanks of 4th Armoured Brigade, of 1st Armoured Division, through the gap and the afternoon of 1 July found them bogged down, in a blinding sandstorm, trying to find a weakness in this fairly solid position.

Farther south however, the combined might of 15th Panzer and 21st Panzer overcame the raw 18th Indian Infantry Brigade in the Deir el Shein. The Panzers had only about 55 tanks between them, but the only available British armour, 22nd Armoured Brigade, had, since dawn when it arrived in the area, withdrawn beyond Ruweisat and did not return to support the Indian brigade box. 22nd Armoured Brigade was, in any case, reported as having only 28 tanks, of which ten were on tow.

Notes

Dedication

1. R. W. Thompson, *The Montgomery Legend*, p. 99.

Preface

1. John Connell, *Auchinleck*.

Introduction

1. I alone bear responsibility for the accuracy of this history, but my objectives would be missed if these pages distorted the truth to any degree and the story would be thin indeed if it did not rest on the testimony of other survivors. Some of these were recorded while memory was still quite fresh, but the heart of the story comes from the memory of men who 25 to 40 years later could not forget Ruweisat.

   The note in 'The Times Diary' on the 25th anniversary led to letters from all sorts and conditions of men from Chelsea Pensioners to the commander of Robcol. This correspondence led to other contacts and in a short time the author's beliefs were to rest on fact or at least on the recorded memories of others who played a more important role on the fateful day. But the readership of *The Times* proved too narrow a base from which to reach the men who actually served the guns. An article in *The Gunner* magazine on the 35th anniversary showed that they too could not forget.

   These men have therefore borne witness to the facts of Robcol:

   50th Division HQ: The Brigade Major, Major Douglas Brown, at the time of writing Major General W. D. Brown, CB, CBE, DSO, a Colonel Commandant of the Royal Artillery.

   Robcol HQ: The Column Commander, Brigadier R. P. Waller DSO, MC.
   His Brigade Major, Major B. A. G Jones, later Brigadier, DSO.

   11th Field Regiment RA:

RHQ: Commanding Officer, Lt. Colonel A. O. McCarthy, MC
2 I/C, Major Pat R. M. Waterfield, later Brigadier, MBE,
Regimental Sergeant Major 'Nobby' J. Clark
Staff Sergeant D. A. N. Tydeman
B Echelon, Sergeant G. Coates
Signals, Lt. 'Pip' Mott.
83rd/85th Field Battery RA:
HQ, Signals, Sergeant G. T. O'Shaughnessy
D Troop Command Post, 2nd Lt. John S. Mayes (Don Troop leader)
AGPO, L/Bdr 'Chalky' Whyte
Sergeant H. 'Tug' Wilson
Chelsea Pensioner, J. Bethell
E Troop, Commander, Captain, later Major L. L. Boyd, MC
Gun Commander, BSM, George Wilkinson, MM
265th Anti-Tank Battery RA: N. Troop, Commander, Lt. later Major M. Budd, MBE
11th HAC: Major G. A. Armstrong, later Colonel
1st/4th Essex: At the All Ranks Reunion in October 1968:
Commanding Officer, Lt. Colonel Arthur Noble, later Colonel Sir Arthur, CB, DSO, TD, DL
C Company Commander, Major Leonard W. A. Chappell
B Company Commander, Major H. Joe Young, MC
13th Platoon, Sergeant Wynn and Pte. Tommy Townsend
Anti-Tank Platoon, Captain D. A. Beckett, later Major General, DSO, OBE, Director of Army Personnel Services
Bren Carriers: Captain J. Watt; Sergeant E. Chapman; Sergeant Barnard
Rifle Companies: Colour Sergeant R. G. Wheeler, MM; CSM F. Wiggs; RQMS N. Croucher

Chapter 1

1. Anthony Eden, *The Eden Memoirs.*
2. *History of the Second World War* Volume III.
3. Gerald Pawle, *The War and Colonel Warden*, based on the recollections of R. C. Thompson, personal assistant to the PM 1940–5.
4. Eden.
5. Pawle.
6. Thompson.

Chapter 2

1. E. Waller (1606–87).
2. History of the 5th Indian Division, *Ball of Fire*, Chapter XVII.

3. Connell.
4. Desmond Flower & James Reeves (Eds), *The Taste of Courage: The War 1939–1945.*
5. Compton Mackenzie, *Eastern Epic.*
6. John Wheeler-Bennett, *King George VI.*
7. David Hunt, *A Don at War.*
8. Before finishing the draft for this chapter, *The Times* carried the obituary of Lt. General Sir Francis Tuker, KCIE, CB, DSO, OBE, commander of 4th Indian Division and one of the war's great divisional commanders.
9. Thompson.

Chapter 3

1. R. H. W. S. Hastings, *The Rifle Brigade in the Second World War 1939–1945,* Chapter X.
2. Hunt.
3. Carver.
4. I. S. O Playfair et al, *The Mediterranean and Middle East: Vol. IV: The Destruction of the Axis Forces in Africa.*
5. Ibid.
6. C. E. Lucas Phillips, *Alamein* (British Battles).
7. Corelli Barnett, *The Desert Generals.*
8. Denis Johnston, *Nine Rivers from Jordan.*
9. Mackenzie.
10. Hunt.
11. J. A. I. Turner & L. C. F. Agar-Hamilton, *Crisis in the Desert May–July 1942,* Chapter 15.
12. Ibid.

Chapter 4

1. Connell.
2. Ibid.
3. Ibid.

Chapter 5

1. This chapter was drafted a few days after the memorial service to that great general, Sir Francis Tuker, and its title is borrowed from the title of his book *Approach to Battle.*
2. *The Salonika History, A History of XI Field Regiment, Royal Artillery, 1939–1946.*
3. J. L. 'Jim' Manning added a tale of the consternation of a young officer who joined 187th Battery in 1943. After reporting to the Adjutant and the CO in the orderly

room, he bumped, for the first time, into the RSM. 'Moustache out, sir,' said the RSM, regarding the new arrival's growth with apparent disfavour. The officer was proud of his lip's demonstration of his surging manhood, but his protestations were cut short by Nobby Clark's definition of Military Law in the 11th Field Regiment: 'Never mind what the CO says, sir, in this regiment no one's allowed to wear a moustache longer than mine!'

4. J. L. Scoullar, *Official History of New Zealand in the Second World War 1939–45: Battle for Egypt*.

5. Ibid.

Chapter 6

1. Maj. Gen. Sir Howard Kippenberger, *Infantry Brigadier*.
2. Paolo Caccia Dominioni, *Alamein 1933–1962: An Italian Story*.
3. The action in the Deir el Shein has received more attention from historians than the fighting on Ruweisat Ridge on the following two days. This chapter draws off a number of sources, including original research. In particular however, acknowledgement is due to the accounts by Lt. Colonel G. R. Stevens OBE, Sir Compton Mackenzie, Lt. General Sir Francis Tuker, KCIE, CB, DSO, OBE, Colonel T. A. Martin MBE, C. E. Lucas Phillips and J. A. I. Turner and L. C. F. Agar-Hamilton, who all appreciate the importance of the 18th Indian Infantry Brigade's stand.

Chapter 7

1. Turner & Agar-Hamilton.
2. It is possible that the Hotbox extended closer to Ruweisat than the Brigadier's approximate position suggests. The cartographer of *Crisis in the Desert* placed it in a little kidney-shaped re-entrant just north of the ridge and just to the east of the bifurcated barrel track which runs down from Alamein station. This re-entrant is not shown on the Brigadier's map, but the 1:250,000 map El Daba shows a re-entrant 2,000 yards farther south – on the little figure 38. If so, nearly four months later, 11th Field joined in the barrage at Montgomery's Alamein, firing from this very depression. Pt 38 marks a *bir* (a well or cistern) at the foot of the 40-foot tower of tubes and hessian which housed Don Troop's observation post.

Chapter 9

1. Thirteen out of the 46 officers photographed that day are recorded in *Regimental Fire* as killed in action. In addition to the seven killed by 2 July 1942, Maj. W. A Sheil, Lt. P. M. Britton, Lt. S. A. C Watt, Lt. T. F. Butler, Lt. Storey, MC, and Lt.

M. V. Boys are known to have lost their lives. *Regimental Fire* page 86 shows that in May and June, 11th HAC lost 20 officers and 210 other ranks killed or wounded plus five officers and 17 other ranks missing.

Chapter 10

1. Imperial War Museum (516.319 (K17794) Ruweisat Ridge – 2 July 1942).
2. 'The Battery Captain', Jimmy Breakell, was by now a prisoner in Mersa Matruh. In this instance, it can only be your author, the Command Post Officer. But who, but me, would gain comfort from such mis-identification?
3. IWM.
4. Ibid.

Chapter 11

1. 3rd RHA did not actually arrive until the next day. The smoke came from 1st or 2nd RHA (or both). B. A. G. Jones's 1,000 yards is probably a measure of the distance that the HQ retired (being in effect, non-combatants) rather than the distance moved by the two troops which were ordered to withdraw.
2. IWM.
3. Ibid.

Epilogue

1. Some people are fated to reap less reward than they deserve. Lt. Col. (Acting Brigadier) R. P. Waller, DSO, MC, was granted the temporary rank of brigadier in the Middle East list of appointments with effect from 27 June 1942.
2. Joan Bright, *The 9th Queen's Royal Lancers*.

Postscript

1. From author's collection.
2. From author's collection.
3. From author's collection.

Bibliography

516.319 (K17794) Ruweisat Ridge – 2nd July 1942, Library of The Imperial War Museum

Allen, J. P., *A Short History of the 57th Light Anti-Aircraft Regiment, Royal Artillery*, Gale & Polden, 1947

Anonymous, *Teheran to Trieste, The Story of 10th Indian Division*, War Department, Government of India, 1947

Armstrong, Geoffrey, DSO, MC, TD, *The Sparks Fly Upward*, Gooday Publishers, 1991

Avon, Rt. Hon. The Earl of, KC, PC, MC, *The Eden Memoirs*, Cassell, 1960

Barclay, Brigadier C. N., CBE, DSO, Ed., *The Regimental History of the 3rd Queen Alexandra's Own Gurkha Rifles (Vol. II)*, W. Clowes & Sons, 1951

Barnett, Corelli, *Britain and Her Army*, Allen Lane/Penguin Press, 1970

Barnett, Corelli, *The Desert Generals*, Cassell, 1983

Beddington, Major General W. R., CBE, *A History of the Queens Bays, 1929–1945*, Warren & Son, 1954

Benevolent Fund, The Royal Artillery, *The Royal Artillery Commemoration Handbook 1939–1945*, G. Bell & Sons, 1950

Brett-James, Antony, *Ball of Fire, Fifth Indian Division in the Second World War*, Gale & Polden, 1951

Bright, Joan, OBE, *History of the Northumberland Hussars Regiment*, Mawson, Swan & Morgan Ltd, 1949

Bright, Joan, OBE, *The 9th Queen's Royal Lancers, 1936–1945, The Story of an Armoured Regiment in Battle*, Gale & Polden, 1951

Bryant, Sir Arthur, *The Turn of the Tide*, Collins, 1957

Caccia-Dominioni, Paolo, *Alamein 1933–1962, An Italian Story*, Allen & Unwin, 1966

Capleton, E. W., *Shabash 149, The War Story of the 149th Regiment, Royal Artillery*, C. Tinling & Co Ltd, 1963

Carrell, Paul, *The Foxes of the Desert*, Bantam, 1960

Carver, Lt. Colonel R. M. P., CBE, DSO, MC, *Second to None, The Royal Scots Greys, 1919–1945*, McCorquodale & Co, 1954

Carver, Lt. Colonel R. M. P., CBE, DSO, MC, *Tobruk*, Batsford, 1972

Chariappa, General K. M., *The Tiger Kills, Traditions in the Indian Army*, HMSO, 1944

Churchill, Sir Winston, *The Second World War, Volume IV, The Hinge of Fate*, Cassell, 1953

Clarke, Brigadier Dudley, *The Eleventh at War, Being the Story of the 11th Hussars (Prince Albert's Own) Through the Years 1934–1945*, M. Joseph, 1952

Clifford, Alexander, *Three Against Rommel*, Harrap, 1943

Clifton, Brigadier G., DSO, MC, *The Happy Hunted*, Cassell, 1955

Connell, John, *Auchinleck*, Cassell, 1959

Dawnay, Brigadier D., DSO, Historical Committee Chairman, *The 10th Royal Hussars in the Second World War, 1939–1945*, Gale & Polden, 1948

de Visscher, Ed., *Wartime in the Middle East, An Anthology*, Brussels, 1945

Denholm-Young, C. P. S., *Men of Alamein*, Schindler (Cairo), 1943

Flowers, Desmond & Reeves, James, *The Taste of Courage*, Harper & Bros, 1960

Flowers, Desmond & Reeves, James, *The War 1939–1945*, Cassell, 1960

Gee, F. W., Ed., *A History of the Essex Yeomanry, 1919–1949, 1950*

Hart, Liddell, Sir Basil. H., Ed, *The Rommel Papers*, Easton Press, *1988*

Hastings, Major R. H. W. S. DSO, OBE, MC, *The Rifle Brigade in the Second World War, 1939–1945*, Gale & Polden, 1950

Historical Committee, *The History of the 7th Medium Regiment, Royal Artillery (later 32nd Medium Regiment, Royal Artillery)*, Loxley Brothers, 1951

Horrocks, Lt. General Sir Brian, *A Full Life*, Collins, 1960

Hunt, Sir David KCMG, OBE, *A Don at War*, William Kimber, 1966

Johnson, Brigadier R. F., *Regimental Fire (The Honourable Artillery Company in World War II)*, Williams Lea & Co. Ltd, 1958

Johnston, Dennis, *Nine Rivers from Jordan*, Little, Brown, 1955

Joslen, Lt. Colonel H. F., *Orders of Battle, Second World War 1939–1945, Volumes 1 & 2*, HMSO, 1960

Kennedy, General Sir John, GCMG, KCVO, KBE, MC, *The Business of War*, Hutchinson, 1957

Kippenberger, Major General Sir Howard, KBE, CB, DSO, ED, *Infantry Brigadier*, Oxford University Press, 1961

Knight, Captain H. R. *Historical Records of the Buffs*, Gale & Polden, 1905

Lewin, Ronald, *The Life and Death of The Afrika Korps*, Batsford, 1977

Lewis, Major P. J., MC, & English, Major I. R., MC, *Into Battle with the Durhams*, The London Stamp Exchange 1990

Lucas Phillips, C. E., *Alamein*, Heinemann, 1962

Mackenzie, Sir Compton, *Eastern Epic, Volume 1*, Chatto & Windus, 1951

Majdalanay, Fred, *The Battle of El Alamein*, Weidenfeld & Nicolson, 1965

Martin, Colonel T. A., MBE, *The Essex Regiment, 1929–1950*, The Essex Regiment Association, 1952

Maxwell, Lt. Colonel W. E., CIE, *Capital Campaigners, History of 3rd Battalion (Queen Mary's Own), The 10th Baluch Regiment*, Gale & Polden, 1948

McCarthy, Lt. Colonel A. O., MC, courtesy of, *The Salonika History, A History of XI Field Regiment, Royal Artillery, 1939–1946*

McCorquodale, Colonel A. D., OBE et al, *History of the King's Dragoon Guards, 1938–1945,* Printed for the Regiment by Messrs. McCorquodale & Co Ltd, 1946

Mellenthin, von, F. W., *Panzer Battles 1939–1945*, Cassell, 1955

Moorehead, Alan, *The Desert War*, Hamish Hamilton, 1965

Morris, Sergeant R. W., *121st Medium Regiment, Royal Artillery, 1939–1946*

Oates, Edward A. *Gunfire Target, Six Years with the Royal Artillery,* The Book Guild Ltd, 1996

Onslow, The Earl of, KBE, MC, TD, *Men and Sand, 22nd Armoured Brigade,* St Catherine Press Ltd, 1959

Parkinson, Roger, *The War in the Desert*, Hart-Davis MacGibbon, 1976

Pawle, Gerald, *The War and Colonel Warden*, Harrap, 1963

Pitt, Barrie, *The Crucible of War, Year of Alamein 1942*, Jonathan Cape, 1982

Pitt-Rivers, J. A., *The Story of the Royal Dragoons, 1938–1945*, Wm. Clowes & Sons Ltd, 1956

Playfair, Major General I. S. O., CB, DSO, MC and Bar, *The Mediterranean and the Middle East, Volume III*, HM Stationary Office, 1960

Prasad, Bisheshwar, Ed., *Official History of the Indian Armed Forces in the Second World War, 1939–1945*, Combined Inter-Services Historical Section (India & Pakistan), 1953–1956

Purnell, *History of the Second World War*, Published in 96 weekly parts, 1975

Schmidt, Heinz Werner, *With Rommel in the Desert*, Harrap, 1973

Scoullar, Lt. Colonel J. L., *Battle for Egypt, Official History of New Zealand in the Second World War*, War History Branch, New Zealand, 1955

Smuts, J. C., *Jan Christian Smuts*, Cassell, 1952

Stevens, Lt. Colonel G. R., OBE, *Fourth Indian Division*, McLaren & Son, 1948

Stewart, Captain P. F., *The History of the XII Royal Lancers*, Oxford University Press, 1950

Synge, Captain W. A. T., *The Story of the Green Howards*, The Green Howards, 1952

Tedder, Lord, Marshal of the Royal Air Force, *With Prejudice*, Cassell, 1966

Thompson, R. W., *The Montgomery Legend*, Allen & Unwin, 1967

Tuker, Lt. General Sir Francis, KCIE, CB, DSO, OBE, *Approach to Battle*, Cassell, 1963

Turner, J. A. I. & Agar-Hamilton, L. C. F., *Crisis in the Desert, May/July 1942*, Oxford University Press, 1952 (This history is now difficult to find in England. The author was fortunate in being able to borrow from Colonel Geoff Armstrong the copy which was presented to him 'With compliments of the Prime Minister, Union of South Africa' in recognition of the great help he gave the authors in 1952.)

Ward, S. G. P., *Faithful, The Story of the Durham Light Infantry*, Thomas Nelson & Son Ltd, 1962

Warner, Philip, *Auchinleck, The Lonely Soldier*, Buchan & Enright, 1981

Wheeler-Bennett, Sir John, *King George VI*, Macmillan, 1965

Young, Desmond, *Rommel*, Fontana, 1972

Permissions

I would like to thank all those involved who provided kind help in tracing the rights owners of extracts from the following works:

Allen, J. P.
205–6:   'The fighting around Mersa Matruh lasted until the 28th June ...'
          'In one heavy Stuka raid on the Chestnut Troop ...'
Reproduced from *A Short History of the 57th Light Anti-Aircraft Regiment, Royal Artillery*, Gale & Polden, 1947, with kind permission.

Avon, Rt. Hon. The Earl of
2:        '[M]any blows fell, during the early months of 1942 ...'
4:        'July 2nd: Winston wound up with one of his most effective speeches ...'
Reproduced from *The Eden Memoirs*, Cassell, 1960, with kind permission.

Beddington, Major General W. R.
195–6:   'The Queen's Bays (2nd Dragoon Guards) were not as such on Ruweisat ...'
Reproduced from *A History of the Queens Bays, 1929–1945*, Warren & Son, 1954, with kind permission.

Bright, Joan
209:      'Rob [Waller] had fostered their traditions and built up ...'
210:      'They had expected a formidable obstacle and were soon disillusioned ...'
Reproduced from *History of the Northumberland Hussars Regiment*, Mawson, Swan & Morgan Ltd, 1949, with kind permission.
151–2:   'That day [3 July] had really marked the end of the danger period. ...'
Reproduced from *The 9th Queen's Royal Lancers, 1936–1945, The Story of an Armoured Regiment in Battle*, Gale & Polden, 1951, with kind permission.

Caccia-Dominioni, Paolo
62:     '… an uninitiated observer would have stood amazed at the sight …'
180:    'If it had not been for Auchinleck, the British would probably have lost Egypt …'
181:    'July 1st 1942. A couple of days previously …'
        'Hill 33. El Alamein, July 4th 1942. …'
        'On July 2nd the confusion was general, circling to and fro …'
Reproduced from *Alamein 1933–1962, An Italian Story*, Allen & Unwin, 1966 with kind permission.

Capleton, E. W.
212:    'If one had to select the Regiment's finest hour …'
        'On the night of July 3rd, his armour rolled through the line. …'
        'As the Regiment pulled out of Khatatba …'
213:    'By July 3rd, some struggling Staff Officer intent on getting support …'
        'At 22.00 hours July 7th, the Regiment was placed under four hours' notice …'
Reproduced from *Shabash 149, The War Story of the 149th Regiment, Royal Artillery*, C. Tinling & Co Ltd, 1963, with kind permission.

Carver, Lt. Colonel, R. M. P.
12:     'Tuker's 4th Indian Division, which had no major part …'
17–18: 'One of the new commander's first steps was to order …'
Reproduced from *Tobruk*, Batsford, 1972, with kind permission of B. T. Batsford, part of Pavilion Books Company Limited.

Chariappa, General K. M.
198:    'From this point onwards no record will be given …'
199:    'The three Indian Cavalry Regiments …'
202:    '… the remainder of the 97th and 121st Field Regiments …'
Reproduced from *The Tiger Kills, Traditions in the Indian Army*, HMSO, 1944, under the Terms of Crown Copyright Policy Guidance issued by HMSO.

Churchill, Sir Winston
xvi: 'For the first six months all went ill …'
2:      'Before Alamein we never had a victory …'
Reproduced from *The Second World War, Volume IV, The Hinge of Fate*, Cassell, 1953, with kind permission of Curtis Brown, London on behalf of The Estate of Winston S. Churchill.

Hart, Sir Basil Liddell, Ed.
23:     '[L]ate in the afternoon I decided to put everything …'
45:     'The 1st British Armoured Division was no longer in a fit state …'

182: 'Dearest Lu, how much I think of you …'
      'Now the battle of Mersa Matruh has also been won …'
      'We planned to get through to the Alamein line …'
      'there had only been a few days during which we could …'
      'At about 0900 hours, the 21st Panzer Division ran up against …'
183: 'At 16.00 hours a report came in from Nehring …'
      'At 2130 hours that evening, I ordered the 90th Light Division …'
      'the struggle for the last position before Alexandria is hard …'
      'Unfortunately, things are not going as well as I should like …'
184: 'After three days vainly assaulting the Alamein line I decided …'
215: 'Late in the afternoon I decided to put everything …'

Reproduced from *The Rommel Papers*, Easton Press, 1988, © 1953 by B. H. Liddell-Hart and renewed 1981 by Lady Kathleen Liddell-Hart, Fritz Bayerlein-Dittmar and Manfred Rommel. Reprinted by permission of Houghton Mifflin Harcourt Publishing Company. All rights reserved.

Hastings, Major R. H. W. S.
15–16: 'It is nonsense to talk of the Alamein "Line". …'
85–6:   'The 9th Battalion … were used to plug every gap in the line …'
Reproduced from *The Rifle Brigade in the Second World War, 1939–1945*, Gale & Polden, 1950, © Major R. H. W. S. Hastings 1950.

Horrocks, Lt. General Sir Brian
174–5: 'Few generals have ever had such a load to bear. …'
175:    'It was the desperate fighting in the first fortnight of July …'
Reprinted from *A Full Life*, Collins, 1960, © Lt. General Sir Brian Horrocks 1960, by kind permission of HarperCollins Publishers Ltd.

Hunt, Sir David
13:     'It was on the night of the 3rd November that the 5th Indian Brigade …'
14:     'In fact it must be clear by now that I am one of those …'
16–17: 'El Alamein was only a name to us then though a very well-known one. …'
21:     'This ridge had always been recognized as one of the keys …'
172:    'The 2nd July 1942 is the day which to my mind …'
Reproduced from *A Don at War*, William Kimber, 1966, © Sir David Hunt 1966, by kind permission of Taylor & Francis Books UK.

Johnston, Dennis
20:     'a small railway station set in the midst of some hundreds of miles of nothing …'
Reproduced from *Nine Rivers from Jordan*, Little, Brown, 1955, with kind permission of The Permissions Company for the Hachette Book Group.

Joslen, Lt. Colonel H. F.
186:     'In March 1942 owing to the paucity of equipment …'
189:     'was employed for the remainder of 1941 in equipping …'
191:     'In June 1942 in Libya, the Brigade suffered heavy casualties …'
208:     'captured by the Germans in Libya. …'
Reproduced from *Orders of Battle, Second World War 1939–1945, Volumes 1 & 2*, HMSO, 1960, under the Terms of Crown Copyright Policy Guidance issued by HMSO.

Kennedy, General Sir John
172:     'Unless the Middle East is reinforced strongly and fast …'
          'From the purely military point of view, the retention of Iraq …'
          'By 1st July, Rommel was only 60 miles from Alexandria. …'
Reproduced from *The Business of War*, Hutchinson, 1957, with kind permission of Penguin/Random House.

Mackenzie, Sir Compton
12:      'A legend has grown up that the Eighth Army …'
21:      'If the enemy could sweep up to the crest …'
73:      'many of the gunners were able to escape capture …'
Reproduced from *Eastern Epic, Volume 1*, Chatto & Windus, 1951, with kind permission of the Society of Authors as the Literary Representative of the Estate of Sir Compton Mackenzie.

Martin, Colonel T. A.
70:      'Two lacked sights, and the accompanying ammunition was very limited. …'
120:     'their endurance, week after week, in the early days …'
Reproduced from *The Essex Regiment, 1929–1950*, The Essex Regiment Association, 1952, by kind permission of the heirs of Colonel T. A. Martin.

Moorehead, Alan
178:     'Rommel's forces were roughly equal to ours …'
178–9:   'Only one barrier lay between them and the Delta …'
179–80: 'Even in the remote villages, the people guessed …'
Reproduced from *The Desert War*, Hamish Hamilton, 1965, by kind permission of Pollinger Limited (www.pollingerltd.com) on behalf of the Estate of Alan Moorehead.

Pawle, Gerald
4:       'the greatest friends Hitler ever had'
          'On the day the Censure debate opened, Rommel's Afrika Korps …'
175:     'Hardly had they reached the White House before the grave news arrived. …'
Reproduced from *The War and Colonel Warden*, Harrap, 1963, with kind permission.

Lucas Phillips, C. E.
19:     'The defence works were of an exiguous nature ...'
72:     '[W]hat was left of the garrison stood fast, the Regiments fighting ...'
73:     'Here the Brigade, all alone ...'
Reproduced from *Alamein*, Heinemann, 1962. *Playfair, Major General I. S. O.*
18:     'three defended localities, about fifteen miles apart ...'
Reproduced from *The Mediterranean and the Middle East, Volume III*, HM Stationary Office, 1960, under the Terms of Crown Copyright Policy Guidance issued by HMSO, with kind permission.

Scoullar, Colonel J. L.
45:     'Auchinleck emphasized that "it is of paramount importance ..."'
214:    'After the initial surprise, followed by humiliation ...'
Reproduced from *Battle for Egypt, Official History of New Zealand in the Second World War*, War History Branch, New Zealand, 1955, with kind permission of the Alexander Turnbull Library, The National Library of New Zealand.

Thompson, R. W.
xiii: 'A battle is many things to many men. ...'
2:      'The loss of Abadan and Bahrain would be "calamitous" ...'
3:      'was the Auk who really saved us all. ...'
4:      'In its way this was a turning-point in the war ...'
4–5:   'Few, if any, in high places harboured doubts ...'
8:      'In the political and military crises of June and July, ...'
10:     'The galaxies of headquarters flags dotting the immense areas ...'
11:     'There had been no certainty in the desert war ...'
12:     'Officially, "the turn of the tide" would be held back ...'
14:     'The worst was his treatment of the 4th Indian Division ...'
171:    'The CIGS knew that a false move ...'
175:    'On June 30th President Roosevelt asked Marshall for an evaluation ...'
Reproduced from *The Montgomery Legend*, Allen & Unwin/Harper Collins, 1967, with kind permission.

Von Mellenthin, F.
183:    'Some ground was gained on Ruweisat Ridge ...'
Reproduced from *Panzer Battles 1939–1945*, Cassell/Orion Books, 1955, with kind permission.

Wheeler-Bennett, Sir John
xvi: 'The actual turning of the tide in the 2nd World War ...'
2:      'After Rommel was repulsed at El Alamein on July 2nd ...'
12:     'By what strange and ugly combination of factors were Auchinleck ...'
Reproduced from *King George VI*, Macmillan, 1965, with kind permission of Pan Macmillan via PLSclear.

All efforts have to contact rights holders for the following quoted material have been unsuccessful:

Clifford, Alexander
177:     'Desperately now Auchinleck needed time, time to unload ...'
         'So Auchinleck kept his army and stole some of the time ...'
177–8:   'Behind the crust of the Alamein line there was ...'
Reproduced from *Three Against Rommel*, Chambers/Harrap, 1943.

Connell, John
10:      'July became the month that was ignored ...'
15:      'the ultimate rampart of Alamein'
27:      'In this sliding, melting world of rout and defeatism ...'
27–8:   'Auchinleck stood in the sand by the roadside, bare-headed ...'
28:      'He resolved to strip the army down to what it needed ...'
173–4:   'On the eve of what may prove to be the turning point ...'
174:     'With all their faults, Auchinleck and Eighth Army ...'
         'These damn British have been taught for too long ...'
         'They presented themselves on July 3rd at Rommel's headquarters ...'
176:     'I hope one day I shall have something more solid to report.'
         'I cannot help liking very much the way things seem to be going.'
Reproduced from *Auchinleck*, Cassell/Orion Books, 1959.

Turner, J. A. and Agar-Hamilton, L. C. F.
23:      'the crucial day in the whole desert campaign'
76:      'The Brigade then learned that a column which the War Diary ...'
194:     'At that time, however, 4th Armoured Brigade was still unable ...'
196:     'the DAK approaching the Alamein line on the evening ...'
197:     'the sweep which Rommel envisaged for the afternoon ...'
197–8:   'I did decide late at night ... That it would be easier ...'
Reproduced from *Crisis in the Desert, May/July 1942*, Oxford University Press, 1952.

Index